COGNITIVE PSYCHOLOGY

Psychology:
Revisiting the Classic Studies

Series Editors:
S. Alexander Haslam, Alan M. Slater and Joanne R. Smith
School of Psychology, University of Exeter, Exeter, EX4 4QG

Psychology: Revisiting the Classic Studies is a new series of texts aimed at students and general readers who are interested in understanding issues raised by key studies in psychology. Volumes centre on 12–15 studies, with each chapter providing a detailed account of a particular classic study and its empirical and theoretical impact. Chapters also discuss the important ways in which thinking and research has advanced in the years since the study was conducted. Chapters are written by researchers at the cutting edge of these developments and, as a result, these texts serve as an excellent resource for instructors and students looking to explore different perspectives on core material that defines the field of psychology as we know it today.

Also available:
Social Psychology: Revisiting the Classic Studies
Joanne R. Smith and S. Alexander Haslam

Developmental Psychology: Revisiting the Classic Studies
Alan M. Slater and Paul C. Quinn

COGNITIVE PSYCHOLOGY

***REVISITING**
THE CLASSIC STUDIES

EDITED BY:
MICHAEL W. EYSENCK
& DAVID GROOME

Los Angeles | London | New Delhi
Singapore | Washington DC | Boston

Los Angeles | London | New Delhi
Singapore | Washington DC

SAGE Publications Ltd
1 Oliver's Yard
55 City Road
London EC1Y 1SP

SAGE Publications Inc.
2455 Teller Road
Thousand Oaks, California 91320

SAGE Publications India Pvt Ltd
B 1/I 1 Mohan Cooperative Industrial Area
Mathura Road
New Delhi 110 044

SAGE Publications Asia-Pacific Pte Ltd
3 Church Street
#10-04 Samsung Hub
Singapore 049483

Editor: Luke Block
Assistant editor: Keri Dickens
Production editor: Imogen Roome
Proofreader: Bryan Campbell
Indexer: Judith Lavender
Marketing manager: Alison Borg
Cover design: Wendy Scott
Typeset by: C&M Digitals (P) Ltd, Chennai, India
Printed and bound by CPI Group (UK) Ltd,
Croydon, CR0 4YY

Editorial arrangement and Chapters 1 and 9 © Michael W. Eysenck
and David Groome 2015
Chapter 2 © Michael W. Eysenck 2015
Chapter 3 © Vicki Bruce and Yoav Tadmor 2015
Chapter 4 © George Mather 2015
Chapter 5 © Glyn Humphreys 2015
Chapter 6 © Colin MacLeod 2015
Chapter 7 © Howard Eichenbaum 2015
Chapter 8 © Robert Logie 2015
Chapter 10 © James Nairne 2015
Chapter 11 © Fernand Gobet and Peter Lane 2015
Chapter 12 © Klaus Fiedler and Momme von Sydow 2015
Chapter 13 © Ben Newell 2015
Chapter 14 © Trevor Harley and Siobhan MacAndrew 2015
Chapter 15 © Max Coltheart 2015

First published 2015

Library of Congress Control Number: 2014951038

British Library Cataloguing in Publication data

A catalogue record for this book is available from
the British Library

ISBN 978-1-4462-9446-8
ISBN 978-1-4462-9447-5 (pbk)

At SAGE we take sustainability seriously. Most of our products are printed in the UK using FSC papers and boards.
When we print overseas we ensure sustainable papers are used as measured by the Egmont grading system.
We undertake an annual audit to monitor our sustainability.

Contents

About the editors

Michael W. Eysenck is Professorial Fellow at Roehampton University and Emeritus Professor and Honorary Fellow at Royal Holloway University of London. He has published 49 books and approximately 160 articles and book chapters. He has written numerous textbooks on cognitive psychology and his main research area is concerned with the relationship between anxiety and cognition. His hobbies include bridge, croquet, travelling, and walking.

David Groome was Principal Lecturer in the Psychology Department at the University of Westminster, London. He retired in 2011, but retains a research connection with the department. His research interests mainly involve cognition and memory, especially memory suppression and the effects of mood disorders on cognition. He is the author/co-author of six cognitive psychology textbooks. In 2009 he was awarded the BPS Award for Excellence in the Teaching of Psychology. His hobbies include running, travel, dogs, and music. In his spare time he is a keen guitarist, and is still waiting for his big break as a rock star.

About the contributors

Vicki Bruce is Professor of Psychology at Newcastle University. She has held posts at the universities of Nottingham, Stirling, Edinburgh and Newcastle. Her main research has been on face recognition and the broader areas of social perception and visual cognition. Some of her most significant publications have been with Andy Young, with whom she helped to develop a theoretical framework that guided a good deal of research in face recognition in the latter part of the 20th century. They also wrote two books together, the most recent being Face Perception (Bruce and Young, 2012, Psychology Press).

Max Coltheart is Emeritus Professor of Cognitive Science at the Centre for Cognition and its Disorders at Macquarie University, Sydney, Australia. He works on acquired and developmental disorders of reading, and on computational modeling of the human reading system. When that gets to be too straightforward, he returns to his other research interest, which is studying patients with delusional beliefs (see the paper on this in Annual Review of Psychology 2011). When that gets too hard, he returns to his research on reading. And so it goes.

Howard Eichenbaum is a University Professor at Boston University, where he is also the Director of the Center for Memory and Brain and Silvio O. Conte Center for Neuroscience Research. He is a Fellow of the Association for Psychological Science of the American Association for the Advancement of Science and served on the Council of the Society for Neuroscience, the US National Advisory Mental Health Council, and as Chair of the Section on Neuroscience at the American Association for the Advancement of Science. He is editor-in-chief of the journal Hippocampus and has published over 240 research papers, reviews, book chapters and books on the hippocampus and memory. Together with his sons, he is a diehard Red Sox fan.

Klaus Fiedler is chair of social psychology at the University of Heidelberg, Germany. His research interests cover various topics, such as language and social cognition, affect and behavior regulation, judgment and decision making, inductive inference, and the analysis of adaptive cognition from a cognitive-environmental theory perspective. In several journal articles, he has also contributed to methodological problems in behavioral science. Klaus has been an associate editor of several journals, including the Psychological Review, the Journal of Experimental Social Psychology and, presently, the Journal of Experimental Psychology: General.

Fernand Gobet is Professor of Cognitive Psychology at the University of Liverpool. He earned his Ph.D. in psychology in 1992 at the University of Fribourg, Switzerland. After a six-year stay at Carnegie Mellon in Pittsburgh, where he collaborated with Nobel Prize winner Herbert Simon, he held research and teaching positions at the University of Nottingham. In 2003, he moved to Brunel University, London, to take up a Chair in cognitive psychology. He moved to his present post at the University of Liverpool in 2013. His research interests concern the psychology of expertise and talent, computational modelling and the acquisition of language. He is the main architect behind CHREST, one of the small number of cognitive architectures in the world. He has (co-)authored nine books, including Foundations of Cognitive Psychology (2011) and Understanding Expertise (2015).

Trevor Harley is Chair of Cognitive Psychology at the University of Dundee, UK. He has worked on difficult moments in speech production for many years; for example, see The Psychology of Language (Harley, 2014). Finding difficult moments too difficult, Harley now works on sleep and dreams. He still occasionally dabbles in language production, feeling that understanding misunderstanding is key to understanding understanding.

Glyn W. Humphreys is Watts Professor and Head of the Department of Experimental Psychology at the University of Oxford. He has published over 600 papers and 15 books in the field of visual cognition. He was won the Spearman medal, The Cognitive Psychology prize and the President's Award from the British Psychological Society, the Freda Newcombe Award from the British Neuropsychological Society and the Donald Broadbent Prize from the European Society for Cognitive Psychology. He is a Fellow of the Academy of Social Sciences, the Association for Psychological Science and the British Academy. He enjoys all forms of music, as well as running and swimming.

Peter Lane is Senior Lecturer in Computer Science at Hertfordshire University. He has published approximately 50 journal articles and conference papers. His research covers various aspects of machine learning, including cognitive modelling and data mining. His hobbies include astronomy and chess.

Robert Logie is Professor of Human Cognitive Neuroscience, Department of Psychology, University of Edinburgh, UK. His research addresses theoretical and applied questions on human memory, and especially working memory in healthy adults (e.g. Logie, 2011), on cognitive decline in healthy ageing (e.g. Johnson, Logie & Brockmole, 2010) and in neurodegenerative disease (e.g. Parra, Abrahams, Logie et al., 2010), and on the design of digital systems to support human cognition (e.g. Wolters, Niven, Logie, 2014). He is a member of the Centre for Cognitive Ageing and Cognitive Epidemiology at the University of Edinburgh, and Chair (in 2015) of the Psychonomic Society.

Siobhan MacAndrew is a cognitive neuropsychologist at the University of Abertay in Dundee, Scotland. She has carried out research in the fields of amnesia, aphasia, dementia and latterly Parkinson's disease. Since the majority of her time is occupied with teaching students she also carries out research on enhancement in teaching and learning. She has contributed to policy and practice via publications, membership of the British Psychological Society accreditation panel, and roles within the Higher Education Academy Psychology Network. Her hobbies are testing Wellington boots to destruction, digging large holes then refilling them, and reducing the slug population in her garden.

Colin M. MacLeod is Professor and Chair, Department of Psychology, University of Waterloo, Ontario, Canada, where he has been for 11 years. For the 25 preceding years, he was Professor at the University of Toronto, Scarborough. His research is in the domain of memory (e.g., Jonker, Seli, & MacLeod, 2013) and attention (e.g., MacLeod, 1991). Apart from memory and attention, his real expertise is in popular music. He loves to travel, swim, and ski.

George Mather is Professor of Vision Science at the University of Lincoln. He has held post-doctoral fellowships at Reading University, UK; York University, Canada; and University College London, UK. He was appointed to a lectureship at Sussex University in 1984, and was Professor of Experimental Psychology there from 2000 until 2011. Since 2011 he has been Professor of Vision Science at the University of Lincoln, UK, and is currently Director of Research in the College of Social Science. His main research area is visual motion perception, and he has received support for his research from a range of funding sources including MRC, SERC (as was), EPSRC, the Wellcome Trust, and ESRC. He has published 60 papers in scientific journals, and is currently on the editorial board of the journals Proceedings of the Royal Society Series B and Perception/i-Perception.

James S. Nairne is the Reece McGee Distinguished Professor of Psychological Sciences at Purdue University. His research specialty is human memory, particularly how evolutionary selection pressures have shaped the human capacity to remember and forget. He is a past editor of Memory & Cognition, past associate editor for the Psychonomic Bulletin & Review and the Journal of Memory and Language. He is a Fellow of the Association for Psychological Science, the

Psychonomic Society, and the Society of Experimental Psychologists. He is also a recipient of the Excellence in Education Award and the Charles B. Murphy Award for teaching excellence from Purdue University. In 2003 Dr. Nairne was inducted into the Book of Great Teachers at Purdue.

Ben R. Newell is Professor of Cognitive Psychology and Australian Research Council Future Fellow in the School of Psychology at the University of New South Wales. His research interests include judgment and decision-making, with particular interest in the cognitive mechanisms underlying multiple cue judgment, and the implicit/explicit distinction in learning, memory, categorization and decision making. For the last of these see his recent (2014) paper with David Shanks in Behavioral and Brain Sciences – a critical review of the notion that unconscious processes influence our decision making. A second edition of his co-authored book Straight Choices: The Psychology of Decision Making will be published in 2015.

Momme von Sydow is based in the Psychology Department of the University of Heidelberg, Germany. He has earned two doctorates, one in Philosophy and one in Psychology. He has been affiliated to the universities of Bonn, Durham (UK), Göttingen, Berlin (TU) and Heidelberg. He has been in charge of two DFG projects on Bayesian hypothesis testing at the intersection of epistemology and empirical psychology. His main research interests concern knowledge-based models of Bayesian rationality. Since 2011 he has been working at the University of Heidelberg in the group headed by Prof. Dr. Klaus Fiedler, while being responsible for his own research project that forms part of the DFG priority program New Frameworks of Rationality.

Yoav Tadmor is a senior lecturer at the School of Psychology, Newcastle University, UK. His main research interests are human spatial vision, eye movement and the statistical properties of natural images. Before taking a position in Newcastle, he worked with David Tolhurst at Cambridge University on the statistical properties of natural scenes, devising novel paradigms for systematically manipulating image statistics during psychophysical experiments.

Preface

Cognitive psychology occupies an increasingly central place within the whole of psychology. At a conservative estimate, the world's research journals publish tens of thousands of articles on cognitive psychology every year. This is unsurprising given that a cognitive perspective is important in understanding every field of psychology, including individuals' social behaviour (social psychology), changes in behaviour with age during childhood (developmental psychology), and the differences between individuals with mental disorder and healthy individuals (abnormal psychology).

Unsurprisingly, there are numerous textbooks covering the main areas within cognitive psychology (e.g., attention, perception, memory, language, problem solving, decision making). Indeed, both of us have made various contributions to the ever-growing pile of such books! However, what most of these textbooks fail to do (in common with many lecture courses in cognitive psychology) is to provide the historical context necessary for a complete understanding of contemporary cognitive psychology. The central reason for producing this book is to fill that gap. In so doing, we have been extremely fortunate to have persuaded prominent cognitive psychologists to contribute chapters relating to their area of expertise.

But this book is not just about the history of cognitive psychology. We have asked our authors to explain the impact of the classic studies on subsequent research, tracing their influence right up to the present day. So this is a book about the past, the present, and even the future of cognitive research. The truly classic studies are the ones that live on in the work of future generations.

We hope that the readers of this book will agree with us concerning the value of applying an historical perspective to cognitive psychology. We are less sanguine that you will agree with all our choices of classic studies. However, since there have been hundreds of thousands of publications in cognitive psychology over the past 60 years or so, it would a remarkable statistical fluke if there were complete consensus!

Michael W. Eysenck and David Groome

Acknowledgements and thanks

We would like to offer our thanks to Alex Haslam, Alan Slater, and Joanne Smith for their help and advice in planning this book, and to Keri Dickens and Michael Carmichael at Sage for putting the book together. We would also like to offer our special thanks to Alan Baddeley and Endel Tulving, who kindly agreed to let us have their comments on the chapters about their work. We are very pleased to include these comments in the book.

1

An introduction to classic studies in cognitive psychology

Michael W. Eysenck (Roehampton University and Royal Holloway University of London) and David Groome (University of Westminster)

THE CLASSIC PAPERS IN COGNITIVE PSYCHOLOGY

Of the hundreds of thousands of papers and other publications on cognitive psychology published over the years, just a few stand out as 'classics'. These are the studies which shaped the way that cognitive psychology would develop in the years to come. They became classics because they introduced some new theoretical framework or experimental procedure which would influence cognitive theory and research in the future.

This book traces the way in which classic studies in cognition have led us to the very latest research going on today. We have chosen 14 studies which in our opinion deserve to be considered classics, because they provided a new approach to some aspect of cognitive psychology. Each study provided the starting point for a wealth of research in subsequent years. We wanted our book to reflect how the classic studies have influenced today's research, so we selected 14 researchers currently among the leaders in the field relating to each study. We then asked them to write a chapter on the relevant classic study, explaining its influence on subsequent research.

Selecting the classic studies obviously involved a certain amount of personal opinion. We are sure there will be other studies you think should have been included, and probably some we have included you think should have been excluded. However, we tried our best to pick the ones we believe have had the most influence on subsequent research. Of course, many important studies and theories have failed to stand the test of time. Many theories were proposed which eventually proved to be incorrect, and many new procedures were introduced which were popular for a time but which have now outlived their usefulness. Such studies have not been included in this book because they are no longer relevant to current research. We have restricted our list of classics to those having contemporary relevance, the key studies which steered cognitive research in a new direction and which still influence research today.

The first scientific experiments in cognitive psychology were performed in the latter part of the nineteenth century. Early pioneers included Wilhelm Wundt, who opened the world's first laboratory of psychology in Leipzig in 1879 and carried out some of the earliest experiments on perception, and Hermann Ebbinghaus (1885), who carried out the first scientific experiments on memory. Many more experimental studies followed, some of which took cognitive psychology in new directions. The Gestalt group added important findings on the perception of shapes and figures (Wertheimer, 1912), and also carried out early studies of thinking and problem solving (Köhler, 1925). Bartlett (1932) contributed key findings about the significance of meaning and knowledge on memory. All these early contributions could be considered classic studies in their time. However, they are mainly of historical interest as they involved theories and methods no longer particularly relevant to current research. For this reason we have excluded them. As we stated above, the aim of our book is to revisit the classic studies which laid the foundations of today's cognitive research, and then to trace the development of that research right up to the present day.

The study of cognitive psychology was initially held back by the prevailing influence of behaviourism, whose protagonists argued that mental processes could not be directly observed and were not therefore open to scientific study. They concluded that mental processes should be excluded from the discipline of psychology altogether (Watson, 1913; Skinner, 1938). However, we must not exaggerate the baleful influence of behaviourism. Some behaviourists (especially, for example, Tolman, 1932) argued that theorists should focus on *intervening variables* referring to internal processes mediating the effects of stimuli on responses. Of special relevance to cognitive psychology was his notion of 'cognitive map' (Tolman, 1948), according to which even rats store away integrated spatial representations of their environment.

It was not until the 1950s that cognitive psychology began to emerge from the shadow of behaviourism and started to establish itself as a truly scientific discipline within mainstream psychology. A new generation of cognitive psychologists devised ways of investigating cognition and mental processes scientifically. This changed the nature and subject matter of our discipline so dramatically that it has often been called the 'cognitive revolution'. It is mainly from this period that we have chosen our first 'classics'.

THE 14 CLASSIC STUDIES

A number of studies published in the 1950s set the stage for today's cognitive research. One of the first was carried out by **Cherry (1953)**, who devised a new method of investigating how we direct our attention. Colin Cherry used a procedure known as dichotic listening, whereby a set of headphones was used to direct different messages to each ear. The participant attended to one message and ignored the other, but Cherry was mainly interested in the fate of the unattended message. He discovered that very little of the unattended message was perceived, as it was apparently processed at only a very basic level, not extending to meaning. Cherry's study began a whole new approach to the study of selective attention, and this research continues to the present day. We have therefore included Cherry's paper in our list of classic studies, and you will find a detailed account of Cherry's work and its influence on subsequent research in Chapter 2.

Another important study of this period was that of **Gibson (1950)**, who was interested in the way we extract information from our surroundings. James Gibson argued that the perceptual system is capable of detecting patterns in the incoming sensory array, which enable the individual to grasp the nature and potential uses of objects in the world around us in the absence of mental interpretation. Gibson's view of perception therefore focused on 'bottom-up' processes, which contrasted with the previously popular view that the organism can only make sense of the world by processing the new input in a schema-driven or 'top-down' fashion. His approach was also strikingly original in that he argued that the main function of perception is to move around the environment and to respond to the actions of others. This differed radically from previous empirical approaches in which participants were required to keep their heads still while visual stimuli were presented. Gibson's study has become a classic, making a lasting impact on the study of perception. Gibson's study and its subsequent influence are discussed in detail in Chapter 3.

Marr (1982) proposed a highly influential theory of object recognition based on a computational approach. He assumed that the brain recognises objects by subjecting them to an information-processing mechanism similar (but not necessarily identical) to the processing carried out by a computer. Marr suggested that a new sensory input is subjected to several different stages of processing and analysis, with each stage producing an increasingly detailed and complete representation of the stimulus. Marr's theory was strongly influenced by analogy with computer programs, and has led to extensive research on the computerised simulation of object recognition. You will find an account of Marr's study in Chapter 4.

Goodale and Milner (1992) demonstrated that perceptual processing actually appears to involve two separate processing mechanisms analysing different aspects of the same visual input. They studied a brain-damaged patient unable to identify objects visually, but who retained a relatively unimpaired ability to identify their location. From this finding, Goodale and Milner concluded that there are two separate pathways from the visual cortex, each having different functions. The ventral pathway (the one damaged in their patient) appears to be concerned with object identification and shape, while the dorsal pathway is concerned with spatial location. Goodale and Milner's study is described in Chapter 5.

Some studies were not recognised as classics when published and so remained largely ignored until rediscovered by later researchers. Such a study was that of **Stroop (1935)**, whose findings received little attention until the 1960s, when his work was finally recognised as a classic demonstration of some basic cognitive processes which had then begun to attract interest. Stroop's experiments had shown that it takes longer to name the ink colour of a word if that word is the name of a different colour (e.g., the word 'blue' written in red ink). Although this finding was largely disregarded at the time, later researchers would return to the

'Stroop effect' (as it became known) because it provided an excellent example of automatic processing (of the word meaning) as well as demonstrating interference between rival inputs. Today, the Stroop effect is used widely as a measure of both automaticity and interference, and consequently Stroop's paper has finally become a classic study after lying dormant for some 30 years. Stroop's study is discussed in Chapter 6.

Our understanding of memory and amnesia underwent a dramatic change with the publication of a paper by **Scoville and Milner (1957)** about a severely amnesic individual known as 'HM'. HM differed from patients studied previously in that his amnesia was caused by a surgical procedure performed on his temporal lobes. As a result, the date of onset of HM's amnesia was precisely known, as was the location of his brain lesions. William Scoville and Brenda Milner discovered that HM had been unable to create and store any new memories since surgery in 1953. However, his ability to retrieve memories from before this date seemed relatively unimpaired. Scoville and Milner therefore concluded that the main impairment suffered by HM was an inability to encode and store new memories, and showed this was associated with lesions in the medial temporal lobe, especially the hippocampus. Scoville and Milner also noted that HM's short-term memory remained unimpaired. Although subsequent research has revealed a rather more complex situation in studies of both HM and other amnesic patients, Scoville and Milner's paper remains a classic and a vital turning point in the study of amnesia. Their paper (and its impact on subsequent research) is discussed in Chapter 7.

Studies of amnesic patients like HM suggested that short-term memory and long-term memory involve quite separate mechanisms, though it was not entirely clear at that stage why there was a need for a separate memory system for storing memories over very short time periods. **Baddeley and Hitch (1974)** performed experiments suggesting that short-term memory actually operates as a mental workspace, which they called 'working memory'. Their study also provided evidence that working memory contains several different components, notably the central executive and memory loops whose function is to retain information very briefly to allow it to be processed. The working memory model proposed by Alan Baddeley and Graham Hitch is discussed and evaluated in Chapter 8.

A study by **Tulving (1972)** suggested that long-term memory could also be divided into sub-components, namely semantic memory (which stores knowledge and facts) and episodic memory (which stores memory for specific events). Endel Tulving demonstrated convincingly (and for the first time) that semantic and episodic memory exhibit different characteristics and have different processing requirements. However, the precise relationship between episodic and semantic memory is still not completely clear. In spite of their different characteristics, it is assumed they must overlap and interact to a considerable degree. Tulving's work on the distinction between episodic and semantic memory is discussed in Chapter 9.

Another important memory study was performed by **Tulving and Thomson (1973)**, who showed that successful retrieval of an episodic memory depends on the degree of match between the information in the retrieval cue and that in the stored trace. This became known as the Encoding Specificity Principle (ESP), and it remains one of the most important theories of how memories are retrieved. ESP can provide an explanation for a number of well-established cognitive phenomena, such as transfer-appropriate processing and context-dependent memory. Tulving and Thomson's study is described in Chapter 10.

Another aspect of cognition involves the study of thinking and problem solving. **Newell, Shaw, and Simon (1958)** pioneered the use of computer simulation to test out theories of human problem solving. They argued that programs enabling a computer to solve problems by using a sequence of information-processing operations suggested possible models of human information-processing and problem solving. Newell et al.'s computer simulation approach was to become influential in many fields of cognitive psychology and is explained in Chapter 11.

Tversky and Kahneman (1974) investigated the strategies used by human beings when making judgements. They discovered people do not always make judgements rationally, as a computer might, but tend to make errors caused by a failure to consider all the relevant evidence. Tversky and Kahneman showed that when people make judgements they tend to apply well-tried strategies and heuristics which have apparently worked in the past, but which are actually prone to systematic biases. These findings have been enormously influential not only in the field of cognition but also in many other fields of psychology. Tversky and Kahneman's study and its subsequent influence is covered in Chapter 12.

In a later study, **Kahneman and Tversky (1979)** demonstrated further biases which occur when human beings make decisions. For example, when the probability of success is very low (e.g., when playing the National Lottery), people tend to be more risk-seeking over possible gains, but more risk-averse over possible losses. However, with high outcome probabilities this situation is reversed, and people tend to be more risk-seeking over possible losses. These findings formed the basis of Kahneman and Tversky's prospect theory, which has proved to be of great value not only to cognitive psychologists but also to economists making financial judgements. This work earned Kahneman the Nobel Prize for Economics in 2002, and it is discussed in Chapter 13.

The use of language is another important function which has interested cognitive psychologists, and the study of language impairment has proved to be particularly informative. **Chomsky (1957)** initiated a completely new approach to the study of language. Previous theories of language acquisition, based on the tenets of behaviourism, assumed that language was acquired by a process of reinforcement. Chomsky showed that reinforcement would be quite inadequate for the learning of complex grammar, and he argued that language acquisition depends upon an innate ability to generate speech and linguistic output from a set of grammatical rules. This theory was enormously influential, and it led to the founding of a new science of psycholinguistics. Chomsky's study is discussed in Chapter 14.

The study of language has also benefited greatly from research on language disorder, and one highly influential early study was that of **Marshall and Newcombe (1973)**. They studied a large number of cases of acquired dyslexia, and concluded that they did not all arise from the same cause. Marshall and

Newcombe realised there were several distinct subtypes of acquired dyslexia, and they constructed a model explaining each subtype as arising from impairments to different components of the model. This approach would subsequently be adopted by many other researchers, and it provided the basis of the new science of cognitive neuropsychology. Marshall and Newcombe's study is described in Chapter 15.

CLASSIC STUDIES: GENERAL LESSONS

There are obvious dangers in drawing general conclusions from the limited sample size (N = 14) of classic studies discussed in this book. However, we believe it is of interest to consider various factors often thought to be relevant to outstanding research.

YOUTHFUL CREATIVITY

Conventional wisdom has it that the most outstanding research (perhaps especially in the hard sciences) is produced by young researchers when creativity is maximal. Famous supporting evidence is provided by Albert Einstein's initial theory of relativity, produced when he was only 26 years old.

Jones and Weinberg (2011) discovered that youthful creativity has apparently become less important than it used to be. They focused on researchers in physics, chemistry, and medicine who won the Nobel Prize before 1905 or after 1985. In the earlier period, the mean ages at which these researchers produced their most outstanding research was 37, 40, and 45, respectively. In the later period, however, the mean ages were 50, 46, and 45, respectively. Thus, there has been a dramatic increase averaging over 8 years in the age at which outstanding research is produced.

Why has the age of outstanding scientific achievement increased? First, the age at which researchers obtain their highest degree has increased considerably. Jones and Weinberg (2011) found that the increased time researchers needed to acquire foundational knowledge predicted the age at which they produced their best research. Second, theorists had their greatest achievements 4.4 years earlier than empiricists, and the percentage of outstanding research that is theoretical has declined.

We turn belatedly to the ages at which cognitive psychologists produced their classic research. The mean age, based on all the authors of each study, was 40.4 years, a higher figure than many would have predicted. In fact, the figure increases to 41.6 years (which rounds up to 42) when we consider only the central researchers and not their co-authors.

During preparation of this chapter, we chanced upon a study by Franses (2014) on the age at which great artists since Goya produced their most outstanding paintings. By coincidence, the mean age was 42 years. Perhaps Douglas Adams (1979) was right when he claimed that 42 was 'the Answer to the Ultimate Question of Life, the Universe, and Everything'!

Most of our classic studies involved theoretical and empirical contributions and so we cannot neatly separate out theorists and empiricists. However, those whose contributions were primarily empirical were slightly younger than the mean age of the researchers as a whole. There was thus no support for Jones and Weinberg's (2011) findings for other scientific disciplines.

As discussed above, Jones and Weinberg (2011) found that the age at which researchers produced their best research had increased over time. We divided our sample into classic studies carried out in the 1950s or earlier (N = 5) and those from the 1970s or later (N = 9) (strangely, there were no studies from the 1960s). Contrary to Jones and Weinberg (2011), the mean age for the earlier period was approximately 1.4 years older.

Finally, we divided the classic studies into broad research areas (perception and attention; memory; language; and thinking and problem solving). The numbers in each category are very small. However, for what it is worth, memory researchers had the oldest mean age (44.2 years) and language researchers were the youngest (mean = 37.7 years).

ORIGINALITY: FIRST VERSUS SECOND MOVERS

We might assume that outstanding research should be almost totally original. This is analogous to the notion of first-mover advantage in economics and marketing. Alternatively, we might assume that outstanding research often involves developing previous theoretical ideas, analogous to the notion of second-mover advantage. Note, however, the notion of 'originality' is somewhat subjective and there is no absolute distinction between first movers and second movers.

When we consider our classic studies, the studies from the 1950s and earlier tend to correspond more obviously to the notion of first mover than those from the 1970s onwards. We have five studies from the 1950s: Gibson (1950); Cherry (1953); Scoville and Milner (1957); Newell et al. (1958) and Chomsky (1957, 1959). In all cases, their studies owed relatively little to previous research or theorising. Gibson discovered the crucial importance of motion to visual perception, and Cherry discovered several of the key properties of selective auditory attention, a topic that had been almost ignored beforehand. Scoville and Milner found that the brain areas of key importance to long-term memory were much more circumscribed than previously believed. Newell et al. showed for the first time that computational modelling could be used to enhance our understanding of human problem solving. Chomsky showed that previous approaches to language (especially behaviourism) were woefully inadequate. He went on to provide an original and powerful theoretical analysis of the processes involved in language.

The situation is different with several studies from the 1970s and afterwards. Consider Tulving's (1972) classic study on the distinction between episodic and semantic memory. This distinction had been proposed by several psychologists and philosophers considerably earlier than 1972 (see Tulving, 1983). In our opinion, however, that does not detract from the importance of Tulving's contribution because he was the first psychologist to develop the distinction and base a programme of experimental research on it.

Kahneman and Tversky's (1979) theoretical account of decision making under risk has deservedly been hugely influential. However, their prospect theory was based on the earlier expected utility theory and incorporated some of its assumptions. Their study is a classic because they eliminated most inadequacies of the previous theory and added powerful new theoretical assumptions.

Another example of a classic study built on a previous influential theory was the one by Goodale and Milner (1992). Mishkin, Ungerleider, and Macko (1983) put forward a theory in which they argued that object and spatial perception depend on separate cortical pathways. Goodale and Milner developed and extended this theory substantially and reported exciting new empirical findings.

Baddeley and Hitch's (1974) working memory model was much influenced by previous conceptualisations of short-term memory, especially that of Atkinson and Shiffrin (1968). However, their model represented a substantial development of earlier theories and involved the crucial insight that short-term memory plays an important role in numerous non-memory tasks (e.g., problem solving, language comprehension).

Overall, it is arguable that nine of our classic studies (Stroop, 1935; Gibson, 1950; Cherry, 1953; Chomsky, 1957, 1959; Scoville & Milner, 1957; Newell et al., 1958; Marshall & Newcombe, 1973; Tversky & Kahneman, 1974; Marr, 1982) illustrate first-mover advantage. In contrast, five classic studies (Tulving, 1972; Tulving & Thomson, 1973; Baddeley & Hitch, 1974; Kahneman & Tversky, 1979; Goodale & Milner, 1992) are examples of second-mover advantage. First-mover studies were published on average in 1960 whereas second-mover studies were published on average in 1978. This is unsurprising because the number of pre-existing influential theories that can be used as the basis for developing major new theories is almost bound to increase over time.

MAJOR APPROACHES

There are four major approaches to understanding human cognition (Groome, 2014; Eysenck & Keane, 2015). First, there is experimental cognitive psychology, which is the traditional approach based on conducting laboratory studies on healthy participants. Second, there is cognitive neuropsychology, which involves laboratory studies on brain-damaged individuals. Third, there is cognitive neuroscience, which involves obtaining measures of brain activity as well as behaviour under various task conditions. Fourth, there is computational cognitive science, which involves constructing computer models that mimic the behaviour of human participants.

It seems plausible to assume that much outstanding research would occur when researchers are among the first to use a given major approach in a particular research area. That is clearly one way in which new insights and original findings can be obtained.

The above notion is at least partially applicable to several of our classic studies. Three (Scoville & Milner, 1957; Marshall & Newcombe, 1973; Goodale & Milner, 1992) owe much of their classic status to findings obtained from one or more brain-damaged patients and thus fall within cognitive neuropsychology. Two others (Newell et al., 1958; Marr, 1982) were the first (or among the first) systematic attempts to develop systematic theoretical accounts in their respective research areas using computational modelling.

That leaves us with the dog that didn't bark in the night-time – cognitive neuroscience. In spite of the dramatic increase in research in cognitive neuroscience, we did not think any cognitive neuroscience studies deserved the status of classic. There are two likely explanations. First, cognitive neuroscience is a more recent approach than the others, having only been used extensively since the 1990s, and it may simply take longer for classic studies in cognitive neuroscience to emerge. Second, although cognitive neuroscience has proved increasingly important in testing pre-existing theories, it has as yet led to the development of very few new theories. This is probably the case because (unlike cognitive neuropsychology), cognitive neuroscience has rarely produced surprising and dramatic findings.

FALSIFICATION, GENERALITY, AND GRANULARITY

Philosophers of science have long argued about the nature of scientific progress (Okasha, 2002). Karl Popper argued that a scientific theory should be falsifiable, that is, it should make definite predictions that can (at least in principle) be shown to be incorrect. This leads to the notion that theories should be rejected when falsifying evidence is obtained.

Theorists agreeing with Popper would presumably develop relatively specific or narrow theories low in granularity or detail. The reason is that such theories would typically be harder to falsify than more ambitious theories.

Popper is correct in arguing that we would have little confidence in a theory whose predictions were consistently falsified. However, Popper's approach is oversimplified. Lakatos (2001) proposed a preferable approach. According to him, every great scientific theory is immediately engulfed in an 'ocean of anomalies' (p. 172). Thus, virtually all theories have been falsified. What, then, determines which theories should be retained? According to Lakatos, two factors are crucial. First, most theorists add auxiliary hypotheses to address problems within their theory. With theories that should be retained, these auxiliary hypotheses are progressive or productive, that is, they enhance the theory's predictive power. Sadly, it often takes a long time before it is clear whether a theory is progressive or degenerative. Second, theories should be retained until they are superseded by a superior theory.

What light do our classic studies shed on the above issues? First, most of the theories contained in these studies were known to be false at the time they were proposed, which is much more in line with Lakatos than Popper. For example, it was always improbable that all of visual perception can be understood in terms of two independent visual processing systems (Goodale & Milner). Another example is Baddeley and Hitch's working memory model. Active haptic and kinaesthetic processing can occur within working memory, but both forms of processing were omitted (and continue to be omitted) from their model.

Second, there is the issue of generality. It is often argued that cognitive psychology is plagued by paradigm specificity (e.g., Meiser, 2011), meaning empirical research and theorising are excessively focused on specific paradigms or experimental tasks. Consider research on visual search. The typical paradigm requires participants to detect a target stimulus presented at a *random* location within a visual display containing several distractors. Excessive use of this paradigm led theorists to ignore completely the most important determinant of target-detect time – the *predictability* of the visual environment. If you are looking for a pedestrian in a street scene, he/she is far more likely to be located on the pavement or street than halfway up a building or in the sky (Ehinger, Hidalgo-Sotelo, Torraiba, & Oliva, 2009).

In spite of the above example, several of our classic studies contain very general theories. For example, Marr (1982) identified the key processes involved in object recognition, Tulving and Thomson (1973) indicated how retrieval from long-term memory occurs, Baddeley and Hitch (1974) proposed a comprehensive theory of short-term memory, Kahneman and Tversky (1979) theorised about risky decision making, Goodale and Milner (1992) proposed an ambitious theory about visual perception, and Chomsky (1957, 1959) provided an overarching theory of language.

Third, there is the issue of granularity or level of detail. It is often assumed (especially by computational cognitive scientists) that theories in cognitive psychology should be fully explicit and detailed in their assumptions and predictions. In fact, that is often an unnecessarily stringent requirement because it makes theories excessively susceptible to falsification. For example, Baddeley and Hitch in their working memory model were deliberately vague about the precise nature of the central executive, which remains the case to a lesser extent 40 years later. Tversky and Kahneman (1974) identified several important heuristics and biases but did not spell out precisely when each one would be in use. Goodale and Milner (1992) did not specify all the characteristics of their two visual processing systems or the details of their interactions, and Tulving (1972) did not identify all the differences between episodic and semantic memory or how they interact.

In sum, at the risk of oversimplification, the most successful theories are those that are *productive* (i.e., leading to much important research) rather than those that have avoided *falsification*. Successful theories also tend to be general in scope and not especially granular.

CONCLUSIONS

We conclude with two final thoughts. First, as you may have been thinking, we probably should have referred earlier to the 'great person' hypothesis – the notion that outstanding research depends on individual genius rather than the context in which research is conducted. The a priori probability was extremely low that one psychologist (Tulving) would account for two of the 14 classic studies and that a team of two psychologists (Kahneman and Tversky) would account for two more.

Finally, of the 20 different names among the authors of the 14 classic studies, only two (Brenda Milner and Freda Newcombe) are female. All the evidence suggests that there would be a much higher proportion of female researchers in a future edition of *Classic studies in cognitive psychology* in, say, 2030. That is our prediction (and hope).

REFERENCES

Adams, D. (1979). *The hitchhiker's guide to the galaxy*. London: Pan.

Atkinson, R. C., & Shiffrin, R. M. (1968). Human memory: A proposed system and its control processes. In K. W. Spence & J. T. Spence (Eds.), *The psychology of learning and motivation* (Vol. 2). London: Academic Press.

Baddeley, A. D., & Hitch, G. J. (1974). Working memory. In G. H. Bower (Ed.), *Recent advances in learning and motivation* (Vol. 8, pp. 47–89). New York: Academic Press.

Bartlett, F. C. (1932). *Remembering: An experimental and social study*. Cambridge, UK: Cambridge University Press.

Cherry, E. C. (1953). Some experiments on the recognition of speech with one and two ears. *Journal of the Acoustical Society of America*, 25, 975–979.

Chomsky, N. (1957). *Syntactic structures*. The Hague/Paris: Mouton.

Chomsky, N. (1959). Reviews: 'Verbal behavior by B. F. Skinner'. *Language*, 35, 26–58.

Ebbinghaus, H. (1885/1913). *Über dan Gedächtnis*. Leipzig, Germany: Dunker. Trans. H. Ruyer & C. E. Bussenius (1913). *Memory*, New York: Teachers College, Columbia University.

Ehinger, K. A., Hidalgo-Sotelo, B., Torraiba, A., & Oliva, A. (2009). Modelling search for people in 900 scenes: A combined source model of eye guidance. *Visual Cognition*, 17, 945–978.

Eysenck, M. W., & Keane, M. T. (2015). *Cognitive psychology: A student's handbook* (7th edn). Hove, UK: Psychology Press.

Franses, P. H. (2014). When do painters make their best work? *Creativity Research Journal*, 25, 457–462.

Gibson, J. J. (1950). *The perception of the visual world*. Boston, MA: Houghton Mifflin.

Goodale, M. A., & Milner, A. D. (1992). Separate visual pathways for perception and action. *Trends in Neuroscience*, 15, 22–25.

Groome, D. (2014). *An introduction to cognitive psychology* (3rd edn). Hove, UK: Psychology Press.

Jones, B. F., & Weinberg, B. A. (2011). Age dynamics in scientific creativity. *Proceedings of the National Association of Sciences*, 108 (47), 18910–18914.

Kahneman, D., & Tversky, A. (1979). Prospect theory: An analysis of decision under risk. *Econometrica*, 47, 263–291.

Köhler, W. (1925). *The mentality of apes* (trans. Ella Winter). New York: Harcourt, Brace and World.

Lakatos, I. (2001). *The methodology of scientific research programmes*. Cambridge, UK: Cambridge University Press.

Marr, D. (1982). *Vision: A computational investigation into the human representation and processing of visual information*. San Francisco, CA: W. H. Freeman.

Marshall, N., & Newcombe, F. (1973). Patterns of paralexia: A psycholinguistic approach. *Journal of Psycholinguistic Research*, 2, 175–199.

McClelland, J. L., & Rumelhart, D. E. (1981). An interactive activation model of context effects in letter perception. Part 1. An account of basic findings. *Psychological Review*, 88, 375–407.

Meiser, T. (2011). Much pain, little gain? Paradigm-specific models and methods in experimental psychology. *Perspectives on Psychological Science*, 6, 183–191.

Mishkin, M., Ungerleider, L. G., & Macko, K. A. (1983). Object vision and spatial vision – 2 cortical pathways. *Trends in Neurosciences*, 6, 414–417.

Newell, A., Shaw, J. C., & Simon, H. A. (1958). Elements of a theory of human problem solving. *Psychological Review*, 65, 151–166.

Okasha, S. (2002). *Philosophy of science: A very short introduction*. Oxford: Oxford University Press.

Scoville, W. B., & Milner, B. (1957). Loss of recent memory after bilateral hippocampal lesions. *Journal of Neurology, Neurosurgery & Psychiatry*, 20, 11–21.

Skinner, B. F. (1938). *The behaviour of organisms*. New York: Appleton-Century-Crofts.

Stroop, J. R. (1935). Studies of interference in serial verbal reactions. *Journal of Experimental Psychology*, 18, 643–662.

Tolman, E. C. (1932). *Purposive behaviour in animals and men*. New York: Century.

Tolman, E. C. (1948). Cognitive maps in rats and men. *Psychological Review*, 55, 189–208.

Tulving, E. (1972). Episodic and semantic memory. In E. Tulving & W. Donaldson (Eds.), *Organisation of memory*. London: Academic Press.

Tulving, E. (1983). *Elements of episodic memory*. Oxford: Clarendon Press.

Tulving, E., & Thomson, D. M. (1973). Encoding specificity and retrieval processes in episodic memory. *Psychological Review*, 80, 352–373.

Tversky, A., & Kahneman, D. (1974). Judgment under uncertainty: Heuristics and biases. *Science*, 185, 1124–1130.

Watson, J. B. (1913). Psychology as the behaviourist views it. *Psychological Review*, 20, 158–177.

Wertheimer, M. (1912). Experimentelle Studien über das Sehen von Bewegung. *Zeitschrift für Psychologie*, 61, 161–265.

2

Attention: Beyond Cherry's (1953) cocktail party problem

Michael W. Eysenck (Roehampton University and Royal Holloway University of London)

BACKGROUND TO THE CLASSIC STUDY

It is crucially important for psychologists to understand attention, as it is the starting point for all subsequent cognitive processing. So far as everyday life is concerned, we all spend much of our time engaged in selective attention, which involves choosing which of the myriad stimuli presented to our senses to attend to. This topic was recognised as being of major significance by the American psychologist William James (1890), who was right on that issue as on so many others.

Research on selective attention continued throughout the first half of the twentieth century. However, this research was limited in scope, as can be seen from a perusal of Woodworth's (1938) highly influential textbook on experimental psychology. He devoted only one chapter out of 30 to attention and considers topics such as the span of apprehension or attention span (the number of objects that can be assessed accurately after a brief presentation) and distractibility. Most of this research involved the visual modality and there was scarcely any mention of selective attention. Overall, it appeared that attention had not been the focus of much research in the almost half-century since William James emphasised its importance.

The dominance of behaviourism played a part in inhibiting researchers from exploring the topic of attention. Why was that the case? Basic behaviourism involved an emphasis on the need to be 'scientific', by which was meant a focus on observable stimuli and responses. The behaviourists had a problem with the concept of 'attention' because it was clearly neither a stimulus nor a response, coupled with the difficulty in measuring it with any precision. This may explain why researchers focused on simple tasks such as span of apprehension and decided not to explore the internal mechanisms underlying selective attention.

It was probably an advantage for Colin Cherry (1914–1979) that he had not trained as a psychologist and so was probably oblivious of the constraints that behaviourism imposed on psychological research. He had a range of professional interests, most of which were of a practical nature. He was a trained electronics engineer and was involved in radar research during the Second World War. When he became a Professor at Imperial College London in 1958, his Chair was in Telecommunications.

There are some interesting parallels between Cherry's experience on the one hand and the early career of Donald Broadbent on the other hand. Broadbent also made substantial contributions to our understanding of selective attention in the 1950s (these contributions are discussed more fully later). Much of Broadbent's interest in attention arose from considering the difficulties that radar operators had during the Second World War in communicating with several pilots at the same time. These difficulties were compounded because the pilots' voices were all heard over the same loudspeaker (Driver, 2001).

Around 1950, Colin Cherry became interested in what is generally known as the 'cocktail party problem' (a phrase that he himself came up with). Suppose you find yourself at a cocktail party (such parties are sadly less common now than in the past) with many people talking loudly at the same time. What is striking (and in some ways surprising) is that it is often possible for individuals to 'tune into' one person's voice and more or less ignore other people's. It is tempting to think that one reason why Cherry decided to focus on such a 'real world' problem was because his background was in solving such problems rather than being confined to the artificiality of the experimental laboratory.

DETAILED DESCRIPTION OF THE CLASSIC STUDY

Colin Cherry decided to investigate the cocktail party problem. This is a more complex and important problem than you might imagine. We can see its complexity in the finding that experts have found it extremely difficult to devise automatic speech recognition systems that can successfully separate out one voice from several concurrent voices (Shen, Olive, & Jones, 2008).

Cherry reported the findings of his initial experiments on this problem in his classic study (Cherry, 1953). His research was relatively straightforward. However, it was hugely important because he was addressing fundamental issues. First, what are the differences between two concurrent auditory messages that are used by listeners to select one and ignore the other? Second, what information do listeners typically extract from the message to which they are not attending?

Cherry (1953) started by presenting two messages recorded by the same speaker on one tape so that both ears received precisely the same input. The participant was instructed to repeat one of the messages (i.e., to shadow it) while ignoring the other simultaneous message and he was permitted to play the tape as often as necessary to perform the task. The most striking finding of this experiment was that the participant found it incredibly difficult to perform the task, and would often shut his eyes to enhance his concentration. Some phrases had to be listened to up to 20 times before he identified them correctly. Some errors were made (no precise numbers are provided!), most of which were words that had a reasonably high probability within the context of the message. Thus, top-down processes played a role.

In the next experiment, Cherry (1953) made it even harder for the listener to discriminate between the two auditory messages. What was done was to present two concurrent auditory messages in the same voice to both ears with each message consisting of a string of unrelated clichés (e.g., 'I am happy to be here today'; 'We are on the brink of ruin'). The listener typically produced complete clichés in what he said; the problem was that he produced comparable numbers of clichés from each message and so showed no ability to distinguish between the two messages. The reason why performance was even worse in this experiment than the previous one was that there were no thematic differences between the two messages. This meant that the listener could not use top-down processes based on knowledge of the theme of the attended message to facilitate selective auditory attention.

Cherry (1953) then moved on to a series of experiments in which two auditory messages in the same voice were presented concurrently. Now, however, one message was presented only to the left ear and the other message only to the right ear. Again, the listener had to repeat back or shadow one of the messages. This is the dichotic listening task and it has been used extensively ever since.

Cherry (1953) was impressed by the substantial differences in the listener's performance by this apparently modest change in what was presented to him. In his own words, 'The subject experiences no difficulty in listening to either speech at will and "rejecting" the unwanted one' (p. 977). However, Cherry was most impressed by the other main finding that emerged from this experiment: 'If the subject is subsequently asked to repeat anything of what he heard in his other (rejected-message) ear, he can say little about it at all' (p. 978).

This last finding prompted Cherry to carry out further experiments in which two auditory messages were presented, one to each ear, with instructions to repeat or shadow the one presented to the right ear. In one experiment, normal male-spoken English was presented on the unattended message, as in previous research. Cherry found that listeners did not realise when the unattended message was in German. Reversed speech was either identified as normal speech or as speech having something odd about it. Listeners in all of these experiments failed to identify any word or phrase presented in the unattended message.

The listeners' performance was better in other experiments. For example, they nearly always identified when the unattended message was in a female voice (the attended message was in a male voice). In addition, they always detected when a 400 cycles per second pure tone was presented on the unattended message.

The overall pattern of findings obtained by Cherry (1953) seemed reasonably clear-cut. Listeners were very effective at using physical differences between the two messages to repeat back or shadow one message. They were remarkably poor at detecting words in the unattended message but were very good at detecting major physical differences between the unattended and attended messages.

A complication arose in another of Cherry's experiments. Listeners were instructed to repeat back or shadow the message presented in a male voice to their right ear. Unknown to them, the identical message was also presented to the left ear at a variable delay to the same message presented to the right ear. Nearly all the participants detected at some point that the message on the unattended ear was the same as that on the attended ear. The time delay of the unattended message compared to the attended message at which detection occurred was typically between two and six seconds. This finding is surprising in that listeners in the previous experiments never identified any words at all in the unattended message. It suggests that there is continuing activation of words presented in the attended message which facilitates their subsequent detection in the unattended message.

There is a final point that needs to be made about Cherry's study. It is very strong in terms of its empirical contribution to selective attention. However, what is perhaps surprising is that Cherry had relatively little to say at a theoretical level. For example, consider the role of top-down processes based on expectations and predictions. Cherry was well aware that some of his findings (e.g., errors involving words highly probable in context; clichés produced rapidly in their entirety) indicated that top-down processes had a role in selective auditory attention. However, he failed to address important theoretical issues, such as the ways in which bottom-up and top-down processes interact to determine what the listener hears.

IMPACT OF THE CLASSIC STUDY

Cherry's (1953) classic study has had an enormous impact. According to Google Scholar, this article has been cited over 2,700 times, which is an exceptionally high figure. I also used *Web of Science* to see the number of citations for the topic of the cocktail party problem. The mean number of citations per annum has been between 350 and 400 in recent years – very few research topics attract that level of interest well over 50 years after their publication.

Cherry's research had a strong influence on the theorising of the British psychologist Donald Broadbent, who was one of the pivotal figures (possibly the *most* pivotal) in the rise of cognitive psychology. As we will see, his filter theory (proposed in the late 1950s), was built squarely on Cherry's findings. Remember that Cherry found that selective attention to one out of two concurrent auditory messages was most efficient when there were clear physical differences between them (e.g., pitch, apparent source). His other major finding was that listeners apparently noticed only simple physical features (e.g., pitch) of the ignored message.

Broadbent's (1958) filter theory incorporated the important insight that the above two findings are related (Driver, 2001). In essence, he argued that two major stages are involved in perception. First, the physical properties of auditory stimuli (e.g., pitch, sound location) are extracted in parallel for all stimuli. Second, the more 'abstract' properties of auditory stimuli (e.g., their meaning) are processed in a serial fashion. The second stage has limited capacity, and so there is a filter which allows only stimuli possessing a given physical property to enter.

It would be difficult to overestimate the influence that Broadbent's filter theory has had. Here are just a few examples. First, Broadbent's theory was one of the earliest attempts to develop an information-processing approach in which there are several successive processing stages. That notion became hugely influential in the following decades and remains so (Eysenck & Keane, 2010).

Second, the limited capacity that Broadbent associated with the second stage of processing overlaps with notions of the limited capacity of short-term memory and the limits of central processing units in computers. Attempts to assess the limited capacity of short-term memory were made during the 1950s. The most famous of such attempts was by Miller (1956), who referred to 'the magic number seven, plus or minus two'.

Third, as Driver (2001) pointed out, numerous subsequent cognitive theorists followed Broadbent in arguing that an initial parallel 'pre-attentive' stage of processing is followed by a serial 'attentive' stage. This is especially clear with respect to research on consciousness. According to global workspace theory (Baars, 1997), initial processing of stimuli involves numerous special-purpose unconscious processors operating in parallel. After that, conscious experience is associated with integrated or synchronous brain activity across several different brain areas. There is much support for this theoretical position (e.g., Melloni, Molina, Pena, Torres, Singer, & Rodriguez, 2007).

We have seen that there is a very direct historical trail from Cherry to Broadbent. The same is true if we consider Broadbent and Treisman. Anne Treisman was one of Broadbent's PhD students, and she went on to make several outstanding theoretical contributions to our understanding of selective attention. Of particular relevance here, Treisman's (1964) attenuation theory represented a revision and extension of Broadbent's filter theory.

It is an interesting historical curiosity that research on selective attention in the 1950s was predominantly on auditory attention whereas ever since it has mostly been on visual attention. Of course, the dominance of auditory attention in the 1950s owed a substantial amount to Cherry's research. The switch to research on visual attention occurred in part because it is easier to exert precise experimental control over visual stimuli than auditory ones (e.g., in terms of exact timing). It also occurred because for most humans vision is the dominant sense.

Cherry's research and Broadbent's theorising had a strong impact on visual attention research in the 1960s. For example, consider research using the Sperling paradigm (Sperling, 1960). Several letters (e.g., four rows of three letters) are presented in an array, followed by full or partial report. Full report requires participants to report all the letters in the array, whereas partial report involves presentation of a cue, indicating that only a subset of the letters (e.g., the bottom row) has to be reported. Participants typically perform better in the latter condition than the former one, suggesting that the rapid decay of information about the letters in the array impairs performance in the former condition. Of most relevance with respect to Cherry's research, selective report is generally better when relevant and irrelevant letters differ in terms of some physical property (e.g., colour) than when they differ in a more abstract property (e.g., digit versus letter) (Von Wright, 1970). This finding clearly resembles the findings Cherry obtained with auditory stimuli.

One of the most striking findings reported by Cherry (1953) was that selective auditory attention can be extremely efficient. It was only many years later that cognitive neuroscientists began to uncover evidence of brain mechanisms associated with this high level of efficiency. Much of what happens within the auditory system is a 'winner-takes-all' situation in which the processing of the attended auditory input (the winner) suppresses the brain activity of the other auditory input or inputs (Kurt, Deutscher, Crook, Ohl, Budinger, Moeller, et al., 2008). This was shown clearly by Horton, D'Zmura, and Srinivasan (2013) in a study in which listeners were instructed to attend to the auditory message on one ear and to ignore the message presented to the other ear. There was enhanced brain activity associated with the attended message combined with reduced or suppressed activity associated with the unattended message.

Impressive evidence of the efficiency of selective auditory attention was reported recently by Mesgarani and Chang (2012). They used multi-electrode arrays implanted within the auditory cortex that allowed them to record activity there in a very direct fashion. Listeners were presented with two messages presented to the same ear but with instructions to attend to only one message. One message was in a male voice and the other in a female voice to facilitate discrimination of the two messages.

What did Mesgarani and Chang find? Responses within the auditory cortex revealed 'the salient spectral [based on sound frequencies] and temporal features of the attended speaker, as if subjects were listening to that speaker alone' (Mesgarani & Chang, 2012, p. 233). Cherry would not have been surprised by these findings.

CRITIQUE OF THE CLASSIC STUDY

As is the case with virtually all research in psychology, Cherry's pioneering study had various limitations, some of which I mentioned previously. For example, researchers nowadays would find it very difficult to publish psychological experiments with remarkably small sample sizes (N = 1). In addition, there was an almost complete lack of detail about precisely how the experiments were carried out, and there was no proper presentation of the data or any formal statistical analyses! Nowadays undergraduate students who carried out and reported the findings of their research in such a slipshod fashion would not expect to receive a high mark.

Cherry (1953) assumed that all the deficiencies in selective attention exhibited by listeners in his experiments were due to the complexities and similarities of the auditory inputs. However, by doing so he neglected the demands of the shadowing task that the listeners had to perform. Performing the shadowing task requires much processing capacity, and this may well have impaired performance on the selective attention task.

We can test the above notion by making the assumption that the processing demands of shadowing would be greatly reduced in someone who had prolonged experience of shadowing. Such a person was Neville Moray, a British psychologist who carried out numerous experiments on the cocktail party problem. He was given the task of detecting digits on the unattended message while he shadowed the attended message. He detected 67% of these digits, which was substantially better than the 8% of digits detected by naïve participants (Underwood, 1974).

Cherry (1953) was specifically interested in listeners' ability to attend to one auditory message while ignoring a second message. As a consequence, he did not consider what would happen if participants shadowed an auditory message while pictures were presented at the same time. Allport, Antonis, and Reynolds (1972) did precisely this and discovered that participants remembered 90% of pictures presented concurrently with a shadowed auditory message. In contrast, recall of auditorily presented words concurrently with a shadowed auditory message was very poor. Thus, the apparently minimal processing of and memory for the unattended message reported by Cherry (1953) is not found when the unattended message is in a different modality to the attended message.

One of the most important limitations of Cherry's research concerned the way in which he assessed the listener's processing of the unattended message. In essence, what Cherry did consisted simply of retrospective questioning: participants were asked at the end of the experiment what they had noticed about the unattended message. This approach may cause an *under-reporting* of what had been processed on the unattended message for two reasons. First, processing of the ignored message of which listeners were consciously aware at the time might have been forgotten by the time that they were questioned retrospectively. Second, as became increasingly recognised in the decades after Cherry's classic study, considerable amounts of processing can occur in the absence of conscious awareness of such processing.

What is really needed is to assess processing of the unattended message online (i.e., while it is occurring). For example, consider the research of Von Wright, Anderson, and Stenman (1975). They instructed their participants to shadow one list of words and to ignore a second list. When a word previously associated with electric shock was presented on the unattended list, there was sometimes a physiological reaction in the form of a galvanic skin response. They observed the same effect when a word similar in sound or meaning to the previously shocked word was presented on the unattended list. Various other techniques have been used (see Driver, 2001). The evidence generally supports the notion that there is partial processing of unattended words and that such processing can extend to the semantic level.

It is important to note that there remains some controversy as to the most appropriate interpretation of the above findings. One possibility is that genuinely unattended stimuli can receive semantic processing. Another possibility was put forward by Lachter, Forster, and Ruthruff (2004). They pointed out that semantic processing of allegedly 'unattended' stimuli may occur because of what they called 'slippage'. By slippage, they meant that attention may occasionally shift from attended to unattended stimuli. The existence of slippage would be consistent with Cherry's (1953) claim that there is minimal processing of unattended stimuli.

There is some support for Lachter et al.'s theoretical position. For example, Dawson and Schell (1982) carried out a study resembling that of Von Wright et al.

(1975) and managed to replicate their findings. However, they also found that most of the increased physiological responses to previously shocked words occurred on trials on which it was likely that the listeners had shifted attention to those words.

Lien, Ruthruff, Kouchi, and Lachter (2010) presented a prime word briefly followed by a target word and instructed participants to decide whether the target word belonged to a specified category (e.g., _sports_). They were especially interested in whether there was a priming effect when the prime word belonged to the same category as the target. There was no priming effect at all when the prime words were not attended, even though these words were each repeated 160 times during the course of the experiment and were highly expected. This finding suggests that (at least in the visual modality) semantic processing requires attention.

Cherry's research suggested that the mechanisms involved in selective auditory attention are relatively simple and straightforward (as can be seen in Broadbent's filter theory). Unsurprisingly, subsequent research has revealed that the actual mechanisms are dramatically more complex. For example, it is correct (but insufficient) to argue that listeners attend to one auditory input and ignore another by focusing on a single difference in their physical properties (e.g., spatial location). In real life, of course, there are often more than two auditory inputs, and these inputs typically differ from each other in several properties.

Shamma, Elhilali, and Micheyl (2011) argued that the physical properties (e.g., timbre, pitch, frequency, spatial location) of any given auditory input tend to display temporal coherence. What that means is that neural responses associated with each of these properties tend to correlate highly with each other. These correlated neural responses provide the basis for grouping together any given auditory input's properties. The process of grouping or binding together an input's properties is facilitated by selective attention. In sum, effective selective auditory attention involves combining information across many stimulus properties in ways that are considerably more complicated than those envisaged by Cherry.

As we indicated earlier, Cherry (1953) obtained evidence indicating that auditory attention depended in part on top-down processes based on using context to predict what words were about to be presented. What Cherry did not do was to distinguish between two contrasting ways in which context might influence auditory attention and perception (Harley, 2013). First, there is the interactionist position, according to which contextual information influences the processing of auditory language at an early stage _prior_ to word recognition. Second, there is the autonomous position, according to which context exerts its influence late in processing _after_ word recognition.

Research in this area has been somewhat inconsistent (Harley, 2013). In general, however, the interactionist position is more applicable to situations in which degraded speech is presented whereas the autonomous position is more applicable when the speech signal is clear.

In sum, Cherry's (1953) classic study is limited in several ways. First, he adopted a crude methodological approach. Second, he did not appreciate the importance of the demands imposed by the shadowing task. Third, Cherry probably underestimated the extent to which the unattended message was processed because of his reliance on retrospective self-report. Fourth, while he realised that top-down processes triggered by expectations were of importance to selective attention, he did not distinguish between early and late effects of such processes. Fifth, Cherry underestimated the complexities involved in focusing attention on one auditory input to the exclusion of all other auditory inputs.

CONCLUSIONS

C herry's (1953) research on the cocktail party problem played a major role in stimulating research into selective attention. Ever since his classic study was published, selective attention has been one of the most active areas within cognitive psychology. In addition, one reason why his research has proved so influential is because he devised a very simple task that nevertheless had direct applicability to the real world. Sad to say, most laboratory research at the time involved the use of very artificial tasks which have no obvious relevance to everyday life.

Lack of ecological validity has plagued cognitive psychology throughout its entire history. A notorious example can be found in research on visual search. Until fairly recently, nearly all research on visual search involved tasks in which the target stimulus was presented at a *random* location within a visual display. This differs radically from everyday life. For example, if you are looking for a friend at a railway station, you do not search the sky or the ceiling of the station but rather focus on the floor and the nearby street. Research (e.g., Ehinger, Hidalgo-Sotelo, Torraiba, & Oliva, 2009) indicates that the single most important factor in real-life visual search (but one totally ignored for many years by researchers!) is the potential relevance or irrelevance of any region in visual space as the location of the target.

In my opinion, the main lesson that Cherry's (1953) classic study has for today's researchers is that he showed them how to maximise the chances of carrying out research possessing ecological validity. What Cherry did was to notice an important psychological phenomenon in everyday life, after which he devised a simple and ingenious way of studying this phenomenon under laboratory conditions. This strategy may sound absolutely obvious. However, tens of thousands of researchers in cognitive psychology fail to adopt this strategy.

FURTHER READING

Cherry, E. C. (1953). Some experiments on the recognition of speech with one and two ears. *Journal of the Acoustical Society of America*, 25, 975–979.

Driver, J. (2001). A selective review of selective attention research from the past century. *British Journal of Psychology*, 92, 53–78.

Harley, T. A. (2013). *The psychology of language: From data to theory* (4th edn). Hove, UK: Psychology Press.

Mesgarani, N., & Chang, E .F. (2012). Selective cortical representation of attended speaker in multi-talker speech perception. *Nature*, 485, 233–U118.

Shamma, S. A., Elhilali, M., & Micheyl, C. (2011). Temporal coherence and attention in auditory scene analysis. *Trends in Neurosciences*, 34, 114–123.

REFERENCES

Allport, D. A., Antonis, B., & Reynolds, P. (1972). On the division of attention: A dis-proof of the single channel hypothesis. _Quarterly Journal of Experimental Psychology_, 24, 225–235.

Baars, B. J. (1997). _In the theatre of consciousness: The workspace of the mind_. New York: Oxford University Press.

Broadbent, D. E. (1958). _Perception and communication_. Oxford: Pergamon.

Cherry, E. C. (1953). Some experiments on the recognition of speech with one and two ears. _Journal of the Acoustical Society of America_, 25, 975–979.

Dawson, M. E., & Schell, A. M. (1982). Electrodermal responses to attended and non-attended significant stimuli during dichotic listening. _Journal of Experimental Psychology: Human Perception and Performance_, 8, 315–324.

Driver, J. (2001). A selective review of selective attention research from the past century. _British Journal of Psychology_, 92, 53–78.

Ehinger, K. A., Hidalgo-Sotelo, B., Torraiba, A., & Oliva, A. (2009). Modelling search for people in 900 scenes: A combined source model of eye guidance. _Visual Cognition_, 17, 945–978.

Eysenck, M. W., & Keane, M. T. (2010). _Cognitive psychology: A student's handbook_ (6th edn). Hove, UK: Psychology Press.

Harley, T. A. (2013). _The psychology of language: From data to theory_ (4th edn). Hove, UK: Psychology Press.

Horton, C., D'Zmura, M., & Srinivasan, R. (2013). Suppression of competing speech through entrainment of cortical oscillations. _Journal of Neurophysiology_, 109, 3082–3093.

James, W. (1890). _The principles of psychology_. New York: Holt, Rinehard & Winston.

Kurt, S., Deutscher, A., Crook, J. M., Ohl, F. W., Budinger, E., Moeller, C. K., Scheich, H., & Schulze, H. (2008). Auditory cortical contrast enhancing by global winner-take-all inhibitory interactions. _PLoS One_, 3, 317–335.

Lachter, J., Forster, K. I., & Ruthruff, E. (2004). Forty-five years after Broadbent: Still no identification without attention. _Psychological Review_, 111, 880–913.

Lien, M.-C., Ruthruff, E., Kouchi, S., & Lachter, J. (2010). Even frequent and expected words are not identified without spatial attention. _Attention, Perception, & Psychophysics_, 72, 973–988.

Melloni, L., Molina, C., Pena, M., Torres, D., Singer, W., & Rodriguez, E. (2007). Synchronisation of neural activity across cortical areas correlates with conscious perception. _Journal of Neuroscience_, 27, 2858–2865.

Mesgarani, N., & Chang, E. F. (2012). Selective cortical representation of attended speaker in multi-talker speech perception. _Nature_, 485, 233–U118.

Miller, G. A. (1956). The magic number seven, plus or minus two: Some limits on our capacity for processing information. _Psychological Review_, 63, 81–93.

Shamma, S. A., Elhilali, M., & Micheyl, C. (2011). Temporal coherence and attention in auditory scene analysis. _Trends in Neurosciences_, 34, 114–123.

Shen, W., Olive, J., & Jones, D. (2008). Two protocols comparing human and machine phonetic discrimination performance in conversational speech. _INTERSPEECH_, 1630–1633.

Sperling, G. (1960). The information that is available in brief visual presentations. *Psychological Monographs*, 74 (Whole No. 498), 1–29.

Treisman, A. (1964). Verbal cues, language and meaning in selective attention. *American Journal of Psychology*, 77, 206–219.

Underwood, G. (1974). Moray vs. the rest: The effect of extended shadowing practice. *Quarterly Journal of Experimental Psychology*, 26, 368–372.

Von Wright, J. M. (1970). On selection in visual immediate memory. In A. F. Sanders (Ed.), *Attention and performance* (Vol. III, pp. 280–292). Amsterdam: North Holland.

Von Wright, J. M., Anderson, K., & Stenman, U. (1975). Generalisation of conditioned G.S.R.s in dichotic listening. In P. M. A. Rabbitt & S. Dornic (Eds.), *Attention and performance* (Vol. V). London: Academic Press.

Woodworth, R. S. (1938). *Experimental psychology*. London: Methuen.

3

Perception: Beyond Gibson's (1950) direct perception

Vicki Bruce and Yoav Tadmor
(Newcastle University)

BACKGROUND TO THE CLASSIC STUDY

Many psychological discoveries and theories of the last century were driven by the exigencies of war. James Jerome Gibson's ideas were shaped during the 1940s by work with the psychological research units in the US Army Air Force. Enormous numbers of young men had to be trained for some kind of flying duty ('something like the equivalent to the entire college population of the country' – Gibson, 1967, p. 15, in Reed & Jones, 1982). Gibson and his colleagues were employed to try to find ways to select and train them. Just before the war, Gibson and Crooks (1938) had worked together to try to analyse the problem of driving – how vision was used to avoid obstacles and in steering. They analysed the task in terms that seem to resonate with some of Gibson's later work. But it was the additional challenge posed by flying and landing planes that stimulated Gibson's initial critique and re-analysis of the topic of 'depth perception'.

'Depth perception' is the term used to describe how we are able to see in three dimensions a world of solid objects and extended surfaces. This solidity and extent in the world is usually seen as something that must be added in, or 'inferred', from a series of clues or correlates of depth in the retinal image which, when considered in a single eye, is often described as though it were a 2D 'picture' of the scene. This conception can be dated to Johannes Kepler's discovery of the retinal image in 1604: 'Thus vision is brought about by a *picture* of a thing seen being formed on the concave surface of the retina' (Crombie 1964, p. 150, in Wade, 1998). Kepler himself struggled to understand how and where this picture was interpreted, using language which in some ways resonates with more contemporary notions of bottom-up versus top-down processing:

> I leave it to natural philosophers to discuss the way in which this image or picture is
> put together by the spiritual principles of vision residing in the retina and in the

nerves, and whether it is made to appear before the soul or tribunal of the faculty of vision by a spirit within the cerebral cavities, or the faculty of vision, like a magistrate sent by the soul, goes out from the council chamber of the brain to meet the image in the optic nerves and retina, as it were descending to the lower court. (Crombie 1964, pp. 147–8, in Wade, 1998)

Others since have struggled too. A central problem of visual perception, once cast as a problem mediated by a retinal image – even a pair of them – is that the third dimension – the solidity of objects and the extent of surfaces – is lost and must somehow be restored. Any particular pattern of excitation on a single retina could have been produced by a multitude of different shapes at different orientations and distances (see Figure 3.1). This fundamental ambiguity of the retinal image has led to the mainstream view that retinal images must be interpreted and that visual perception involves cognitive mediation.

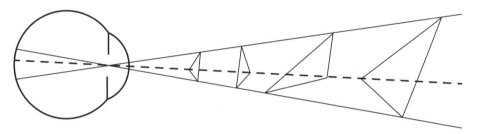

Figure 3.1 The traditional depiction of ambiguity of size/orientation and distance for any single retinal projection (reproduced from Bruce, Green, & Georgeson, 2003, Figure 10.3, p. 304)

Now the problem of interpreting a two-dimensional retinal 'picture' in terms of depth can be seen as closely related to the problem faced by an artist who must depict depth on a flat canvas. Artists during the Renaissance made explicit the rules of perspective that enable an impression of distance to be obtained. These rules of perspective can be demonstrated quite well if we look at a simple picture of a railway line (see Figure 3.2; ignore the arrows in this picture – we will return to them later). We see that in a picture of a railway line, the parallel lines from the world converge in the picture. The railway sleepers of constant size in the world have pictorial sizes related to their distance. The sleepers that lie on the same horizontal plane in the world are higher up in the picture the further the way they are, and so forth. The convergence of parallel lines and the changes in relative size and height of objects depicted at different distances are among the devices that an artist can use to make a picture depict a three-dimensional world. And they are some of the 'cues' or 'clues' that the brain uses, according to conventional theory,

Figure 3.2 Perspective view of railway tracks. The arrows drawn on the picture show the pattern of optical flow for an observer looking down the track as the train recedes from the depicted horizon (reproduced from Bruce, Green, & Georgeson, 2003, Figure 10.7, p. 307)

to infer depth from a 2D image. In addition to these 'static' pictorial cues, there is the 'cue' of motion parallax: when the observer moves relative to a scene, the images of nearer objects would sweep across their retina faster than those of objects that are further away. And of course an observer has two laterally separated eyes and these two slightly different views of the world are combined to provide a 3D world through stereopsis at close range.

Flying (particularly landing) a plane requires that the pilot knows how the plane is oriented with respect to objects and surfaces. Since approaching an airfield involves understanding distance and orientation and how they are changing over time, it seems reasonable to assume that skills of interpreting depth 'cues' (relative size, height, and so forth) might be useful, particularly as the distances generally exceed those that can exploit stereopsis. But Gibson found that screening or training with 'depth cue' tests did not help the selection or preparation of pilots. This led him to reformulate the problem of 'depth perception'. In 1950, he published the first of his three theoretical volumes on perception. This first book, *The perception of the visual world*, deserves to be listed as one of the most interesting and significant contributions to the study of perception in the past century. Unfortunately, however, Gibson's theories, as developed over his three books (and numerous papers), have divided people. Some scientists have been extraordinarily critical of Gibson's ideas and others have simply ignored him. For many of the enthusiasts, however, Gibson's work and theories have acquired a cult status and triggered a radical but often marginalised school of thought.

In the remainder of this chapter we will provide a brief outline of Gibson's own intellectual journey – since it is some of his later work that may have led to the neglect of his – to our minds – more important early work, the 1950 book in particular. We will then describe and evaluate the wider impact specifically of his early work.

DETAILED DESCRIPTION OF THE CLASSIC STUDY

GIBSON'S 'CLASSIC' CONTRIBUTIONS: TEXTURE GRADIENTS AND OPTIC FLOW

Each of Gibson's three books contained (at least) one 'big' idea. It seems important to note all three before focusing on the contribution made in the 1950 work since so many commentators, and Gibson himself, conflate his contributions. But it is his later work that is the more controversial.

The three big ideas are:

1. The total structured pattern of visual input and the way it changes as a result of movement provides information about the visual world. When conceived in this way, the third dimension was never 'lost' and need not be restored (Gibson, 1950).

2. There is a reciprocity of perception and action. The senses should be construed as 'perceptual systems', not as passive recipients of stimuli (Gibson, 1966).

3. The meanings of things – affordances – are directly specified in the structured patterns of light (Gibson, 1979).

In developing his theoretical ideas, Gibson was strongly influenced by the philosopher-psychologist E. B. Holt, a former student of William James (Charles, 2011). Holt was part of a group espousing a 'New Realism' which denied the separation of the mental/representational from the world. The meanings of things were 'in' the world, not the head. Moreover, Holt was a behaviourist, but for him, animals were propelled by purpose rather than prodded by 'stimuli'. In Holt we can see several elements that come together in Gibson's central work – his middle book – *The senses considered as perceptual systems* (1966).

Gibson described and developed an ideological position termed 'direct realism'. He claimed, most forcefully in his later works, that perception was not mediated by any kind of interpretation. There was no unconscious inference about what must be 'out there'. What is out there is 'just' seen, because there is sufficient information when we understand the nature of that information properly. Gibson believed that the study of perception, in artificial laboratory settings, of impoverished stimuli devoid of context, misled scientists into thinking that internal inference – cognitive or computational processes, in today's terminology – was necessary to mediate between the reception of light and the perception of the world.

At least in his earlier works, Gibson did not assert that 'real world' perception was always without error: 'Although it is true that everyday perception tends to be selective, creative, fleeting, inexact, generalised, stereotyped, and to have all the other defects so commonly ascribed to it, the best hope of understanding these defects is first to understand the respects in which perception is adequate and exact' (Gibson, 1950, p. 10). Nor did he deny the physiological processes that are involved in perception and he did *not* deny the importance of image formation on the retina – what he did deny is that the starting point for explanation is a static 'retinal image' as though this was a pictured snapshot of the scene.

Gibson's position on the retinal image has led him to be often misunderstood and occasionally ridiculed by other scientists, but it is worth examining what he actually said. In 1950 he argued that the projection from retina to brain should not be thought of as an 'image': 'It is an event composed not of light but of nerve-cell discharges' (p. 50). And later in the same volume: 'The image is a *projection* of the world ... not a *replica* of the world' (p. 53), the 'object does not have a copy in the image but a *correlate*' (p. 54).

Gibson is not denying that perception is mediated by activity in the pathway from eye to brain, including the retinal image. But he is denying that a static snapshot of this activity provides the correct place to start to understand how we see a world of solidity and extent.

WHAT, THEN, IS THE CORRECT PLACE TO START?

TEXTURE GRADIENTS

For Gibson (1950), the place to start in understanding perception is not the projection of an isolated object in the air (see Figure 3.1), but the ground on which people and animals move: 'visual space, unlike abstract geometrical space, is perceived only by virtue of what fills it' (Gibson, 1950, p. 5). Indeed, Gibson raises the possibility that 'there is literally no such thing as a perception of space without the perception of a continuous background surface' (Gibson, 1950, p. 6). This forms the foundation of his global psychophysics, in which he spells out the relationship between our perception and the totality of patterned light we receive. This is a different approach from the elemental psychophysics introduced by Weber and Fechner in the nineteenth century and which formed the foundation of much twentieth-century methodology in vision research.

The ground is comprised of surfaces which generally have some kind of texture to them, which may be blades of grass or pebbles on a shingle beach in the natural world, clods of earth in the farmed world, or paving stones in the manufactured one. The important thing about textures – whatever they comprise – is that they have a kind of regularity and so in an image of a textured surface receding from a viewer there is a gradient of projected size of texture elements – a texture gradient. (This is not to imply that all elements of texture are identical to each other, but that they have a statistical regularity). Such gradients provide a continuous scale to specify distance and orientation (see Sinai, Ooi, & He, 1998, for some evidence supportive of Gibson's assertion, and see Figures 3.3a and 3.3b for some examples). And texture gradients on ground surfaces allow a completely different take on the classic problem of depth perception:

'The puzzle of the third dimension can be much better understood if we first examine the scenes we actually see and the ones which are of practical importance for human behaviour' (Gibson, 1950, p. 2). According to Gibson, we don't see depth, we

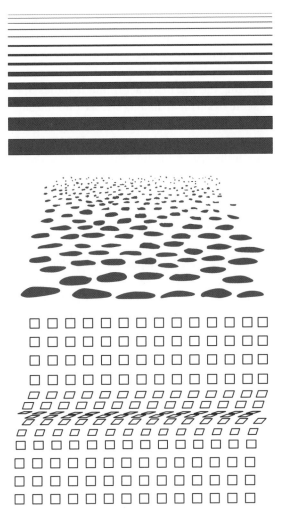

Figure 3.3 Texture gradients specifying distance (a) and changes in surface orientation (b) (reproduced from Bruce, Green, & Georgeson, 2003, Figures 10.1 and 10.2, p. 303)

see surface layout. We don't use cues but correlates of layout. If there is no gradient in texture elements, then the surface is oriented perpendicular to the viewer. If there is a gradient of projected texture elements, then there is a surface extended away from the viewer. The texture gradient itself specifies the slant of a surface. And so on.

One of the most powerful illustrations of the contrast between Gibson's 'ground' theory of perception and the traditional 'air' theory of depth perception (Figure 3.1) comes with the treatment of size constancy. Size constancy is the observation that things seem to appear to be of constant size despite changes in distance from the observer. The size of the retinal image of an object decreases as its distance from the observer increases. In traditional accounts, the brain must take account of the apparent distance of an object (which is done by using depth cues) and 'scale up' its apparent size.

For Gibson, though, the object does not appear to shrink precisely because it *does* stay the same size at different distances. This constancy of size means that the object will always conceal or occlude the same amount of background texture at its base. Imagine the texture is that of the clods of earth in a ploughed field and the observer is contemplating the size of a tractor that trundles up and down the field. The tractor doesn't seem to shrink to half its size as it doubles its distance, and that is because, according to Gibson, the wheels of the tractor (for example) are always seen to conceal the same number of clods. Gibson (1947) conducted experiments on size constancy with observers judging the sizes of stakes placed at different distances away in just such a field. He suggested that the traditional model would predict that at great distances size constancy would fail because precise distance could not be used in the scaling up of apparent size. What he observed, however, was that as distance was increased, size judgements became more variable, but not, overall, less accurate.

There are situations where size constancy does break down, and that is when we look at objects from a great height (as in an aeroplane or very high building). On a traditional account, this is because looking from a great height does not provide the depth cues we usually use. For Gibson, it is because there is no 'ground', texture, and horizon to provide the scale against which sizes can be judged.

There is a famous and curious illusion of size constancy which is the Ames distorted room. In this, a person appears to shrink in size as they walk across an apparently normal rectangular room. Of course the room is far from normal – it has been cleverly constructed to appear to be rectangular from a single point of observation. On the traditional view – the person's size is judged against their apparent distance. Due to the room's construction, the person who walks across the room appears to be closer than they really are – so their size is not scaled up enough. They seem to shrink. How would Gibson explain this? First, he would note that, as in many (though not all) 'illusions', there is an artificiality about the situation. The illusion works only when the observer looks through a peephole with a single eye (so no stereo vision is possible) and does not move (so there is no motion parallax either). Moreover, to the extent that the room provides any 'texture', it has been doctored to provide a misleading view of scale, and the apparent sizes of the people are consistent with this.

OPTIC FLOW

Texture gradients alone don't help much with the problem faced by the pilot, who must orient and guide the plane safely in to land. Here we need to think how the rich information provided in texture gradients *changes* as we move in the world, and this introduces the idea of optical flow, one of the most important ideas developed from Gibson's war-work with pilots.

Once we conceive of the input to vision being the totality of information from textured surfaces as it impinges on the viewer (the optic array, as Gibson termed it in his later work), then it is easy to understand how there are systematic changes at the level of this total input as we move in the world. If we approach a point in the world, there is optical outflow – images of texture in the periphery of the visual field stream past us, while those in the place we are heading stay still. So, outflow specifies approach (see Figure 3.4, for Gibson's classic illustration of this). If we recede from a point (see Figure 3.2), there is inflow. The projections of texture elements from the periphery stream into the field of vision (inflow) with their direction focused on the point from which we are receding. The rate of optical flow depends on speed of travel. Thus optical flow patterns can specify both direction and speed of travel. Moreover, the total pattern of optical movement can disambiguate its source. If we consider the 'traditional' situation with an isolated eye viewing a single object suspended in space, then there is ambiguity – motion on the retina could arise from movement of the object or of the eye. However, when we think of the input reaching an observer viewing objects and surfaces in the real world, then there is no ambiguity. Movement by the observer is always accompanied by some global transformation in the optic array, while movement of an object within the world provides a local perturbation, allowing visual disambiguation of the question of whether self or object gives rise to motion of the 'image'.

Figure 3.4   The optic flow field for a pilot landing an aeroplane (from Gibson, 1950). Copyright © by Houghton and Mifflin Company. Reprinted with permission

IMPACT OF THE CLASSIC STUDY

One of the greatest impacts of Gibson's analysis of optic flow fields has been work developed by David Lee and his colleagues (see Lee, 1980) on the use of *optic flow* to guide action in humans and other animals. One of Lee's earliest and most powerful demonstrations was of the 'swinging room', where posture can be affected by subtle movements of the walls of an experimental 'room' in which the observer stands (e.g., Lishman & Lee, 1973). If you stand facing the solid wall of a real room and there is optical flow of the texture you are looking at, this must result from your own movement, and requires a postural adjustment to compensate. In the swinging room, the floor is solid and stable but the walls are made of a bottomless box suspended over the unsuspecting participant, which can be moved slightly towards or away from the person standing there. Body sway can be 'driven' by movements of the room, and babies learning to walk, or adults balancing on one leg, can be 'knocked over' by consciously imperceptible movements of the room (Lee, 1980).

If an expanding optic flow pattern specifies approach to a surface, its _rate_ of expansion can easily be shown to specify how soon the surface will be contacted, assuming approach at a constant velocity. Time to contact a surface to which you are moving, or an object approaching you, is, of course, an event-related analogue of 'distance' – now cast in action-related terms. A person or animal could use this parameter, which Lee calls 'tau', in order to control actions such as landing (birds, or pilots again) or steering (to avoid obstacles) or grasping (to catch a ball).

Lee and his colleagues used a variety of sources of evidence to argue that across species, and in various situations, actions were indeed timed in ways consistent with the use of a strategy based upon detecting tau. Lee and Reddish (1981), for example, made measurements on films of gannets diving for fish in the North Sea. The gannet must streamline its wings on entry to the sea, to avoid injuring them, but needs the control of flight from outstretched wings for as long as possible. How does it know when to pull in its wings? Measurements made of the time-to-contact at which streamlining occurred for different durations of dive suggested that a strategy based upon tau (complicated due to acceleration of the diving bird) gave a better fit to the recorded data than other possible strategies. Lee, Young, Reddish, Lough, and Clayton (1983) looked at timing by humans asked to punch volleyballs dropped from various heights – so also accelerating under gravity. A tau strategy, given this acceleration, should lead to punches initiated sooner for balls dropped from greater heights. Measurements of the flexion of the actors' knees and ankles again appeared consistent with the use of tau in this situation.

Gibson's impacts go well beyond such investigations of the use of optic flow, however, and here we briefly mention three more areas.

First, Gibson's realisation that _natural scenes_ are the ecologically valid stimulus that should be used for the study of vision was of fundamental importance. His new way of thinking about perception led to a change in our thinking about the constraints on neuronal representations and the actual _goals_ of sensory processing, but this change in thinking was not instantaneous. Nonetheless, although not often credited for his pioneering views, Gibson would probably be pleased if he were able to browse through the great flurry of studies published during the last three and a half decades on the interrelationship between the statistical properties of natural scenes and visual perception. Few would disagree nowadays with the notion that a fuller understanding of the functional architectures and response properties of sensory, perceptual, and cognitive systems requires that we concurrently study, understand, and characterise the information that they have evolved to process.

For example, by determining the statistics of local luminance contrasts in natural scenes it was possible to show that mammalian visual neurons, despite their limited dynamic response ranges, do provide an optimal representation of those contrasts (e.g., Tadmor & Tolhurst, 2000). Similarly, by determining the statistics of natural colour signals it was possible to show that the particular spectral tuning of primate L and M photoreceptors makes them suitable for the detection of ripe fruit against foliage (Osorio & Vorobyev, 1996; Regan et al., 2001; Parraga, Troscianko, & Tolhurst, 2002). Further studies of the spatial and the temporal luminance statistics of natural scenes were able to show how cortical neurons and circuits may exploit such correlations and redundancies to achieve an efficient representation of our natural diet and how local image features can drive our eye-movements (for reviews, see Simocelli & Olshausen, 2001; Geisler, 2008).

Second, Gibson's (1950 and later) emphasis on understanding *natural activities* in the real world and how observers guide their actions with appropriate information pick-up is an early forerunner of intriguing work recording eye movements by active observers doing everyday tasks. Several studies of eye movements during natural behaviour agree that it is the actual information needed for the immediate task that determines where observers look. Furthermore, there are similarities in 'where' and 'when' different individuals look at any informative locations while engaged in natural behaviours. For instance, different drivers all look consistently at or close to the tangent point of a bend in the lane ahead (Land & Lee, 1994). Similarly, when cutting a sandwich, participants initially fixate the point of contact with the knife and then move their gaze along the locus of the cut, just ahead of the knife (Hayhoe, Shrivastava, Mruczek, & Pelz, 2003). Likewise, the pattern and the fixation sequences of three different individuals engaged in the task of filling a kettle and making tea are all remarkably similar (Land, Mennie, & Rusted, 1999; and Tatler, Hayhoe, Land, & Ballard, 2011, for a comprehensive review).

Such consistencies would agree with Gibson's assertion that the observer samples an optic array which directly specifies all that is needed to guide action. Different observers sample this rich naturalistic information in similar ways.

And finally there was the impact that Gibson's work had on the development of a broader, radical *'ecological' psychology*, within but also well beyond the field of perception. This movement was described well by Michaels and Carello (1981). Within perception, for example, there have been interesting attempts to describe the 'invariants' in patterns that specify complex dimensions, such as age of faces. And beyond the field of perception, Gibson's work came to influence a wider range of theorists who argued that the artificiality of laboratory settings was limiting our understanding of how attention, thinking, and memory worked in real situations. For example, Ulric Neisser's (1976) text *Cognition and Reality*, provided a critique of cognitive psychology and was strongly influenced by Gibson's work.

CRITIQUE OF THE CLASSIC STUDY

While Gibson's work stimulated investigations of what information *could* be used to guide action, in general there are rather few convincing demonstrations that such information *is* actually used, or used in the way that Gibson and followers suggested. Take 'tau' (time to contact an approaching surface or object), for example. Wann (1996) reanalysed the data used by Lee and his colleagues and showed in some cases that the use of tau was not proven, and in other cases quite obviously not supported by the data originally published. Wann argues that the data are better described by the animal or human action being triggered when there is a threshold *change in distance* to the target. And distance, as we began this chapter, is deciphered by a range of 'cues' which include, but are not limited to, texture gradients. Recent approaches (see Bruce, Green, & Georgeson, 2003, for a summary) have described how optical flow patterns specifying approach may be used *alongside* other sources of information about distance, including binocular disparity. This does not deny the importance of understanding how optical flow can provide useful information about an observer's motion, but considerably undermines the notion that observer action is directly guided by this information alone.

Flexible use of information determined by circumstances and experience also seems to be the hallmark in other situations too. For example, a racing driver driving on a familiar track seems to adopt a different looking strategy from regular drivers (Land & Tatler, 2001). Similarly, a study in an immersive virtual reality environment demonstrated that fixations on identical objects in a fixed environment varied considerably if participants were attempting to approach or to avoid the same object. This result highlights the importance of understanding the function of each fixation for understanding fixation placement (Rothkopf, Ballard, & Hayhoe, 2007). Thus, there are cases where a different task in the very same natural environment affects the way that the information is sampled. Such variation is not necessarily at odds with Gibson's later analyses of purposive action: 'The perceptual systems, however, are clearly amenable to learning. It would be expected that an individual, after practice, could orient more exactly, listen more carefully ... and look more perceptively than he could before practice' (Gibson, 1966, p. 51). But variations in looking 'strategy' and shifts in observer 'attention' do seem easier to accommodate within a framework that permits cognitive mediation.

And this brings us to the most significant criticism of Gibson's work, which comes from his assumption that specifying the information that could be used to guide action relegated the problem of how the information was 'picked up' to that of trivial physiological detail. Marr (1982) admired Gibson's contribution to understanding the right kind of questions to ask about perception, yet clearly expressed this frustration well:

> Although one can criticise certain shortcomings in the quality of Gibson's analysis, its major, and, in my view, fatal shortcoming lies at a deeper level and results from a failure to realize two things. First, the detection of physical invariants, like image

surfaces, is exactly and precisely an information-processing problem, in modern terminology. And second, he vastly underrated the sheer difficulty of such detection. (Marr, 1982, p. 30)

Gibson was clearly concerned with high-level visual information processing when he proposed immediate and direct perception of the natural environment, but in doing so may have failed to appreciate that low-level sensory visual and perceptual mechanisms must have also, by definition, been optimised by evolution and adaptations. Thus, his impression of a seemingly effortless and 'direct perception from the ambient array of light' may simply be a reflection of the very fact that from the earliest stages our visual system has evolved for optimised processing of the statistical structures in our natural environment.

CONCLUSIONS

G ibson's work has been extraordinarily important in getting a wide variety of vision scientists to think clearly about the sources of information that might be available to guide activities in the *natural* world. He should be credited for being one of the first to realise the necessity of moving away from artificial laboratory stimuli to the natural environment for the study of our sensory and perceptual apparatus.

Owing to this revolutionary move, we can now begin to understand *why* some our sensory components have evolved the particular properties that they have (e.g., the retinal centre-surround and the elongated cortical receptive field organisation, the particular forms of contrast response functions given the limited dynamic response ranges of those neurons and the specific chromatic tuning of L and M cone photoreceptors that are suited for detecting fruit against foliage), and thus why our perceptual and cognitive networks function as they do. Such a visual-neuro-ecological awareness is a prerequisite for an appreciation that other species occupying the very same ecological niches as us may, in fact, live in different perceptual worlds (e.g., insects and birds can process visual signals in the ultraviolet range, and snakes in the infra-red).

As well as sophisticated analyses of how biological visual systems evolved to process natural information, there has been enormously productive work developing *artificial* systems that can analyse optic flow patterns for a range of applications, including robotics. Indeed, paradoxically, Gibson's greatest lasting impact is probably in the field of biologically-inspired robotics.

FURTHER READING

Lee, D. N. (1980). The optic flow field: the foundation of vision. *Philosophical Transactions of the Royal Society of London*, 290, 169–179.

Describes how ideas which were stimulated by Gibson (1950, 1966) were developed to provide an overarching framework for understanding how optical flow patterns provide information to guide action.

Bruce, V., Green, P., & Georgeson, M. (2003). *Visual Perception* (4th edn, and earlier editions too). Hove, UK: Psychology Press.

This textbook, in four successive editions, attempts to describe how different approaches to the study of vision – particularly those of David Marr and J. J. Gibson – provide frameworks to help us account for how people and other animals perceive their visual worlds. It therefore places Gibson's work and impacts into a wider context.

Geisler, W.S. (2008). Visual perception and the statistical properties of natural scenes. *Annual Review of Psychology*, 59, 167–192.

This is a comprehensive review illustrating the diversity of studies of different statistical properties, such as luminance, colour, spatial and temporal regularities, and correlations in natural scenes.

Marr, D. (1982). *Vision: A computational investigation into the human representation and processing of visual information*. San Francisco, CA: W. H. Freeman.

This presents a ground-breaking framework for vision that takes a very different approach from that of Gibson but which nonetheless demonstrates an appreciation of Gibson's own contributions.

Michaels, C., & Carello, C. (1981). *Direct perception*. Englewood Cliffs, NJ: Prentice Hall.

Argues coherently for the 'ecological' approach to perception and sets it out clearly in contrast to the traditional theories. Describes research on the invariants regarding, for example, ageing. The manuscript is available online at: http://ione. psy.uconn.edu/docs/MC.pdf

REFERENCES

Bruce, V., Green, P., & Georgeson, M. (2003). *Visual Perception* (4th edn, and earlier editions too). Hove, UK: Psychology Press.

Charles, E. P. (2011). *A new look at New Realism: The psychology and philosophy of E. B. Holt*. New Brunswick, NJ: Transaction.

Crombie, A. C. (1964). Kepler: De Mondo Visionis. In *Melange Alexandre Koyre L'Aventure de la Science* (pp 135–172). Paris: Hermann.

Geisler, W. S. (2008). Visual perception and the statistical properties of natural scenes. *Annual Review of Psychology*, 59, 167–192.

Gibson, J. J. (1947). *Motion picture testing and research*. AAF Aviation Psychology Research Report, No. 7. Washington, DC: Government Printing Office.

Gibson, J. J. (1950). *The perception of the visual world*. Boston, MA: Houghton Mifflin.

Gibson, J. J. (1966). *The senses considered as perceptual systems*. Boston, MA: Houghton Mifflin.

Gibson, J. J. (1967). Autobiography. Reprinted (pp. 7–22) in E. Reed & R. Jones (1982 eds) *Reasons for Realism*. Hillsdale, NJ: Lawrence Erlbaum Associates.

Gibson, J. J. (1979). *The ecological approach to visual perception*. Boston, MA: Houghton Mifflin.

Gibson, J. J., & Crooks, L. E. (1938). A theoretical field analysis of automobile-driving. *American Journal of Psychology*, 51, 453–471.

Hayhoe, M. M., Shrivastava, A., Mruczek, R., & Pelz, J. B. (2003). Visual memory and motor planning in a natural task. *Journal of Vision*, 3, 49–63.

Land, M. F., & Lee, D. N. (1994). Where we look when we steer. *Nature*, 369, 742–744.

Land, M. F., & Tatler, B. W. (2001). Steering with the head: the visual strategy of a racing driver. *Current Biology*, 11, 1215–1220.

Land, M. F., Mennie, N., & Rusted, J. (1999). The roles of vision and eye movements in the control of activities of daily living. *Perception*, 28, 1311–1328.

Lee, D. N. (1980). The optic flow field: The foundation of vision. *Philosophical Transactions of the Royal Society of London*, 290, 169–179.

Lee, D. N., & Reddish, P. E. (1981). Plummeting gannets: A paradigm of ecological optics. *Nature*, 293, 293–294.

Lee, D. N., Young, D. S., Reddish, P. E., Lough, S., & Clayton, T. M. H. (1983). Visual timing in hitting an accelerating ball. *Quarterly Journal of Experimental Psychology*, 35A, 333–346.

Lishman, J. R., & Lee, D. N. (1973). The autonomy of visual kinaesthesis. *Perception*, 2, 287–294.

Marr, D. (1982). *Vision: A computational investigation into the human representation and processing of visual information*. San Francisco, CA: W. H. Freeman.

Michaels, C., & Carello, C. (1981). *Direct perception*. Englewood Cliffs, NJ: Prentice Hall.

Neisser, U. (1976). *Cognition and reality*. San Francisco, CA: W. H. Freeman.

Osorio, D., & Vorobyev, M. (1996). Colour vision as an adaptation to frugivory in primates. *Proceedings of the Royal Society of London*, B263, 593–599.

Parraga, C. A., Troscianko, T., & Tolhurst, D. J. (2002). Spatiochromatic properties of natural images and human vision. *Current Biology*, 12, 483–487.

Reed, E., & Jones, R. (1982). *Reasons for realism: Selected essays of J. J. Gibson*. Hillsdale, NJ: Lawrence Erlbaum Associates.

Regan, B. C., Julliot, C., Simmen, B., Vienot, F., Charles-Dominique, P., & Mollon, J. D. (2001). Fruits, foliage and the evolution of primate colour vision. *Philosophical Transactions of the Royal Society of London*, B356, 229–283.

Rothkopf, C. A., Ballard, D. H., & Hayhoe, M. M. (2007). Task and context determine where you look. *Journal of Vision*, 7 (14), 16, 1–20.

Simoncelli, E. P., & Olshausen, B. A. (2001). Natural image statistics and neural representation. *Annual Review of Neuroscience*, 24, 1193–1216.

Sinai, M. J., Ooi, T. L., & He, Z. J. (1998). Terrain influences the accurate judgement of distance. *Nature*, 395, 497–500.

Tadmor, Y., & Tolhurst, D. J. (2000). Calculating the contrasts that retinal ganglion cells and LGN neurons encounter in natural scenes. *Vision Research*, 40, 3145–3157.

Tatler, B. W., Hayhoe, M. M., Land, M. F., & Ballard, D. H. (2011). Eye guidance in natural vision: Reinterpreting salience. *Journal of Vision*, 11 (5), article 5. DOI: 10.1167/11.5.5.

Wade, N. J. (1998). *A natural history of vision*. Cambridge, MA: The MIT Press.

Wann, J. P. (1996). Anticipating arrival: Is the tau margin a specious theory? *Journal of Experimental Psychology: Human Perception and Performance*, 22, 1031–1048.

4

Computational approaches to perception: Beyond Marr's (1982) computational approach to vision

George Mather (University of Lincoln)

BACKGROUND TO THE CLASSIC STUDY

The influential Gestalt approach to perception identified a number of organising principles or laws which describe how visual patterns appear to be structured. According to the law of proximity, for example, elements in a pattern which are close together tend to be grouped perceptually. The general theme of Gestalt laws is that pattern elements which share some property in common, such as proximity, orientation, motion direction or collinearity, are perceived as a cohesive group. Gestalt Psychology was primarily descriptive in that it did not attempt to explain why or how its laws are applied to images. In the late 1950s, new discoveries in neuroscience promised to answer at least some of these questions. Hubel and Wiesel (1959) discovered individual neurons in the brains of cats and monkeys which seemed to represent simple visual features such as contour orientation and movement direction. During the following decade or so cognitive psychologists and computer scientists attempted to develop and implement models of human perception based on constructing assemblages of simple visual features, each of which was supposedly encoded by activity in cortical neurons. However, by the early 1970s it had become clear that this project was doomed to fail. Early attempts to build computer models of perception had shown that feature detection was much harder than it seemed from Hubel and Wiesel's experiments. Moreover, perception involves far more than feature assemblages. So computer models had to confine themselves to simple toy domains or 'blocks worlds' (line-drawn scenes containing arrangements of geometric solids) in which the features were already identified and the range of possible objects was highly constrained. Theories to explain perceptual phenomena such as illusions and after-effects tended to lack generality, and had little to say about the broader functional context of perception.

So the prospects for a truly general-purpose theory of vision looked bleak when David Marr joined the MIT Artificial Intelligence (AI) laboratory in 1973.

Nevertheless, Marr set himself the ambitious task of developing new computational solutions to vision which could be treated as serious candidate models for explaining available biological and psychophysical data on human perception. Once Marr and his collaborators had set to work, his theory emerged rapidly in the form of a series of AI Memos, which were the basis for several highly influential journal papers. Marr began with a manifesto for his entire theoretical project, based on the idea (described in detail below) that vision could be understood at three distinctly different levels of description (Marr & Poggio, 1976). This was followed by a series of detailed papers, mostly published by the Royal Society of London between 1976 and 1979. Marr's entire theoretical approach was summarised in a book entitled *Vision*, finished by colleagues following his untimely death from leukaemia in 1980 at the age of 35 and first published posthumously in 1982. It is important to recognise that major contributions to Marr's theories were made by his collaborators, including Ellen Hildreth, Ken Nishihara, Tomaso Poggio, and Shimon Ullman. *Vision* constitutes the classic study which is the subject of this chapter.

I have a flashbulb memory of meeting one of my old undergraduate tutors, Professor John Frisby, by chance on a train journey to London in the late 1970s while I was a graduate student at Reading University in England. John had been reading Marr's papers and was an early convert; he saw in them the future of vision research. John firmly believed that Marr's approach represented a paradigm shift in vision science, and indeed is still committed to Marr's philosophy (see Frisby & Stone, 2010). Frisby was a highly influential figure both personally and in the wider research community, so it was clear to me at the time that I needed to learn a lot more about Marr's work (though the first priority was to finish a thesis). Fortunately, in the year that *Vision* was published I arrived as a postdoc at York University in Toronto, where the vision research group had just embarked on a page-by-page, chapter-by-chapter reading of the text. The same exercise was probably taking place in many other vision labs around the world at the time. Fortuitously, the first desktop personal computers became available during this period (the Apple II appeared in 1977 and the first IBM PC in 1981), so many vision researchers began to learn programming and were inspired by Marr to use computational modelling routinely in their work. All in all, it is difficult to overestimate the impact that Marr's approach had on the field of vision science in the late 1970s and succeeding decades.

DETAILED DESCRIPTION OF THE CLASSIC STUDY

MARR'S THESIS

Marr's thesis can be divided into two parts. The first is a general framework for studying and understanding visual perception, based on the aforementioned distinction between three levels of description. The second part of his thesis proposed a specific theory of visual processing, in the form of a series of visual representations created in the brain. The starting point of the process is a primitive description of the constituents of the input image, and its culmination is a three-dimensional description of the objects in the scene.

MARR'S FRAMEWORK

Marr proposed that any machine carrying out an information-processing task can be understood at three levels (Marr, 1982, p. 25):

- Computational theory – 'What is the goal of the computation, why is it appropriate, and what is the logic of the strategy for carrying it out?'

- Representation and algorithm – 'How can this computational theory be implemented? In particular, what is the representation of the input and output, and what is the algorithm for the transformation?'

- Hardware implementation – 'How can the representation and algorithm be realised physically?'

We can use stereo vision to illustrate the distinction between the three levels. The two eyes form slightly different images of the world, which means that a given point in the world occupies slightly disparate positions in the two images. This positional disparity can be used to estimate distance. But there is a matching or 'correspondence' problem: how can the brain decide which points in each eye match up with each other? Marr's computational theory of stereopsis defined three constraints on allowable matches which guarantee correct matches, and can be described in simple terms using images that contain only black dots and white dots:

- *Compatibility* – Black dots can match only black dots.

- *Uniqueness* – A black dot from one image can match only one black dot from the other image.

- *Continuity* – The disparity of the matches varies smoothly almost everywhere over the image.

Marr then went on to describe two different algorithms for solving the stereo correspondence problem using these constraints, the second of which involved a process of initially matching coarse, widely separated features in each image and using those matches to guide matching at successively finer scales. Finally, Marr suggested two possible neural implementations of the second algorithm, though neurophysiological data available at the time could not rule out either of them.

As indicated in this example, in Marr's view the three levels of description are only loosely related. A specific computational theory could be implemented using different algorithms, and realised in different physical forms. For him, computational theory had conceptual priority; only by considering the task being performed, at an abstract computational level, can one hope to develop truly general functional theories of vision. Without computational theory any attempt to explain perception would ultimately be misguided. He took a swipe at the empirical neurosciences, as follows:

> ...trying to understand perception by studying only neurons is like trying to understand bird flight by studying only feathers: It just cannot be done. (p. 27)

According to Marr, a crucial aspect of the computational theory of a processing problem is the identification of constraints on computations which allow a solution to be achieved. Once constraints have been identified they can be used in different algorithms and implemented by different hardware. His specific theory divides visual processing into a series of consecutive stages, each of which is grounded in specific computational constraints.

MARR'S THEORY OF PROCESSING

Marr's theory of processing was very much of its time. AI in the 1970s was dominated by the use of symbolic computations. The MIT AI Lab where Marr developed his theory used a programming language called LISP (LISt Processing), which was designed for symbolic computation – the creation and manipulation of logical assertions. Programs were composed of functions which manipulated symbolic descriptions of, for example, features in a 'blocks world', in order to make new logical assertions about the data. In keeping with this approach to AI, Marr made symbolic descriptions of image features or 'primitives' the building blocks of his entire theory, which comprises three separate stages. Each stage of processing involves the creation and manipulation of a limited vocabulary of symbols which constitute primitive assertions about the content of the image:

- *Primal sketch* – Describes the intensity changes in the image, and their geometrical distribution and organisation.

- *2½-D sketch* – Describes the orientation and rough depth of the visible surfaces and contour discontinuities in the image.

- *3-D model representation* – Describes shapes and their spatial organisation in an object-centred coordinate system.

The theory is a 'bottom-up' theory in which information flows in one direction only, from lower stages of processing to higher stages. At the first stage, the purpose of the primal sketch is to make explicit important information about the image, using a small set of symbolic primitive features which are extracted from the intensity image. These include edges, bars, blobs, and terminations. Certain assumptions or constraints allow the image to be broken up or grouped into regions which represent the geometry of the visible surfaces. For example, one assumption which aids in grouping primitives into regions is called 'spatial continuity':

...markings generated on a surface by a single process are often spatially organised –
they are arranged in curves or lines and possibly create more complex patterns. (p. 49)

These grouping assumptions are highly reminiscent of the Gestalt principles
described earlier, of course, but set in a rigorous functional context.

The second stage of processing is the 2½-D sketch, which creates a dense depth
map of all the visible surfaces in the image, using primitives that represent local
surface orientation as 'needles' which protrude from the surface perpendicular to
it. Marr proposed that the map combined information from 'a number of different
and probably independent processes that interpret disparity, motion, shading,
texture, and contour information' (p. 129). He presented detailed models of these
modules, each with its own computational theory based on specific constraints.
The stereo disparity module was outlined earlier.

The topmost stage of processing, 3-D model representation, describes shapes
and their spatial organisation in an object-centred coordinate frame. In other
words, the representation is completely independent of the observer's viewpoint
(the previous two levels contain viewer-centred or image-based representations).
The primitives used at this level represent volume and shape using simple
three-dimensional ('volumetric') geometrical forms. The representation is rather
schematic and hierarchical, being composed of cylindrical parts arranged into an
object, rather like pipe-cleaner human figures or twisted balloon models of animals. The task of object recognition then involves matching an active 3-D model
description against a stored catalogue of 3-D models.

IMPACT AND CRITIQUE OF THE CLASSIC STUDY

Although Marr's approach has been hugely influential, his 'three levels' framework has come under attack and is not widely used in contemporary research.
Furthermore, many of his specific theoretical proposals have not stood the test of
time well. This critique will evaluate Marr's framework and theory separately.

FRAMEWORK

A major focus of criticism of Marr's framework centres on the particular computational goals and constraints he identified. Where did he get them from, and how
can they be justified? The computations performed by biological information-
processing systems are often inferred from observed behaviours or neural
structures and their functions. In a flowchart at the end of *Vision*, Marr observed
that computational goals can be suggested by everyday experience or 'coarse
psychophysical observations' (1982, p. 332). He admitted that 'there is no real
recipe for this type of research – even though I have sometimes suggested that
there is' (p. 331). So the claim that computational theory has priority over the
other two levels is undermined. It is not completely independent of algorithm and
implementation, but is closely connected to these levels right from the outset;

ideas about computation may emerge from a consideration of the other levels in the framework. The presence of two eyes working together to create binocular images and psychophysical observations of depth perception suggest a processing task, namely stereo vision. But it does not necessarily follow that the goal of stereo vision is the computation of a dense depth map. The system may compute only depth discontinuities.

Marr contrasted the computations he proposed for the human visual system with those performed by systems in simpler organisms such as frogs and houseflies. He argued that:

> 'the frog does not detect *flies* – it detects small, moving black spots of about the right size. Similarly, the housefly does not represent the visual world about it, it merely computes a couple of parameters ... which cause it to chase its mate with sufficiently frequent success. We, on the other hand, very definitely do compute explicit properties of the real visible surfaces out there...' (p. 340)

In general, he claimed, simpler systems, such as those of frogs and houseflies, do not produce objective properties of the world like the human visual system does, but make do with simpler subjective descriptions which are just sufficient for the frog or housefly to survive; neither needs to see 'the truth' because natural selection depends only on fitness. There is a hint of hubris in this characterisation. One must allow for the possibility that humans and simpler organisms are more similar than we think; our perceptual representations may be no closer to objective truth than are those of frogs and flies. A fundamental issue with Marr's computational theories, as noted by Stevens (2012), is that we lack a methodology for discovering and testing the tasks that underlie vision.

THEORY OF PROCESSING

We are still far from a complete understanding of the computations performed by the visual cortex, but it has become clear in recent years that they do not operate autonomously in the bottom-up fashion that Marr envisaged. Furthermore, while it is not disputed that cognitive processing must become symbolic at some point (see Quiroga, 2012), most researchers do not accept Marr's claim that symbolic representations are created at the very earliest stages of visual analysis in the primal sketch. In current theories, bottom-up and top-down processes interact to create inferences about image content. Recent research indicates that early visual measurements of image properties are represented by continuous distributions of activity in large populations of cells, rather than stored as a small set of discrete, symbolic primitives (population coding; see Pouget, Dayan, & Zemel, 2000). The notion of perception as unconscious inference has a long history that goes back at least to Hermann von Helmholtz, and has modern advocates in the writings of Irvin Rock and Richard Gregory. Marr disliked this kind of problem-solving approach to vision because 'the additional knowledge or hypothesis that is brought to bear is not general but particular and true only of the scene in question' (p. 271). While acknowledging that 'top-down information is sometimes used and necessary' (p. 101), he was inclined towards the view that it was only of secondary importance, and focused primarily on bottom-up processes. However, research in the last 15 years disputes this view. It has become more apparent that many of the problems faced by image-processing systems are intractable without the interaction of prior knowledge with incoming sensory information (sometimes called 're-entrant processing' in computer science). Bayesian inference offers a rigorous way of combining current input with past experience, and this approach is now deeply embedded in the computational neuroscience of vision. Modern theoretical approaches also recognise the need for flexibility in processing which can accommodate variations in the reliability of different information sources. One such use of Bayesian inference is to modulate the weight attached to different visual cues during task execution (which Marr assumed were extracted by independent modules).

Many of Marr's specific proposals have been superseded by more recent research, as one might expect in a rapidly expanding and dynamic research field. For instance, there are several alternatives to Marr's theory and algorithm for encoding spatial features at the primal sketch stage, with empirical evidence to support them (see Morgan, 2011). In the case of motion detection, the current 'industry-standard' model, known as the Adelson-Bergen motion energy sensor, is quite different from that proposed by Marr and Ullman and described in _Vision_. Similarly, models of stereopsis have moved on from Marr and Poggio's approach to the problem. Marr's assumption that the goal of mid-level vision is to create a dense depth map of the metric distance to all visible surfaces (Euclidean structure) is now viewed as incorrect. Perceptual studies have shown that the human visual system in not good at recovering accurate Euclidean structure (Warren, 2012).

Marr did not consider the computational complexity of the processes he proposed (Tsotsos, 1990). Measures of computational complexity deal with the cost of reaching a solution to a processing problem, in terms of time (number of programming steps) and space (memory or processor size). The computations required to produce view-independent 3-D object models are now thought by many researchers to be too complex; no one has yet succeeded in generating 3-D models from image-based representations in the general way proposed by Marr. So research on visual recognition after _Vision_ has largely been dominated by debates between advocates of 3-D object-based and 2-D view-based representations of objects (Hayward, 2003). Notice that Marr's 3-D object models are, by definition, 'objective' descriptions, in keeping with his assumption mentioned earlier that vision tells humans the truth about what is out there, whereas the view-based representations used in current theories are more akin to the 'subjective' descriptions used by frogs and houseflies.

Despite these major issues concerning the details of Marr's theory, it was inspirational to an entire generation of vision researchers. It set them off on a new research program to test the plausibility of Marr's computations and algorithms. In the process, many become adept at developing and testing their own computational models. _Vision_ was the architect of its own downfall, in providing rigorous testable theories for many aspects of visual processing as well as the conceptual tools for building alternatives. For instance, Pollard, Mayhew, and Frisby (1985) found psychophysical evidence for a stereo matching constraint that Marr and Poggio (1976) did not even consider.

CONCLUSIONS

Many of Marr's specific theories have been discarded, so his three-levels framework is perhaps his most substantial legacy. Marr's framework emphasised that adequate theories of perception must be based on computational analysis of tasks, and require algorithmic proof that they can be implemented successfully. His attempts to implement his algorithms exposed the inherent complexity of even the earliest computations required for visual analysis, demonstrating in the process that vision is much more difficult than it appears.

Marr's emphasis on computational theory has changed the way researchers think about theoretical issues in perception. Due weight is now given to the computational goal of proposed algorithms or neural architectures. Even so, Marr's approach, though often cited, has not been widely adopted as a methodology for developing theories of perception (with a few exceptions, such as Frisby and Stone, 2010). Perhaps a fundamental reason behind this lack of enthusiasm is that Marr had no 'silver bullet' with which researchers could nail a theory. He did not supply a methodology for developing and testing computational-level theories. Researchers still have to rely on an *ad hoc* mix of phenomenology, neuroscience, and psychophysics to suggest, and even test, computational problems and solutions. This state of affairs nevertheless represents significant progress, because it brings computational considerations to the fore in vision research.

FURTHER READING

Frisby, J. P., & Stone, J. V. (2010). *Seeing: The computational approach to biological vision*. Cambridge, MA: The MIT Press.

Marr, D. (1982). *Vision: A computational investigation into the human representation and processing of visual information*. San Francisco, CA: W. H. Freeman.

REFERENCES

Frisby, J. P., & Stone, J. V. (2010). *Seeing: The computational approach to biological vision*. Cambridge, MA: The MIT Press.

Hayward, W. G. (2003). After the viewpoint debate: where next in object recognition? *Trends in Cognitive Sciences*, 7 (10), 425–427.

Hubel, D. H., & Wiesel, T. N. (1959). Receptive fields of single neurons in the cat's striate cortex. *Journal of Physiology*, 148, 574–591.

Marr, D. (1982). *Vision: A computational investigation into the human representation and processing of visual information*. San Francisco, CA: W. H. Freeman.

Marr, D., & Poggio, T. (1976). From understanding computation to understanding neural circuitry. *MIT AI Memo*, 357.

Morgan, M. J. (2011). Features and the 'primal sketch'. *Vision Research*, 51 (7), 738–753.

Pollard, S. B., Mayhew, J. E., & Frisby, J. P. (1985). PMF: A stereo correspondence algorithm using a disparity gradient limit. *Perception*, 14 (4), 449–470.

Pouget, A., Dayan, P., & Zemel, R. (2000). Information processing with population codes. *Nature Reviews Neuroscience*, 1 (2), 125–132.

Quiroga, R. Q. (2012). Concept cells: The building blocks of declarative memory functions. *Nature Reviews Neuroscience*, 13 (8), 587–597.

Stevens, K. A. (2012). The vision of David Marr. *Perception*, 41 (9), 1061–1072.

Tsotsos, J. K. (1990). Analyzing vision at the complexity level. *Behavioral and Brain Sciences*, 13, 423–469.

Warren, W. H. (2012). Does this computational theory solve the right problem? Marr, Gibson, and the goal of vision. *Perception*, 41 (9), 1053–1060.

5

Perception and action: Beyond Goodale and Milner's (1992) separate visual pathways

Glyn W. Humphreys (University of Oxford)

BACKGROUND AND DESCRIPTION OF THE CLASSIC STUDY

PERCEPTION AND ACTION: THE CASE FROM NEUROPSYCHOLOGY

In 1991 David Milner and colleagues published the first empirical report of a patient, DF, who had poor visual recognition of objects following carbon monoxide poisoning (Milner et al., 1991). DF was very poor at naming objects and at making judgements about even some of the basic aspects of shape, such as whether an edge had a particular orientation. She had problems in copying simple line drawings and she could not judge whether visual elements grouped together. Despite these severe visual impairments, Milner et al. reported that DF showed a remarkably good ability to use visual information to guide her hand actions. For example, she was able to post a letter through a slot positioned at different orientations – yet, in contrast, she was unable to turn the letter to match the orientation of the slot when asked to make a perceptual judgement about how the slot was oriented. Milner et al. argued that DF had a lesion that disrupted access to higher-order visual representations for object recognition, affecting the transition of information along a 'ventral' visual pathway, going from the primary site of visual input to the brain (the occipital cortex) into the temporal cortex where recognition was thought to take place. Importantly, this ventral lesion spared access from at least some shape attributes (e.g., edge orientation) to other systems that used the visual information to direct action. There was access still to the neural structures determining the use of visual information for action, with these structures being used when the task involved actually posting the letter.

In their 1991 paper, Milner et al. also noted the contrast between DF's case and patients with optic ataxia. Optic ataxic patients classically have damage to a 'dorsal' visual pathway, involving the transmission of information from the occipital cortex into the posterior parietal cortex at the top of the brain. These patients show good clinical recognition of objects but are poor at guiding hand movements to interact with the object (Perenin & Vighetto, 1988). The contrast between DF and the optic ataxic patient represents a double dissociation in which one process (object recognition) is impaired and another (action) spared in one patient (DF), while another patient shows the opposite pattern (spared object recognition but impaired action, as in optic ataxia). Such double dissociations are classically taken to indicate that there is both functional and neural separation between the underlying processes – here, vision for object recognition and vision for action, subserved respectively by the ventral and dorsal streams in the cortex.

The findings reported by Milner et al. (1991), together with those of other researchers, led to major theoretical developments. Goodale and Milner (1992) discussed these theoretical developments in a very influential article that emphasised the crucial distinction between the ventral and dorsal streams. This distinction was also discussed and subsequently developed by Milner and Goodale in their 1995 book, *The visual brain in action*. They argued that the ventral visual route supported visual pattern and object recognition, with lesions along this route leading to visual agnosia. However, this could leave the dorsal visual route spared, which was used for on-line guidance of action. In contrast, lesions of the dorsal route would disrupt the use of visual information to guide action while leaving preserved visual object recognition – as is found in optic ataxia. The distinction between these two cortical visual streams is illustrated in Figure 5.1. Interestingly, Milner and Goodale also suggested that the ventral stream was associated with conscious awareness of the visual stimulus while the dorsal stream was unconscious, as DF was (at least initially) unaware of her ability to use visual information for action.

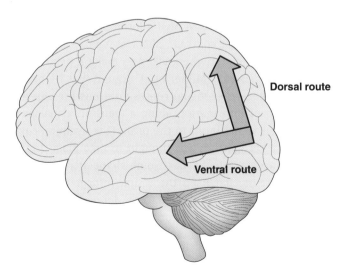

Figure 5.1 The dorsal and ventral routes

The distinction between the ventral and dorsal streams in the cortex was not itself new. Previously, a number of authors had argued that visual processing in the brain could be decomposed, with different functional processes operating in contrasting brain regions (see Ettlinger, 1990; Ingle, 1973; Schneider, 1969; Trevarthen, 1968, for this argument). Perhaps the best known argument relating to the ventral and dorsal visual streams was made by Mishkin and Ungerleider (1982). These authors proposed that the ventral visual stream supported object recognition (they termed this the 'what' system; an idea similar to the account of Milner and Goodale), but they argued that the dorsal stream coded spatial position. Thus monkeys with a lesion of their ventral cortex had problems responding to the identity of an object to gain a reward but could respond to the position. In contrast, monkeys with a lesion of their dorsal cortex differentiated between different objects to gain a reward but had difficulty in learning position-based rewards. The argument from Milner and Goodale, however, went beyond this. They noted that DF was not only able to respond to the location of stimuli (e.g., pointing correctly to the position of a visual target), but also to the orientation of the object that fell there and she could use that orientation information to shape her hand for reaching and grasping. These extra abilities fit with the idea that the dorsal stream is doing more than coding object position, and that it is involved in the visuo-motor control of action.

ADDITIONAL PROPERTIES OF THE VENTRAL AND DORSAL STREAMS

Not content with simply documenting their dissociations between vision and action, Milner and Goodale (1995) went on to characterise other contrasting properties of the systems. One important argument concerned the temporal properties of the streams. They argued that the dorsal visual stream was specialised for the on-line guidance of action. As actions must happen fast and in real-time in relation to the object present (imaging grasping a moving object), so the dorsal stream would need to react rapidly to visual cues. The ventral visual stream, on the other hand, may operate more slowly in order to support stable object recognition over time. This time difference would hold even if there were some conditions when the ventral route could contribute to action – for example, imagine making an action when given the name of an object – when ventral regions concerned with recognition of the learned properties of the object (its known size and shape) may be recruited to support the retrieval of these properties. This kind of 'off-line' control of action would likely be slow and not reactive to the on-line properties of the object.

This contrast between on-line and off-line control of action has been examined by contrasting actions when an object is directly present and actions when there is some delay between when the visual information is available and when the action had to be made – immediate versus delayed action. Interestingly, DF, the prime case of a patient operating with a dorsal but not a ventral visual route, was drastically impaired when she had to make delayed actions and to reach and grasp based on her memory of the stimulus. This clearly contrasted with her immediate actions, when objects were directly available. The result fits with the idea that the dorsal stream is not involved in such delayed actions and that, then, the ventral stream is needed to maintain the properties of the stimulus in memory.

Now one might object to this argument based on the grounds of task difficulty. Note that reaching and grasping objects that are remembered rather than physically present is more difficult than direct reaching for all of us. Perhaps, then, the data arise because DF shows an abnormal effect of difficulty as the action task becomes harder – it is not that delayed actions depend on the ventral route and are not supported by the fast, dorsal route. However, this argument is overruled by data on patients with optic aphasia, who again present a double dissociation in relation to DF. In this case, the double dissociation is based on the effects of delay on action. Milner et al. (1999) reported a highly counter-intuitive result which is that, in contrast to both DF and normal participants, optic ataxic patients actually *improved* in their reaching and grasping actions when objects were removed relative to when the objects were present. That is, there cannot be a general effect of task difficulty that leads to the difference between DF and the optic ataxic patients, since the optic ataxic patients do better with the apparently more difficult task. From this, Milner and Goodale (1995) argued that off-line, delayed reaching and grasping was supported by the ventral visual stream (spared in optic ataxic and impaired in DF). In contrast, the dorsal visual route (impaired in optic ataxia and spared in DF) is specialised for on-line guidance of reaching and grasping and does not support delayed action.

Converging evidence from normal participants

Milner and Goodale (1995) also went beyond the evidence from neuropsychology to argue that their distinction between the ventral and dorsal visual streams should have important implications for normal perception and action. Notably, the ventral visual stream should support conscious perceptual judgements about stimuli while the dorsal route may operate unconsciously and may even be unaffected by some forms of information that infiltrate conscious perceptual judgements. Notable examples here are visual illusions. From the earliest empirical work on human perception it has been noted that our conscious perceptual judgements can sometimes reflect perceptual illusions. One example is the Ebbinghaus illusion (Figure 5.2), in which judgements about the size of a central circle are affected by the size of the items surrounding the circle: we judge the central circle as smaller when it is surrounded by small circles and larger when it is surrounded by smaller circles. Are these perceptual illusions a property of the ventral visual stream and is the dorsal visual stream immune to the illusion – as it is concerned only with the direct use of visual information about the central circle in the control of action?

An early report of the contrast between perception and action in normal participants, using visual illusions, came from Bridgeman, Kirch, and Sperling (1981). They noted that a stationary dot presented against the background of a moving frame appears to drift in the opposite direction to the frame – an illusion produced by the movement of the frame. Despite consciously perceiving the illusion, however, when asked to make a ballistic pointing response to the actual location of the

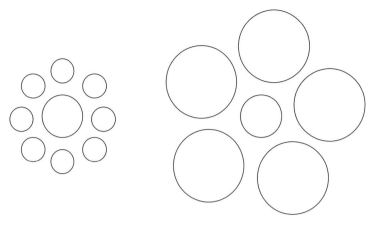

Figure 5.2   The Ebbinghaus illusion

dot, participants are accurate. Apparently, the 'action system' is not fooled by the change in people's conscious perceptual judgements, that the dot is moving. There is a dissociation between vision for conscious perceptual judgements and vision for action even in normal observers.

Aglioti, DeSouza, and Goodale (1995) reported a similar result with the Ebbinghaus illusion. They contrasted two conditions: when participants made conscious perceptual judgements about stimuli, and when they had to act by reaching and grasping the central stimulus. Conscious perceptual judgements were affected by the context in which the target circle was placed (judged bigger with a smaller context and smaller with larger contextual items). In contrast, grasp apertures were tuned to the actual size of the stimulus (e.g., the grasp aperture was the same to the central circle irrespective of whether it was positioned among small or large contextual items). These data support the contention arising from Milner and Goodale's 'two visual streams' account of visual processing in the brain. The 'perceptual system' takes visual context into account and so can be fooled by these contextual illusions. The 'action system', however, is more analytic and responds directly to the local information critical for setting the parameters of the action (e.g., the aperture of the hand as a grasp is made).

The evidence from normal participants here provides important 'converging evidence' for the dual stream account, showing that it does not solely depend on one line of evidence (and in particular from a single neuropsychological patient) but gains support from other lines of evidence that point to the same distinction between conscious perception and action.

IMPACT OF THE CLASSIC STUDY

M ilner and Goodale's (1995) characterisation of the ventral and dorsal visual streams, and the linked distinction between conscious perception and action has undoubtedly had a major impact on the field. The 1992 review paper in _Trends in Neurosciences_ (Goodale & Milner, 1992) has had over 2,000 citations at the time of writing (_Web of Science_). The neuropsychological studies have provided a framework for discussing a wide range of other disorders, including visual extinction (when patients can consciously report a single item presented to their contralesional field but fail to notice it when a second item appears simultaneously in the visual field ipsilateral to their lesion) and visual neglect (e.g., when a patient fails to notice even a single item on the contralesional side of space, or to notice the contralesional side of an object). For example, patients with visual extinction have been found to show better report of the contralesional stimulus if it can invoke an action than if it does not. Di Pelligrino, Rafal, and Tipper (2005) showed this in a study using cups in which the handle of a cup in the contralesional field was oriented to the contra- or ipsilesional side (e.g., respectively to the left or right for a patient with a right hemisphere lesion showing left-side extinction). There was less extinction when the handle was oriented to the contralesional (left) side, when it might better invoke an action to the left. The same did not hold when a non-functional handle-like stimulus was placed on the side of the cup. Di Pellegrino and colleagues argued that vision-for-action was maintained in such patients, despite their impairment in conscious perceptual judgements. Similarly, neglect patients can show less neglect when making actions rather than conscious perceptual judgements. For example, Robertson, Nico, and Hood (1995, 1997) had patients (1) use conscious perceptual judgements to point to the centre of a bar, or (2) make a direct action to reach and grasp the bar. Conscious perceptual judgements were systematically biased to the ipsilesional side, indicating neglect of contralesional space. On the other hand, reaching and grasping actions were more central and based around the centre of gravity of the bar. Again, the results can be interpreted as indicating the perception-for-action is relatively preserved when conscious perceptual judgements are disrupted (in this case, spatially biased) by the brain lesion.

Like the neuropsychological studies, the work on susceptibility to illusions has also generated very many additional experiments, trying either to establish whether differences between perceptual judgements and action truly reflect a 'perception-action' distinction, or to demonstrate the generality of the results across different illusions. There has also been considerable fMRI research with normal participants, trying to establish whether perception and action operate independently in the ventral and dorsal cortical streams. For example, the contrast between pointing and reaching and grasping is correlated with stronger activity for reaching and grasping in the dorsal parietal cortex, consistent with the dorsal parietal cortex being recruited for on-line reaching and grasping (Culham et al., 2003). Much of the work based around this important perception-action distinction can thus be accommodated within the dual-stream account (e.g., see Goodale, 2014, for a recent review). However, there have also been important caveats as research has progressed. These caveats place new constraints on the relations between perception and action in the brain.

CRITIQUE OF THE CLASSIC STUDY

CAVEAT 1: DF

The perception-action distinction was initially based around an argument that the agnosic patient DF had a largely preserved ability to use visual information for action, contrasting with her major impairment in pattern recognition. However, is DF's vision-for-action normal? Further work has shown that DF's use of visual information for action has some limitations. For example, Dijkerman, Milner, and Carey (1998) reported that DF was impaired at making reach and grasp actions that required her fingers to be positioned relative to one another – as when you reach and grasp to pick up a 10-pin bowling ball (with three hole openings). It appeared that this more complex action demanded information coded within the ventral visual stream, for instance concerning the spatial relations between the visual targets of the action. Even if an on-line action was required, this was not accomplished by the dorsal stream alone.

Hesse, Ball, and Schenk (2012) contrasted DF's ability to reach and grasp to objects presented in central vision and her ability to make similar actions to peripheral targets. They found that her actions to peripheral targets were impaired, again contradicting the idea that vision for action is fully controlled through a dorsal stream that is preserved in DF's case. Himmelbach, Boehme, and Karnath (2012) also reassessed DF's reaching and grasping in central vision, taking stringent assessments of her performance relative to controls. Like Hesse et al. (2012), Himmelbach et al. documented that DF's visually guided actions were impaired and not fully preserved. Thus DF does not present a perfect dissociation in which one ability is completely preserved (action) and the other is not (conscious perception). Both abilities are impaired, but to different degrees. Given the vagaries of neurological insult (e.g., DF suffered carbon monoxide poisoning which can generate multiple disseminated lesions in the brain), this might be expected if the dorsal stream was affected along with the ventral system.

CAVEAT 2: OPTIC ATAXIA

The second main set of neuropsychological data that have been used to support the perception-action distinction have been derived from optic ataxic patients. As with patient DF, though, concerns have been raised about how closely the data fit the strict dual stream account.

Jeannerod, Decety, and Michel (1994) examined reaching and grasping in optic ataxia and contrasted actions to unfamiliar objects versus those to familiar items (reaching and grasping a wood block versus a tube of lipstick). They found that actions were substantially improved when actions were made to familiar objects. In this case, the on-line actions appeared to be driven by the spared ventral recognition system and not by the impaired dorsal stream.

Other researchers (see Pisella et al., 2009, for a review) have reported that the reaching deficit apparent in optic ataxic patients is primarily for peripheral targets, while actions to central targets are largely spared (note here the similarity to the data reported by Hesse et al. (2012) for DF). Pisella et al. (2009) suggest that there are distinctions between the use of central and peripheral information for action, which may be separately impaired. Indeed, one of the functions of the dorsal regions lesioned in optic ataxic patients may be to de-couple the normally interlocked eye and hand movement systems so that the eyes can be maintained on one central location while a pointing action is made to a peripheral position.

Other studies have examined whether perceptual abilities are necessarily spared in optic ataxia. Pisella, Rossetti and colleagues (Pisella et al., 2007; Rossetti et al., 2005) examined the ability of optic ataxic patients to detect a change in a peripheral target and found that there were impairments in detecting when the location, size or orientation of the stimulus was altered (see also Perenin & Vighetto, 1988). Pisella et al. (2009) additionally report that these patients are impaired at covertly allocating their attention to peripheral locations when cued to attend there. Kitadono and Humphreys (2007) further showed that when their optic ataxic patient was cued to make an action to the location where a target could be presented, perceptual report of the target decreased. They suggested that the impairment in programming action to visual stimuli decreased processing resources and worsened perceptual report.

These different sets of results provide evidence that optic ataxia is not easily conceived as representing spared perception along with impaired on-line control of action.

CAVEAT 3: ILLUSIONS AND ACTIONS

Although the original work emphasised a dissociation in the effects of visual illusions on perceptual judgements and reaching and grasping, subsequent results have generated more conflicting results, with some groups reporting common illusion effects (e.g., Franz, Fahle, Bulthoff, & Gegenfurtner, 2001; Franz & Gegenfurtner, 2008; Franz, Scharnowski, & Gegenfurtner, 2005). The argument here has been that reaching and grasping impose different attentional constraints to perceptual judgements (reaching and grasping often requiring more focused attention to local elements, so reducing effects of surrounding contexts), and that reaching and grasping benefit from the presence of visual feedback as the action is made (Foster, Kleinholdermann, Leifheit, & Franz, 2012). Others, however, maintain that dissociations remain when attempts are made to control for such factors (e.g., Goodale, 2014).

Functional imaging studies of illusion effects in normal participants suggest that some illusion effects are represented in early visual areas (V1) (Schwarzkopf & Rees, 2013), that activity in regions of the dorsal stream is modulated by contextual illusions (Plewan, Weidner, Eickhoff, & Fink, 2012), and that connectivity between ventral and dorsal regions may be critical (Plewan et al., 2012). More work may need to be done to tie down exactly how and when illusions affect action as well as perception, and which brain regions may subserve these effects.

CAVEAT 4: PERCEPTION IN THE DORSAL STREAM AND ACTION IN THE VENTRAL

Functional brain imaging provides one way to assess the specialisation of processing with cortical regions. Though there is overwhelming evidence for object recognition being mediated by the ventral cortical stream, and reaching and grasping via the dorsal stream (Culham et al., 2003), there are complexities to this. For example, Konen and Kastner (2008) used fMRI adaptation, where neural signals decrease in strength when stimuli are repeated, to examine the sensitivity of different cortical areas to object identity. They found object-specific tuning, independent of the specific location or viewpoint, in dorsal as well as ventral visual regions, and the results were not confined to action-related stimuli. Konen and Kastner suggest that neurons in the dorsal stream may serve to integrate spatial and object codes and the object-specific responses do play a functional role in perception.

Other evidence for the necessary involvement of dorsal cortex in pattern recognition has been reported by Lestou et al. (2014). This study required both control participants and neuropsychological patients to discriminate 'glass

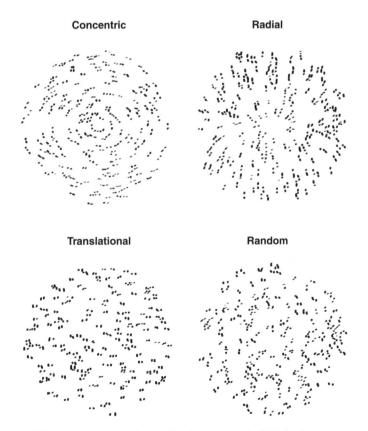

Figure 5.3 Glass pattern stimuli used by Lestou et al. (2014): the concentric, radial and translational stimuli have global patterns, the random stimuli do not

patterns' where local dots were either randomly positioned or were aligned to form concentric rings, radial or translational patterns (see Figure 5.3). When normal participants viewed the patterned displays (versus the random displays), there was activation on both ventral and dorsal visual areas. One agnostic patient, with bilateral lesions of the ventral cortex, could detect the patterned displays and showed normal activity in the dorsal regions. The other patient, an optic ataxic individual with dorsal brain lesions, was poor at detecting the patterned displays and showed no discrimination between patterned and random displays in brain activity in the ventral regions activated in controls – regions that the authors also demonstrated were structurally and functionally intact in the patient. These data indicate that discrimination of the patterned displays was supported by the dorsal region impaired in the optic ataxic patient, and that, when this area was damaged, there was no longer pattern discrimination within the ventral visual cortex. The evidence indicates a necessary role for the dorsal cortex in pattern recognition within the ventral visual stream.

As well as functional imaging evidence pointing to object coding within the dorsal stream, there is also evidence for 'action coding' in ventral visual areas. Roberts and Humphreys (2010) presented participants with displays such as those shown in Figure 5.4. Participants either attended to the two scenes and made a decision about whether they were indoors or outdoors, or to the objects and decided if the objects were related or not. When the objects were positioned to interact with one another, there was increased activity within the ventral visual stream, compared to when the objects were not positioned to interact. This result occurred irrespective of whether the objects were attended (i.e., it occurred even when scene judgements were made) and it did not necessarily depend on whether the objects were familiar as a pair – the objects just had to appear to interact. This suggests that the result was not due to learned (semantic) relations between the objects but to whether the objects together 'afforded' an action. The results

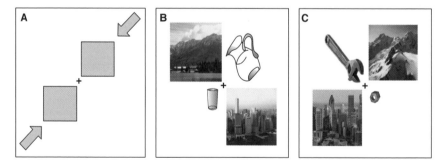

Figure 5.4 Example stimuli used by Roberts and Humphreys (2010). In A, participants were pre-cued to attend to stimuli along one of the two diagonals in the display, making their decision to those stimuli while ignoring the others. In B, participants would attend to the jig and cup and have to decide if the stimuli were related. In C, participants attend to the scenes while ignoring the objects

meshed with other results on patients with dorsal parietal lesions who remain sensitive to the presence of action relations between objects in their perceptual report (Riddoch et al., 2003). The functional imaging data suggest that perceptual report in such cases may be dependent on the activation of preserved regions of the ventral visual stream that register the potential actions that can occur between objects. Moreover, preparing an action that is congruent with the objects can facilitate their perception (Humphreys & Riddoch, 2001), illustrating interactions with the motor system.

CONCLUSIONS

T he distinction between the dorsal and ventral cortical streams, and their roles in (respectively) perception and action, has been a major tenet of visual cognition for the past 20 years. The work that has followed the original arguments, however, has indicated a more complex picture than was perhaps initially proposed. Notably, the ventral visual stream may support on-line action to familiar objects (Jeannerod et al., 1994) and it registers action relations between objects (Robert & Humphreys, 2010). Likewise, the dorsal visual stream is sensitive to pattern and object information (Konen & Kastner, 2008; Lestou et al. (2014) and dorsal lesions can disrupt aspects of perception as well as the on-line visual control of action (Pisella et al., 2009). There are also arguments about whether there is indeed a single dorsal visual stream and whether there may be functionally independent streams in the posterior parietal cortex (e.g., see Rizzolatti & Matelli, 2003). McIntosh and Schenk (2009) argued that the perception-action distinction has served as a useful heuristic for directing research but work needs to focus on the interactions between these streams in order to understand the detailed dynamic processes that determine how we see and act upon the visual world. Exactly how these interactions operate, at both functional and neural levels, is a key issue for future research.

FURTHER READING

Useful references that document the current state of play on many of the issues described here are:

Goodale, M. A. (2014). How (and why) the visual control of action differs from visual perception. *Proceedings of the Royal Society of London*, B281, 20140337.

McIntosh, R. D., & Schenk, T. (2009). Two visual streams for perception and action: Current trends. *Neuropsychologia*, 47 (6), 1391–1396.

Pisella, L., Sergio, L., Blangero, A., Torchin, H., Vighetto, A., & Rossetti, Y. (2009). Optic ataxia and the function of the dorsal stream: Contributions to perception and action. *Neuropsychologia*, 47, 3033–3044.

Schenk, T., & McIntosh, R. D. (2010). Do we have independent visual streams for perception and action? *Cognitive Neuroscience*, 1 (1), 52–62.

REFERENCES

Aglioti, S., DeSouza, J. F., & Goodale, M. A. (1995). Size-contrast illusions deceive the eye but not the hand. *Current Biology*, 5, 679–685.

Bridgeman, B., Kirch, M., & Sperling, A. (1981). Segmentation of cognitive and motor aspects of visual function induced motion. *Perception & Psychophyscs*, 29, 336–342.

Culham, J. C., Danckert, S. L., DeSouza, J. F. X., Gati, J. S., Menon, R. S., & Goodale, M. A. (2003). Visually guided grasping produces fMRI activation in dorsal but not ventral stream brain areas. *Experimental Brain Research*, 153 (2), 180–189.

Dijkerman, H. C., Milner, A. D., & Carey, D. P. (1998). Grasping spatial relationships: Failure to demonstrate allocentric visual coding in a patient with visual form agnosia. *Consciousness and Cognition*, 7, 438–453.

di Pellegrino, G., Rafal, R., & Tipper, S. P. (2005). Implicitly evoked actions modulate visual selection: Evidence from parietal extinction. *Current Biology*, 15, 1469–1472.

Ettlinger, G. (1990). 'Object vision' and 'spatial vision': The neuropsychological evidence for the distinction. *Cortex*, 26, 319–341.

Foster, R. M., Kleinholdermann, U., Leifheit, S., & Franz, V. H. (2012). Does bimanual grasping of the Muller-Lyer illusion provide evidence for a functional segregation of dorsal and ventral streams? *Neuropsychologia*, 50, 3392–3402.

Franz, V. H., Fahle, M., Bulthoff, H. H., & Gegenfurtner, K. B. (2001). Effects of visual illusions on grasping. *Journal of Experimental Psychology: Human Perception and Performance*, 27, 1124–1144.

Franz, V. H., & Gegenfurtner, K. R. (2008). Grasping visual illusions: Consistent data and no dissociation. *Cognitive Neuropsychology*, 25, 920–950.

Franz, V. H., Scharnowski, F., & Gegenfurtner, K. R. (2005). Effects on grasping are temporally constant not dynamic. *Journal of Experimental Psychology: Human Perception and Performance*, 31, 1359–1378.

Goodale, M. A. (2014). How (and why) the visual control of action differs from visual perception. *Proceedings of the Royal Society of London*, B281, 20140337.

Goodale, M. A., & Milner, A. D. (1992). Separate visual pathways for perception and action. *Trends in Neurosciences*, 15, 20–25.

Hesse, C., Ball, K., & Schenk, T. (2012). Visuomotor performance based on peripheral vision is impaired in the visual form agnostic patient DF. *Neuropsychologia*, 50, 90–97.

Himmelbach, M., Boehme, R., & Karnath, H. O. (2012). 20 years later: A second look on DF's motor behaviour. *Neuropsychologia*, 50, 139–144.

Humphreys, G. W., & Riddoch, M. J. (2001). Detection by action: Evidence for affordances in search in neglect. *Nature Neuroscience*, 4, 84–88.

Ingle, D. (1973). Two visual systems in the frog. *Science*, 181 (Sept.), 1053–1055.

Jeannerod, M., Decety, J., & Michel, F. (1994). Impairment of grasping movements following a bilateral posterior parietal lesion. *Neuropsychologia*, 32, 369–380.

Kitadono, K., & Humphreys, G. W. (2007). Interactions between perception and action programming: Evidence from visual extinction and optic ataxia. *Cognitive Neuropsychology*, 24, 731–754.

Konen, C. S., & Kastner, S. (2008). Two hierarchically organized neural systems for object information in human visual cortex. *Nature Neuroscience*, 11, 224–231.

Lestou, V., Kourtzi, Z., Humphreys, K. L., Lam, J., & Humphreys, G. W. (2014) The necessary role of the dorsal visual route in the heterarchical coding of global visual pattern: Evidence from neuropsychological fMRI. *Journal of Cognitive Neuroscience*, 26, 1154–1167.

McIntosh, R. D., & Schenk, T. (2009). Two visual streams for perception and action: Current trends. *Neuropsychologia*, 47, 1391–1396.

Milner, A. D., & Goodale, M. A. (1995). *The visual brain in action*. New York: Academic Press.

Milner, A. D., Paulignan, Y., Dijkerman, H. C., Michel, F., & Jeannerod, M. (1999). A paradoxical improvement of misreaching in optic ataxia: New evidence for two separate neural systems for visual localization. *Proceedings of the Biological Sciences*, 142, 225–242.

Milner, A. D., Perrett, D. I., Johnston, R. S., Benson, P. J., Jordan, T. R., Heeley, D. W., Bettucci, D., Mortara, F., Mutani, R., Terazzi, E., & Davidson, D. L. W. (1991). Perception and action in visual form agnosia. *Brain*, 114, 405–428.

Mishkin, M., & Ungerleider, L. G. (1982). Contribution of striate inputs to the visuospatial functions of parieto-preoccipital cortex in monkeys. *Behavioral Brain Research*, 6 (1), 57–77.

Perenin, M. T., & Vighetto, A. (1988). Optic ataxia: A specific disruption in visuomotor mechanisms. I. Different aspects of the deficits in reaching for objects. *Brain*, 111, 643–674.

Pisella, L., Sergio, L., Blangero, A., Torchin, H., Vighetto, A., & Rossetti, Y. (2009). Optic ataxia and the function of the dorsal stream: Contributions to perception and action. *Neuropsychologia*, 47, 3033–3044.

Pisella, L., Striemer, C., Blangero, A., Gaveau, V., Revol, P., Salemme, R., & Rossetti, Y. (2007). Perceptual deficits in optic ataxia? In P. Haggard, Y. Rossetti, & M. Kawato (Eds.), *Attention and performance XXI: Sensorimotor foundations of higher cognition* (pp. 47–71). Oxford: Oxford University Press.

Plewan, T., Weidner, R., Eickhoff, S. B., & Fink, G. R. (2012). Ventral and dorsal stream interactions during the perception of the Muller-Lyer illusion: Evidence derived from fMRI and dynamic causal modelling. *Journal of Cognitive Neuroscience*, 24, 2015–2029.

Riddoch, M. J., Humphreys, G. W., Edwards, S., Baker, T., & Willson, K. (2003). Seeing the action: Neuropsychological evidence for action-based effects on object selection. *Nature Neuroscience*, 6, 82–89.

Rizzolatti, G., & Matelli, M. (2003). Two different streams form the dorsal visual system: Anatomy and functions. *Experimental Brain Research*, 153, 146–157.

Roberts, K. L., & Humphreys, G. W. (2010). Action relationships concatenate representations of separate objects in the ventral visual system. *Neuroimage*, 42, 1541–1548.

Robertson, I. H., Nico, D., & Hood, B. (1995). The intention to act improves unilateral left neglect: Two demonstrations. *Neuroreport*, 7, 246–248.

Robertson, I. H., Nico, D., & Hood, B. (1997). Believing what you feel: Using proprioceptive feedback to reduce unilateral neglect. *Neuropsychology*, 11, 53–58.

Rossetti, Y., Revol, P., McIntosh, R., Pisella, L., Rode, G., Danckert, J., Tilikete, C., Dijkerman, H. C., Basson, D., & Vighetto, A. (2005). Visually guided reaching: Bilateral posterior parietal lesions cause a switch from fast visuomotor to slow cognitive control. *Neuropsychologia*, 43, 162–177.

Schneider, G. E. (1969). Two visual systems. *Science*, 163 (3870) February, 895–902.

Schwarzkopf, D. S., & Rees, G. (2013). Subjective size perception depends on central visual cortical magnification in human v1. *PLoS One*, 8, e60550.

Trevarthen, C. B. (1968). Two mechanisms of vision in primates. *Psychologische Forschung*, 31 (4), 299–348.

6

Attention: Beyond Stroop's (1935) colour–word interference phenomenon

Colin M. MacLeod (University of Waterloo, Ontario, Canada)

BACKGROUND TO THE CLASSIC STUDY

At the dawn of experimental psychology, conducting his dissertation research under Wilhelm Wundt, James McKeen Cattell demonstrated that words were faster to read than objects or colours were to name, concluding that 'This is because, in the case of words and letters, the association between the idea and name has taken place so often that the process has become automatic, whereas in the case of colours and pictures we must by a voluntary effort choose the name' (Cattell, 1886, p. 65). Thus was born the modern concept of automaticity, so influential today in our thinking about cognitive processing (see Moors & De Houwer, 2006, for a review). Of course, the idea of automaticity of behaviour has a much longer history: it is evident in the writings of the Greek philosophers, as in Aristotle's analysis of virtue.

Over the next 50 years, researchers tested the idea of differential practice as the mechanism underlying Cattell's finding, usually contrasting it with the principal alternative – differential interference or competition – that 'One particular response habit has become associated with each word while in the case of colours themselves a variety of response tendencies have developed' (Peterson, Lanier, & Walker, 1925, p. 281). This alternative, first expressed by Woodworth and Wells (1911), was championed by Joseph Peterson but 50 years passed from the time of Cattell's report until one of Peterson's students combined the two dimensions – word and colour – into a single task. The result was to become the best known phenomenon in all of psychology – the Stroop effect (see MacLeod, 1991a, for more background).

DETAILED DESCRIPTION OF THE CLASSIC STUDY

In his dissertation research, John Ridley Stroop set out to explore the phenomenon of interference (for a biographical sketch of Stroop, see MacLeod, 1991b).

Until that time, interference had most often been studied in the context of memory, where previously learned information sometimes disrupted remembering or new learning. Stroop (1935) wanted to study what we would now call 'on-line' processing. He set out to do so by examining interference, where one dimension of a stimulus competed with another simultaneously displayed dimension, more in keeping today with the study of attention than with the study of memory. He had been exploring word reading and colour naming with Peterson, and his simple but powerful insight was to print words in colour, and then to pit the two dimensions against each other.

Although the essence of Stroop's study is widely known, exactly what he did is often incorrectly reported, so it is worthwhile to précis his study. He set out to answer two questions: what effect each dimension of a compound stimulus has on responding to the other dimension (Experiments 1 and 2), and what effect practice has on the interaction of dimensions (Experiment 3). I will omit discussion of his considerably more complicated Experiment 3 concerned with practice, emphasising the first two experiments that set out the famous phenomenon that now bears his name.

In Experiment 1, he measured the effect of incongruent ink colours on the task of reading words aloud (e.g., for the word RED printed in green ink, the correct response would be 'red'). He used five words and their corresponding ink colours: red, blue, green, brown, and purple. In the experimental condition, each word appeared equally often in each of the other four ink colours on one 10 × 10 stimulus card; the stimuli appeared in reverse order on a second card. The control cards were each identical to an experimental card but all of the words were printed in black ink only. Subjects were to read the words aloud as quickly as possible, correcting errors as they read. The data from the 70 subjects tested in Experiment 1 are shown in the top row of Table 6.1. Although subjects averaged 2.3 seconds longer to read the 100 words on the experimental cards, this 5.6% increase was far from significant.

In Experiment 2, the task was naming the colours aloud (e.g., in the above example, saying 'green'). The control cards substituted solid colour squares for the coloured words. The experimental cards and the procedure were otherwise identical to those of Experiment 1, the critical change being the switch from word reading to colour naming. The data from the 100 subjects tested in Experiment 2 are shown in the bottom row of Table 6.1. Subjects averaged 47 seconds longer to name the ink colours of the incongruent words than of the colour squares, a highly significant 74% increase. A replication almost 60 years later (MacLeod, 1991a) produced results almost identical to Stroop's.

Stroop's study is often described in textbooks and article introductions as if there was a single experiment examining colour naming – or a single experiment contrasting word reading and colour naming – but he actually carried out two separate experiments. Quite often, his word-reading findings (Experiment 1) are not even mentioned. Most egregious, perhaps, is that he is sometimes credited with including a congruent condition (e.g., the word RED in red, say 'red'), which he did not do, likely because he realised that subjects would 'cheat' and simply read the words even if they were instructed to name the colours, given that the responses would be the same in the two cases. The congruent condition had to

Table 6.1 The data from the original Stroop (1935) experiments; mean total response times (in seconds) for 100 items on a card

Experiment	Experimental condition	Control condition
Experiment 1: Reading words	43.30	41.00
Experiment 2: Naming colours	102.27	59.76

Note: In Experiment 1, the experimental condition involved reading words printed in incompatible colours and the control condition involved reading words printed in ordinary black font. In Experiment 2, the experimental condition involved naming colours of words with incompatible names and the control condition involved naming colours of colour patches.

await the advent of single-trial recording; it was actually introduced 30 years later by Dalrymple-Alford and Budayr (1966).

Stroop simply and elegantly explored an interference phenomenon. Overall, he saw differential practice as explaining the asymmetrical interference pattern across his two experiments, with reading words being much more practised than naming colours. He agreed with Peterson et al. (1925) that words evoked a single reading response whereas colours evoked multiple responses, an idea he saw as confirmed when he put it to further test three years later (Stroop, 1938). The reliability, size, and apparent simplicity of the effect named after him have continued to pique the interest of investigators for almost 80 years.

IMPACT AND CRITIQUE OF THE CLASSIC STUDY

It would be hard to overestimate the impact of Stroop's hallmark task, in that it is featured in virtually every introductory and cognitive textbook in the discipline and is that rarest of phenomena – one whose influence has increased rather than declined over time. As evidence of this influence, according to the *Web of Science*, the topic of the Stroop effect appears in 2,800 articles and has attracted over 70,000 citations. I have noticed that many articles involving the Stroop effect do not even cite his classic article, no doubt because 'everybody knows the Stroop effect', so these numbers, high as they are, likely represent a considerable underestimate. The number of articles on the topic of the Stroop effect increased from 42 in the 1980s, to 462 in the 1990s, to 1,350 in the 2000s. The corresponding citations for articles published in these three decades are 1,406, 25,813, and 38,765. That is a truly extraordinary impact.

Yet it did not start out that way. Indeed, for 30 years after the study was published, almost no research pursued the phenomenon or its explanation, with its visibility almost entirely confined to use as a component of psychometric tests (e.g., Thurstone, 1944). But just when Jensen and Rohwer (1966) reviewed this applied use of the Stroop task, it was beginning to attract attention in the realm of basic cognitive research on attention and learning.

Three factors were crucial in reviving interest in what we now know as 'Stroop interference' as a way to explore basic cognitive processes such as attention and learning. The first was a systematic study exploring the phenomenon and reintroducing it to a new generation. That study was published by Klein (1964). In his article, Klein showed that the degree of interference with colour naming caused by the to-be-ignored verbal item was a function of the nature of the verbal item: interference was greatest when the irrelevant words were incongruent members of the set of colours to be named, dropped by 50% as he moved to other colour words not in the response set, and then gradually declined further across high frequency words, low frequency words, and non-words. Klein's study was well timed to reignite interest because its publication coincided with the emergence of the second key factor – a new method. With the appearance of computer-controlled experiments came the possibility of presenting individual Stroop trials to obtain trial-by-trial response times, a procedure that Dalrymple-Alford and Budayr (1966) demonstrated to be viable and that has become by far the dominant paradigm since then. Indeed, the rapid growth in interest in the 1960s shortly led to the third key factor – the appearance of the first comprehensive review article on the Stroop effect as a basic cognitive phenomenon, published by Dyer (1973). Since that time, there has been no looking back: thousands of studies involving the Stroop effect have been published in the past 40+ years.

For a decade or so following the Klein (1964) study, the focus of much of the research on the Stroop effect was on where in the sequence of processing the interference arose. This fit with the then prevailing view of processing as a sequence of serially executed stages (cf. Sternberg, 1969). Interference was widely viewed as the consequence of relative speed of processing, essentially ratifying the ideas of Cattell (1886) and Stroop (1935) that the word dimension was processed faster than the colour dimension, resulting in a race in which, when the task was colour naming, the wrong dimension won. This was often referred to as a 'horse race' model. But where exactly did interference arise in the race? For some, the problem was near the start, during encoding, making it a problem of 'early selection'. In their perceptual-encoding account, Hock and Egeth (1970) argued that the encoding of ink-colour information was slowed by the incompatible information from a colour word (as opposed to a neutral control). But much evidence around the same time and certainly later conflicted with this account. The most influential explanation came to be the response selection account, viewing interference as a 'late selection' problem (e.g., Morton & Chambers, 1973; Posner & Snyder, 1975). Posner and Snyder (1975, p. 57) put this very clearly:

> First, the usual Stroop effect arises because of response competition between vocal responses to the printed word and the ink color. ... Second, the direction of interference depends upon the time relations involved. Words are read faster than colors can be named, thus a color naming response receives stronger interference from the word than the reverse. ... Third, words often facilitate the vocal output to colors with which they share a common name. ... These three results suggest that color naming and reading go on in parallel and without interference until close to the output.

By the mid-to-late 1970s, the idea that processing was quite strictly sequential had lost currency in cognitive psychology, and parallel processing ideas came to hold sway, as seen in the work of Townsend (1976), Taylor (1977), and others. The parallel view – that word and colour were processed simultaneously with cross-talk throughout processing, meshed much better with the Posner and Snyder (1975) automaticity account, and this has been the dominant perspective ever since, whether processing of the response-irrelevant word is seen as 'automatic' or simply as more fluent than processing of the response-relevant colour.

A couple of studies illustrate results that fit well with this parallel view and not with the sequential view. Consider first a study by Glaser and Glaser (1982). Using the individual item procedure and separating the word from the colour, they directly tested the sequential speed of processing idea. They varied the stimulus onset asynchrony, presenting the word prior to the colour or the colour prior to the word over a range of temporal gaps. Their critical finding came from the situation where the task was to read the word but the colour information came first. Surprisingly, there was no evidence of interference with word reading even when an incompatible colour appeared 400 milliseconds before the word. Under any version of the sequential speed of processing account, a reversed Stroop effect – that is, incompatible colours interfering with word reading – should have appeared with such a long lead time for the colour, so finding no interference at all in this situation contradicted this type of account.

Shortly thereafter, Dunbar and MacLeod (1984) took a different approach, manipulating the ease of reading words by spatially transforming them, for example, turning them upside down and backwards. Time to read colour words aloud increased radically when they were presented in unusual orientations. Yet even when reading a colour word became substantially slower than naming the colour in which the word was printed, robust Stroop interference – virtually undiminished – was still observed. Perhaps most striking, when word reading was extremely slow, a reversed Stroop effect co-occurred with the standard Stroop effect. Like the Glaser and Glaser (1982) findings, this pattern of data is thoroughly inconsistent with the sequential speed of processing account. Indeed, research using the Stroop task was instrumental in changing the prevailing view of the stream of processing from a sequential to a parallel framing.

The 1970s and 1980s saw immense growth in research on the Stroop task and its many variants, as reviewed by MacLeod (1991a). As just a few illustrations, the Stroop task was used to test theories not only of attention (e.g., Neill, 1978) and automaticity (e.g., Kahneman & Chajczyk, 1983; MacLeod & Dunbar, 1988), but also of semantic memory (e.g., Klein, 1964; Warren, 1972), bilingual memory organisation (e.g., Mägiste, 1984; Preston & Lambert, 1969), and reading (e.g., Martin, 1978), among others. For the centenary of the establishing of the American Psychological Association, Stroop's (1935/1992) article was selected as one of the classics worthy of republication, and was identified as the 'gold standard' of measures of attention, one of the few widely-known tasks where related research has continued to grow as opposed to declining with the passage of time (MacLeod, 1992).

In the past 20 years, interest in Stroop interference has not abated. Indeed, the task has become a favourite of cognitive neuroscientists interested in basic brain processes and in the disruption of normal brain processes caused by a variety of disorders. This was already true in 2000 (see MacLeod & MacDonald, 2000), but Stroop-related research on basic brain mechanisms of cognition has accelerated since then, with interference used as a measure of inhibition (e.g., Mitchell, 2005) or episodic memory retrieval (e.g., Egner & Hirsch, 2005) and, more often, cognitive control (e.g., Carter et al., 2000; Herd, Banich, & O'Reilly, 2006) processes in brain regions identified by fMRI and other imaging techniques. The clinical work is even more extensive, including research on such diverse diagnoses as schizophrenia (e.g., Minzenberg, Laird, Thelen, Carter, & Glahn, 2009) and ADHD (Bush et al., 1999), where investigators have sought to identify the brain regions affected by the disorder.

NEW EXPLANATIONS

Theoretical work has also developed in the past quarter-century, with notable new theories coming forth from different cognitive domains. The first and best known was the connectionist theory of Cohen, Dunbar, and McClelland (1990). As a starting point, they took the findings of MacLeod and Dunbar (1988) – that interdimensional interference was a direct function of training or practice on each dimension, implying that automaticity is continuous, not all or none. Then, in a parallel distributed processing framework, Cohen et al. argued that automaticity depends on the strength of a processing pathway, with strength increasing over extended training. When the model, a neural net, was trained more on reading words, it was able to produce many of the key findings in the Stroop literature. Automatic word reading did appear to be continuous, emerging gradually with practice. This model has stimulated a great deal of theoretical development since its introduction, both in the Stroop domain and beyond.

Roelofs (2003) disputed this association-based approach, instead building his model on the foundation of a psycholinguistic theory of word production and the idea of production system rules. Essentially, he argued that the Stroop effect is the result of processing interactions within the language-production system and of goal-referenced control processes. In his view, attentional selection in the Stroop task is in fact selection for responding verbally. This selection is based on the individual's goals for action, specifically for verbal action, with the model incorporating both automatic and expectancy-based elements of verbal responding. This model also was very successful in encompassing many of the findings that MacLeod (1991a) had identified as critical for any theory to capture.

In yet another approach, Melara and Algom (2003) built their model on fundamental perceptual principles, arguing that attentional selection results from two memory-based structures that accomplish selection by processing information within and across stimulus dimensions dynamically and without the need for consciousness. The result is that memories of presented and even unpresented dimensional values are retrieved from trial to trial, such that the recent past – and even the more distant past – both influence the present. One of these structures is _dimensional uncertainty_, reflecting the degree of correlation of the dimensional values and the degree to which co-occurrences of those values are unexpected based on memory. The other is _dimensional imbalance_, reflecting the degree of salience of the dimensional values: typically, experimenters specify colour naming as the task, but subjects are vastly more experienced with reading words. Each of these structures plays a role in governing the excitation accruing to the target dimension as well as the inhibition applied to the distractor dimension and to the memories of prior episodes.

The Melara and Algom (2003) model grew out of empirical work by Melara and Mounts (1993) demonstrating that Stroop interference is to a considerable extent the result of episodic history – experience with the various possible stimuli in the experiment. This was the source of the dimensional imbalance structure in the model. Basically, their claim is that the word-colour contingency matters a great deal, a fact that has been under-appreciated in the literature. A major implication is that individual stimuli seen more frequently will be responded to faster than those seen less frequently, other factors being equal. This may well explain why congruent trials are faster than incongruent trials in the Stroop task. Researchers ordinarily design their experiments to have an equal number of trials in each condition, but this necessarily means that there are more incongruent than congruent stimuli across trials (e.g., given four colours, there are four congruent colour–word combinations but 12 incongruent combinations). Consistent with this idea, when Melara and Mounts (see also Sabri, Melara, & Algom, 2001) equated stimuli rather than conditions, the response time advantage for congruent items sharply decreased. As for the dimensional salience structure, they argued that words typically are more discriminable than colours, making words more salient despite instructions to devote attention to colours. When they manipulated dimensional discriminability, they found that making the colours more discriminable or the words less discriminable again sharply reduced Stroop interference. In addition to being consistent with their theory, these results suggest that considerably more thought needs to be given to how Stroop experiments are constructed.

HOW THE CLASSIC STUDY ADVANCED THINKING

Stroop could not have known the continuing prevalence and impact that his task would have – interestingly, when Jensen (Jensen & Rohwer, 1966) spoke to him in the mid-1960s, Stroop was not very interested (see MacLeod, 1991b). At the time of his dissertation, Stroop's project was far removed from the ethos of the day, dominated as the times were by behaviourism. Quite obviously, the size of the behavioural effect – it is one that we can feel almost as soon as we begin performing the task – and the simplicity of the paradigm have been strong attractors for researchers. As well, interference of one type or another is among the few real tools that we have available to explore cognitive mechanisms, and Stroop interference is without doubt the best-known measure of interference.

As already noted, the Stroop task has been put to a wide variety of uses, particularly if its many variants are included. Among the most prevalent variants are the picture–word task (where the task is to name a simple picture, ignoring a word printed on top of the picture; see Dell'Acqua, Job, Peressotti, & Pascali, 2007; van Maanen, van Rijn, & Borst, 2009, on the debate concerning how closely these two tasks are related) and the counting Stroop task (where the task is to ignore a set of digits while counting how many of them there are; see, for example, Bush et al., 1999). But probably the most frequently used variant comes from the clinical literature: the emotional Stroop task (see Williams, Mathews, & MacLeod, 1996, for a review). Here, words related to one's psychopathology (e.g., spider-related words for someone with arachnophobia) are found to be slower to colour name than are control words. This version of the task has been heavily used to explore a host of clinical diagnoses, although whether it is really a true Stroop analogue is a subject of debate. I am inclined to agree with Algom, Chajut, and Lev (2004) who maintain, based on a conceptual analysis and a series of experiments, that the interference observed for the emotion words relative to the control words in the emotional Stroop task reflects a generic slowdown resulting from the threat embodied in the emotional words, not the selective attention influence underlying the classic colour–word Stroop effect. People respond very slowly in the emotional Stroop task, as if they are watching for the emotion-related words. Moreover, the response competition so integral to the classic Stroop effect is absent in the emotional Stroop task.

A reasonable question to ask at this juncture would be: 'What exactly does the Stroop task measure?' Despite its widespread and frequent use, the answer to that question is not straightforward. It is most widely seen as a measure of attentional selectivity, or more properly of its failure (e.g., Melara & Algom, 2003). But it is also frequently taken to be a measure of inhibition, even of neural inhibition (e.g., Brittain et al., 2012). My colleagues and I have argued against the inhibition perspective (e.g., MacLeod, Dodd, Sheard, Wilson, & Bibi, 2003), and the work of Miyake, Friedman, and colleagues (e.g., Friedman & Miyake, 2004) has argued that the concept of inhibition may be over-extended. Some have argued that it is simply an index of extent of learning (e.g., MacLeod & Dunbar, 1988), as even Stroop (1935) himself maintained. And in the past 20 years or so, it has become widely used as an indicator of executive or cognitive control (e.g., Meier & Kane, 2013). Certainly, one goal for future research will be to try to ascertain what Stroop interference actually measures in cognitive processing, which in turn will help us to better understand cognitive processing more generally.

CONCLUSIONS

This very simple task has given us a great deal of insight into the operation of mind. Often, to capture thought in action, we need to see how it fails – what makes it slower or more error-prone. No situation provides a more obvious illustration of this failure than the Stroop task. Better learned information gets in the way of less well learned information, automatic responses trump more controlled ones, and we must keep at bay a more familiar response to be able to make a more novel response. The Stroop task is a reflection of all of these situations, and so continues to provide a valuable tool for exploring basic cognitive functioning as well as disruptions of that functioning.

FURTHER READING

(Complete citations are in the References section.)

MacLeod (1991a) presents the most comprehensive review of the voluminous Stroop literature to that point, although a great deal of research has been published in the over 20 years since then.

MacLeod (1991b) presents a brief biography of John Ridley Stroop, the man whose dissertation launched his eponymous task.

Cohen, Dunbar, and McClelland (1990) present the first detailed model of the Stroop task, also a landmark article in the world of connectionist modelling.

Melara and Algom (2003) offer an alternative, more perceptual account of the Stroop effect, pointing out some critical problems of method and interpretation.

Stroop (1935/1992) is the classic article, containing his dissertation research and written in a clear and engaging fashion, with straightforward analyses and good connections to the 'big picture' relevant to attention, learning, and memory.

REFERENCES

Algom, D., Chajut, E., & Lev, S. (2004). A rational look at the emotional Stroop phenomenon: A generic slowdown, not a Stroop effect. *Journal of Experimental Psychology: General,* 133, 323–338.

Brittain, J.-S., Watkins, K. E., Joundi, R. A., Ray, N. J., Holland, P., Green, A. L., Aziz, T. Z., & Jenkinson, N. (2012). A role for the subthalamic nucleus in response inhibition during conflict. *The Journal of Neuroscience,* 32, 13396–13401.

Bush, G., Frazier, J. A., Rauch, S. L., Seidman, L. J., Whalen, P. J., Jenike, M. A., Rosen, B. R., & Biederman, J. (1999). Anterior cingulate cortex dysfunction in attention-deficit/ hyperactivity disorder revealed by fMRI and the Counting Stroop. *Biological Psychiatry,* 45, 1542–1552.

Carter, C. S., Macdonald, A. M., Botvinick, M., Ross, L. L., Stenger, V. A., Noll, D., & Cohen, J. D. (2000). Parsing executive processes: Strategic vs. evaluative functions of the anterior cingulate cortex. *Proceedings of the National Academy of Sciences of the United States of America*, 97, 1944–1948.

Cattell, J. M. (1886). The time it takes to see and name objects. *Mind*, 11, 63–65.

Cohen, J. D. Dunbar, K., & McClelland, J. L. (1990). On the control of automatic processes: A parallel distributed processing account of the Stroop effect. *Psychological Review*, 97, 332–361.

Dalrymple-Alford, E. C., & Budayr, B. (1966). Examination of some aspects of the Stroop Color-Word Test. *Perceptual and Motor Skills*, 23, 1211–1214.

Dell'Acqua, R., Job, R., Peressotti, F., & Pascali, A. (2007). The picture–word interference effect is not a Stroop effect. *Psychonomic Bulletin & Review*, 14, 717–722.

Dunbar, K., & MacLeod, C. M. (1984). A horse race of a different color: Stroop interference patterns with transformed words. *Journal of Experimental Psychology: Human Perception and Performance,* 10, 622–639.

Dyer, F. N. (1973). The Stroop phenomenon and its use in the study of perceptual, cognitive, and response processes. *Memory & Cognition,* 1, 106–120.

Egner, T., & Hirsch, J. (2005). Where memory meets attention: Neural substrates of negative priming. *Journal of Cognitive Neuroscience,* 17, 1774–1784.

Friedman, N. P., & Miyake, A. (2004). The relations among inhibition and interference control functions: A latent-variable analysis. *Journal of Experimental Psychology: General,* 133, 101–135.

Glaser, M. O., & Glaser, W. R. (1982). Time course analysis of the Stroop phenomenon. *Journal of Experimental Psychology: Human Perception and Performance,* 8, 875–894.

Herd, S. A., Banich, M. T., & O'Reilly, R. C. (2006). Neural mechanisms of cognitive control: An integrative model of Stroop task performance and fMRI data. *Journal of Cognitive Neuroscience,* 18, 22–32.

Hock, H. S. & Egeth, H. (1970). Verbal interference with encoding in a perceptual classification task. *Journal of Experimental Psychology,* 83, 299.

Jensen, A. R., & Rohwer, W. D., Jr. (1966). The Stroop Color-Word Test: A review. *Acta Psychologica,* 25, 36–93.

Kahneman, D., & Chajczyk, D. (1983). Tests of the automaticity of reading: Dilution of Stroop effects by color-irrelevant stimuli. *Journal of Experimental Psychology: Human Perception and Performance,* 9, 497–509.

Klein, G. S. (1964). Semantic power measured through the interference of words with color-naming. *American Journal of Psychology,* 77, 576–588.

MacLeod, C. M. (1991a). Half a century of research on the Stroop effect: An integrative review. *Psychological Bulletin,* 109, 163–203.

MacLeod, C. M. (1991b). John Ridley Stroop: Creator of a landmark cognitive task. *Canadian Psychology,* 32, 521–524.

MacLeod, C. M. (1992). The Stroop task: The 'gold standard' of attentional measures. *Journal of Experimental Psychology: General,* 121, 12–14.

MacLeod, C. M., & Dunbar, K. (1988). Training and Stroop-like interference: Evidence for a continuum of automaticity. *Journal of Experimental Psychology: Learning, Memory, and Cognition,* 14, 126–135.

MacLeod, C. M., & MacDonald, P. A. (2000). Inter-dimensional interference in the Stroop effect: Uncovering the cognitive and neural anatomy of attention. *Trends in Cognitive Sciences,* 4, 383–391.

MacLeod, C. M., Dodd, M. D., Sheard, E. D., Wilson, D. E., & Bibi, U. (2003). In opposition to inhibition. In B. H. Ross (Ed.), *The psychology of learning and motivation* (Vol. 43, pp. 163–214). New York: Elsevier Science.

Mägiste, E. (1984). Stroop tasks and dichotic translation: The development of interference patterns in bilinguals. *Journal of Experimental Psychology: Learning, Memory, and Cognition,* 10, 304–315.

Martin, M. (1978). Speech recoding in silent reading. *Memory & Cognition,* 30, 187–200.

Meier, M. E., & Kane, M. J. (2013). Working memory capacity and Stroop interference: Global versus local indices of executive control. *Journal of Experimental Psychology: Learning, Memory, and Cognition,* 39, 748–759.

Melara, R. D., & Algom, D. (2003). Driven by information: A tectonic theory of Stroop effects. *Psychological Review,* 110, 422–471.

Melara, R. D., & Mounts, J. R. (1993). Selective attention to Stroop dimensions: Effects of baseline discriminability, response mode, and practice. *Memory & Cognition, 21,* 627–645.

Minzenberg, M. J., Laird, A. R., Thelen, S., Carter, C. S., & Glahn, D. C. (2009). Meta-analysis of 41 functional neuroimaging studies of executive function in schizophrenia. *Archives of General Psychiatry, 66,* 811–822.

Mitchell, R. L. C. (2005). The BOLD response during Stroop task-like inhibition paradigms: Effects of task difficulty and task-relevant modality. *Brain and Cognition, 59,* 23–37.

Moors, A., & De Houwer, J. (2006). Automaticity: A theoretical and conceptual analysis. *Psychological Bulletin, 132,* 297–326.

Morton, J., & Chambers, S. M. (1973). Selective attention to words and colours. *Quarterly Journal of Experimental Psychology, 25,* 387–397.

Neill, W. T. (1978). Decision processes in selective attention: Response priming in the color–word task. *Perception & Psychophysics, 23,* 80–84.

Peterson, J., Lanier, L. H., & Walker, H. M. (1925). Comparisons of white and negro children in certain ingenuity and speed tests. *Journal of Comparative Psychology, 5,* 271–291.

Posner, M. I., & Snyder, C. R. R. (1975). Attention and cognitive control. In R. L. Solso (Ed.), *Information processing and cognition: The Loyola symposium* (pp. 55–85). Hillsdale, NJ: Lawrence Erlbaum Associates.

Preston, M. S., & Lambert, W. E. (1969). Interlingual interference in a bilingual version of the Stroop color-word task. *Journal of Verbal Learning and Verbal Behavior, 8,* 295–301.

Roelofs, A. (2003). Goal-referenced selection of verbal action: Modeling attentional control in the Stroop task. *Psychological Review, 110,* 88–125.

Sabri, M., Melara, R. D., & Algom, D. (2001). A confluence of contexts: Asymmetric versus global failures of selective attention to Stroop dimensions. *Journal of Experimental Psychology: Human Perception and Performance, 27,* 515–537.

Sternberg, S. (1969). The discovery of processing stages: Extensions of Donders' method. *Acta Psychologica, 30,* 276–315.

Stroop, J. R. (1935). Studies of interference in serial verbal reactions. *Journal of Experimental Psychology, 18,* 643–662. [Reprinted in 1992 in the *Journal of Experimental Psychology: General, 121,* 15–23.]

Stroop, J. R. (1938). Factors affecting speed in serial verbal reactions. *Psychological Monographs, 50,* 38–48.

Taylor, D. A. (1977). Time course of context effects. *Journal of Experimental Psychology: General, 106,* 404–426.

Thurstone, L. L. (1944). *A factorial study of perception.* Chicago, IL: University of Chicago Press.

Townsend, J. T. (1976). Serial and within-stage independent parallel model equivalence on the minimum completion time. *Journal of Mathematical Psychology, 14,* 219–238.

van Maanen, L., van Rijn, H., & Borst, J. P. (2009). Stroop and picture–word interference are two sides of the same coin. *Psychonomic Bulletin & Review, 16,* 987–999.

Warren, R. E. (1972). Stimulus encoding and memory. *Journal of Experimental Psychology, 94,* 90–100.

Williams, J. M. G., Mathews, A., & MacLeod, C. (1996). The emotional Stroop task and psychopathology. *Psychological Bulletin, 120,* 3–24.

Woodworth, R. S., & Wells, F. L. (1911). Association tests. *Psychological Review Monograph Supplements, 13* (57).

7

Amnesia: Beyond Scoville and Milner's (1957) research on HM

Howard Eichenbaum (Center for Memory and Brain, Boston University)

BACKGROUND TO THE CLASSIC STUDY

In the years leading up to Scoville and Milner's (1957) landmark paper, progress in localising memory as a distinct psychological faculty within the brain was stuck. Studies on brain-damaged patients had shown that lesions localised to anatomically distinct cortical areas resulted in highly specific memory deficits. For example, damage in the temporal-parietal cortex resulted in forgetting the names of common objects. But these material-specific memory deficits were considered secondary to disruption of information processing within the relevant modality rather than loss of memories *per se*, and damage to no cortical area produced a 'global' (material-general) memory deficit. Furthermore, a highly influential programme of experiments on maze learning in rats by Karl Lashley (1950) had concluded that memory could not be localised by destroying any particular pathway or area within the cerebral cortex (see Eichenbaum & Cohen, 2001). Instead, Lashley's findings led him to conclude that the amount of cortical damage, rather than the locus of damage, determined the degree of memory loss.

So, when William Scoville and Brenda Milner reported that damage to the hippocampal region caused a selective and severe global memory loss, it was a game-changer. As acknowledged in their paper, there had been previous reports of memory loss following hippocampal region damage. However, the previous cases did not provide a conclusive and unambiguous link between the hippocampus and memory. The Scoville and Milner paper was the first compelling description of persistent global amnesia without any perceptual or intellectual impairment attributable to damage within a specific brain area, and it revolutionised the study of memory. It is not an overstatement to characterise this paper as the origin of modern neuroscience research on memory.

DETAILED DESCRIPTION OF THE CLASSIC STUDY

The Scoville and Milner (1957) paper was a multiple case study that related the locus and extent of surgical removal of the hippocampal region to subsequent performance of the patients on standard Wechsler intelligence and memory scales. They described ten cases of bilateral resection of the medial temporal lobe that included the amygdala, differing extents of the hippocampus, and some of the cerebral cortex surrounding these structures. Seven of these cases were schizophrenics, one had major depression, and another had a tumour in the medial temporal region, and two of the surgeries involved undercutting of the orbitofrontal cortex as well as medial temporal resection. One of those patients was Henry Molaison and, until his death, was identified in scientific publications only by his initials H.M. (Figure 7.1). H.M. had a chronic seizure disorder that was not ameliorated by anti-convulsive medication and for which a specific seizure focus could not be localised. It is this case that has taken on so much importance because the surgery that was localised bilaterally to the hippocampal region resulted in a near-complete loss of the ability to remember any type of new materials, and the impairment was entirely selective to memory without any possible confounding contributions that could be attributed to psychiatric disorder or other pathology or surgical damage.

At the time of his surgery H.M. was a 29-year-old motor winder with a high school education. His seizures had begun when he was 10 and grew gradually worse until he was having multiple grand mal seizures daily and could no longer work. On 1 September 1953, the surgery was performed and, following the initial

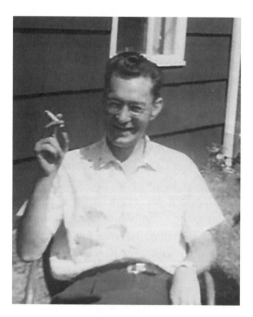

Figure 7.1　Henry Molaison. Copyright Suzanne Corkin by permission of The Wiley Agency (UK) Limited.

recovery, the striking impairment in maintaining recently acquired memories was immediately obvious. Following repeated examinations by his doctors and others, H.M. would immediately forget having met them and would have no recollection of the meeting. His memories acquired remotely prior to the surgery – general world knowledge and personal boyhood memories – were intact, although he exhibited a total retrograde amnesia for events that occurred 19 months before the surgery and partial loss of memories dating three years back. In formal testing, H.M.'s Wechsler-Bellevue full-scale IQ was normal, and indeed had risen slightly from his pre-operative scores, likely due to the reduction in seizure frequency following the surgery. By contrast, his score on the Wechsler memory scale was exceedingly low. For example, his score in learning difficult paired associates was zero and did not increase with practice and, as soon as he was distracted from that task, he completely forgot the experience of the testing session.

The findings on the other nine patients were useful as comparisons, despite limitations of interpretation given their additional psychological and anatomical findings. Scoville and Milner grouped the patients into three categories based on the severity of memory impairment. Most severely impaired were H.M., a 47-year-old paranoid schizophrenic patient, and a 55-year-old manic-depressive patient. In this group, the damage to the hippocampus reached posteriorly 5.5–8 cm from the anterior end of the hippocampus (see Figure 7.2). A group with moderately severe amnesia was composed of five schizophrenic patients who had damage to

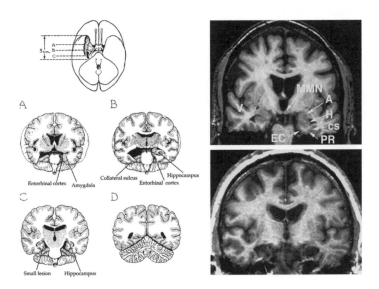

Figure 7.2 Left: A reconstruction of the lesion in H.M., shown only on the right side of the brain; the left side is similarly damaged but here left intact to visualize the normal hippocampus. Right: MRI scans of the normal brain (top) and H.M.'s brain; note lesions in the hippocampal region. MMN: mammillary nuclei; A: amygdala; H: hippocampus; cs: collateral sulcus; PR: perirhinal cortex; EC: entorhinal cortex. Revised from Corkin et al., 1997.

the hippocampus reaching 5–5.5 cm from the anterior end. Finally, they also described a group of patients with no persistent memory deficit, composed of a schizophrenic with damage reaching 4 cm from the anterior end of the hippocampus and the tumour patient with damage reaching 9 cm from the anterior end of the hippocampus but the removal was unilateral.

The clear relationship between severity of the amnesia and extent of hippocampal damage led Scoville and Milner to tentatively conclude that radical excision including at least 8 cm of hippocampal tissue was sufficient to result in a severe impairment in remembering newly learned material (anterograde amnesia) and a partial loss of long memories acquired prior to the surgery (retrograde amnesia). The anterograde memory loss was characterised by an inability to place newly acquired information in long-term memory, even though H.M. had an intact short-term memory capacity. Thus, he could encode and hold new information in mind, supporting a capacity to participate in psychological testing (short-term memory). But as soon as his attention was diverted, memory for the testing experience and its contents were lost (deficient retrieval of long-term memories). The anterograde memory impairment was accompanied by a time-limited retrograde amnesia, such that memories that were acquired shortly before the surgery were lost, but those acquired years before were spared. Furthermore, even the most radical excisions of hippocampal region tissue spared perception, intellect, and personality, as measured by a neurological exam and standard intelligence tests. Finally, with regard to the role of the hippocampus itself, Scoville and Milner included their identification of the critical area included not only the hippocampus, but also neighbouring cortical areas of the uncus and hippocampal gyrus. They noted that the amygdala was damaged in all of the cases, but also pointed out that cases with the same amygdala damage and less hippocampal damage were not impaired in memory. These observations suggested that damage to the amygdala itself was not sufficient to cause amnesia, although combined hippocampal and amygdala damage might have been required to produce the memory loss.

IMPACT OF THE CLASSIC STUDY

The observations on H.M. had a major impact both on the clinical practice of neurosurgery for epilepsy and psychiatric disorders and on experimental studies of memory in humans and animals. With regard to clinical practice, Scoville, who was the neurosurgeon who operated on H.M., made the findings highly public, ensuring that the bilateral medial temporal resection was never subsequently performed. Since the publication, the surgery has been performed only unilaterally, which does not result in severe memory impairment.

Considerable additional study of H.M. has expanded our understanding about the nature and scope of his memory deficit (Corkin, 2013). Over a large range of tests, H.M. exhibited intact perception, short-term and working memory, and other aspects of cognition and general intellect. The global scope of his anterograde memory impairment has been included in a very large domain of verbal and non-verbal materials. His retrograde impairment has been studied in detail and has been extended as a partial loss of memories up to 16 years prior to the surgery, suggesting the hippocampus plays a key role in a prolonged process of the permanent consolidation of memories. However, the extensive retrograde period dating to nearly the time of his first seizures confounds the characterisation of his retrograde amnesia with possible anterograde memory loss due to the progressively increasing frequency of seizures over that period.

In addition, many neuropsychological studies on other patients with damage to the medial temporal lobe and other subcortical brain areas followed. These studies have confirmed that damage to the hippocampal region, or to subcortical areas connected with the hippocampus, including the medial thalamus and mammillary bodies, produce global amnesia whereas unilateral damage in the same areas results in more modest and selective verbal (left-side damage) or non-verbal (right-side) memory impairments (see Andersen et al., 2007; Corkin, 2013). In addition, there are now numerous cases where transient anoxia and viral encephalitis have resulted in damage that is entirely selective to the hippocampus, leaving intact both the amygdala and surrounding cortex. These more limited lesions result in a global amnesic syndrome that is qualitatively similar to that in H.M. but with less severity and a briefer retrograde memory loss. Also, structural brain imaging in clinical studies typically reveals shrinkage of the hippocampus associated with memory loss in mild cognitive impairment. Studies on patients with medial temporal damage limited to the amygdala have confirmed that this structure is not required for memory. So, the main conclusions of Scoville and Milner (1957) have largely been confirmed and extended by standard tests of perception, intellect, and memory, and their focus on the hippocampal region as essential for memory is also confirmed.

Furthermore, the report on H.M. inspired a generation of research on animals aimed at identifying the effects of lesions selective to specific medial temporal lobe areas that can be made in experimental animals, and to characterise the nature of memory representations formed in hippocampal circuits (see Eichenbaum & Cohen, 2001). Progress in modelling global amnesia consequent to hippocampal damage in animals was slow, in that the first studies on monkeys and rats did not reveal a global memory deficit following selective hippocampal damage. Indeed, a mixture of reports indicating impairment or intact performance on a large variety of tests led to suggestions that the hippocampus supports behavioural inhibition or flexibility important to learning in particular tasks, rather than memory itself. In addition, early studies on the firing patterns of hippocampal neurons in behaving rats revealed the existence of 'place cells', neurons of the hippocampus that fire when the animal is in a particular location in an environment (O'Keefe, 1976). Combined with reports of spatial learning and memory impairments following hippocampal damage, these observations led to a prominent view that the hippocampal region plays a dedicated role in spatial navigation, at least in animals (O'Keefe & Nadel, 1978).

Despite these apparent distractions, progress over years of research using animal models have brought the findings on human amnesia and on the effects of hippocampal damage in animals into closer alignment in support of a global memory function. In both humans and animals, the hippocampus is essential to organise memories in time and space and in association with one another. There remains a major schism in the literature on hippocampal function in memory and spatial navigation, despite evidence that hippocampal neurons encode non-spatial stimuli and behaviours and support a temporal as well as spatial organisation of memories (Eichenbaum, 2013). Overall, the road to a convergence of views on hippocampal function in memory in humans and animals has been tortuous, but has still considerably improved our understanding of how the hippocampus supports memory, as will be discussed below.

CRITIQUE OF THE CLASSIC STUDY

ALTERNATIVE INTERPRETATIONS OF THE FINDINGS

Key aspects of the main conclusions of Scoville and Milner have been called into question by several new lines of experimental evidence. These findings have led to alternatives to the conclusions that the perception and cognition are unaffected by damage to the hippocampal region, that the hippocampus is not involved in short-term and working memory, that the amnesic deficit is 'global' across domains of memory, that damage to the hippocampus itself, as opposed to the neighboring cortex, was the cause of the memory deficit, and that the retrograde amnesia resulting from hippocampal damage is temporally limited. Specifics on these challenges and progress resulting from them were recently reviewed (Eichenbaum, 2012) and highlights of the main findings will be outlined and briefly discussed in the following sections.

DAMAGE TO THE HIPPOCAMPAL REGION SPARES PERCEPTUAL AND COGNITIVE CAPACITIES

Some recent studies have suggested that the hippocampus may be involved in the perceptual processing of complex object stimuli. In some experiments, amnesic patients are impaired in performing perceptual judgement and learning tasks that require the discrimination of stimuli that contain overlapping features. Most impressive is evidence that amnesic subjects are impaired in discriminating virtual reality scenes composed of slight changes in the contents of the scenes (Graham et al., 2006). While surely this impairment is an exception to memory loss *per se*, it remains poorly understood what perceptual or cognitive processing is impaired. One possibility is that disambiguation of complex stimuli that share overlapping elements and, conversely, association of ambiguous elements to compose unique representations, may reflect on-line information processing of relations among elements of a declarative memory.

Consistent with this idea, recent studies have shown that amnesic subjects have abnormal exploration strategies when viewing multi-stimulus arrays where individual elements of the array can be seen only in isolation (Voss, Warren, et al., 2011). During exploration of successive elements, normal subjects frequently return to previously viewed stimuli and this 'spontaneous revisitation' engages the hippocampus. Amnesic patients are deficient in spontaneous revisitation, even though the demand for memory of these stimuli is within the range of working memory that is typically intact in amnesic patients (Voss, Gonsalves, et al., 2011). Furthermore, normal subjects benefit in subsequent memory for stimulus arrays by volitional control of their scanning, but amnesic subjects do not, suggesting that they are deficient in composing a complete memory by combining its independent elements.

In addition, the conclusion that cognition is intact in amnesia has been challenged by the observation that the ability to construct future scenarios is impaired in amnesia. In these studies, subjects were asked to imagine new experiences based on brief cues about the nature of those experiences. Whereas normal subjects could easily generate rich scenarios for everyday events, amnesic individuals could not. Thus, for example, when asked to imagine lying on a white sandy beach on a beautiful day, normal subjects imagined an elaborate arrangement of objects on the beach, a boat moving by, and personal feelings of the sun and sand. By contrast, an amnesic patient could only imagine blue sky and white sand without an elaborate array of objects or events contained in the scene (Hassabis, Kumaran, Vann, & Maguire, 2007). These observations suggest a role of the hippocampus that lies outside memory *per se*, but can be viewed as offering insight into a fundamental function of the hippocampal region in creatively interrelating memory fragments from the past to compose a novel future event.

AMNESIA SPARES SHORT-TERM AND WORKING MEMORY

Another major observation on H.M. from the early neuropsychological assessments was that he had a normal digit span and other capacities reflecting intact immediate memory. He could carry on a normal conversation and participate in psychological testing as long as he was not required to reference information left behind earlier in the same experience. However, several recent functional imaging studies have shown strong engagement of the hippocampus during working-memory tasks, and this activation predicts subsequent memory performance. Other studies have revealed impairments in memories for visual scenes well within the period of working memory. These experiments exploit the observation that eye-movements are normally preferentially directly towards locations where stimuli have been manipulated in familiar scenes to show that amnesic patients fail to focus their eye-movements on the manipulated areas even when exposed to the scenes very shortly before (Hannula, Tranel, & Cohen, 2006). These findings suggest that the hippocampus may begin memory processing at the outset of the study, and other brain areas can also support declarative memory within the working memory period but not long-term memory. Consistent with this interpretation, a wealth of functional imaging studies has shown hippocampal activation during the *encoding* of stimuli that predicts long-term memory for those stimuli – a phenomenon known as the 'subsequent memory effect' that is the gold standard evidence for hippocampal involvement in memory (Brewer et al., 1998; Wagner et al., 1998). A major implication of the subsequent memory effect is that the hippocampus begins information processing that supports long-term memory during the learning experience itself, even though other brain areas can support short-term memory performance in amnesic patients.

In addition, many studies on animals have described hippocampal neurons that are activated on-line as animals investigate their environment, and highly specific spatial firing patterns of these neurons develop rapidly (Eichenbaum, 2004). In addition, as animals learn about critical events in various tasks, hippocampal neurons develop robust representations that reflect associations between events and where they occur in parallel with learning and predictive of performance (Komoroski, Manns, & Eichenbaum, 2009). Furthermore, hippocampal neuronal activity in rats and humans during study carries information about the temporal organisation of events, and these representations predict performance in animals and humans (Eichenbaum, 2013). The findings on neural activity during learning provide compelling evidence that the hippocampus is involved during learning experiences and its memory processing contributes to subsequent long-term memories.

AMNESIA DUE TO HIPPOCAMPAL DAMAGE IS 'GLOBAL' ACROSS DOMAINS OF MEMORY

Scoville and Milner (1957) characterised the scope of amnesia in H.M. as spanning all domains of memory, by which they meant that the memory deficit encompassed both verbal and a broad domain of non-verbal materials. However, a major extension of this characterisation is the discovery that the amnesic deficit is limited to a particular form of memory, called declarative or explicit memory, the memory for everyday facts and events that can typically be brought to conscious recollection and used flexibly and creatively to solve all manner of daily problems. This kind of memory is, of course, what most of us would consider 'real' memory. But, there are also several other types of learning and memory, including the acquisition of habits, preferences, familiarities, and dispositions – types of memory that are typically acquired during performance of various tasks and for which the specific contents of memory are not subject to conscious recall, and many studies have shown that these types of memory do not depend on the hippocampus.

Studies immediately following the report by Scoville and Milner revealed an exception to his otherwise severe memory impairment, specifically intact learning of motor skills, and this was followed by discoveries of other exceptions to amnesia, including intact perceptual learning and cognitive skills (Corkin, 2013). In addition, H.M. showed intact 'priming' for recognising fragments of pictures recently viewed. It has become clear that amnesia associated with damage to the hippocampal region is selective to the ability to recall facts and events, and for H.M. the deficit includes the complete absence of episodic memory, defined as the ability to remember specific personal experiences (Steinvorth, Levine, & Corkin, 2005). By contrast, other brain structures and systems support different types of memory performance, including perceptual learning and memory and the acquisition of skills and emotional memories (reviewed in Eichenbaum & Cohen, 2001). These and other studies on subjects with severe deficits in declarative memory led to the largely consensual view that there are multiple memory systems, each with distinct information-processing characteristics and each supported by distinct brain pathways. In addition, recent studies have shown that the components of memory systems may also interact with one another, such that modules within memory systems contribute to, oppose, or operate in parallel with one another in supporting overall memory function (Cabeza & Moscovitch, 2013).

THE HIPPOCAMPUS IS THE CORE BRAIN STRUCTURE SUPPORTING MEMORY

A key conclusion from Scoville and Milner (1957) was that damage to the hippocampus was central to the amnesic disorder. Subsequent case studies that involve damage isolated to the hippocampus in humans and animals have confirmed the observation of amnesia following damage limited to the hippocampus, but the memory deficit is less severe (Zola-Morgan et al., 1986; Bartsch et al., 2010). In particular, which parts of the medial temporal lobe area are critical to memory has been investigated thoroughly in studies on recognition memory in non-human primates. These studies have replicated the finding of severe deficits in memory following large medial temporal lobe lesions, including the hippocampus, the amygdala, and surrounding cortical areas (Mishkin, 1978; for a review see Eichenbaum & Cohen, 2001). However, subsequent studies on the remaining medial temporal lobe components showed that lesions limited to the hippocampus produced, at most, a modest memory deficit (Zola et al., 2000; Murray & Mishkin, 1998). By contrast, damage to the cortex surrounding the hippocampus resulted in severe recognition memory deficits in multiple versions of the task. These findings are consistent with the view that the hippocampus and the surrounding cortical areas interconnected with the hippocampus support distinct roles in memory. Studies across species have shown that damage to the amygdala does not contribute to the deficit in declarative memory characteristic of medial temporal lobe damage. In addition, considerable subsequent research on humans using functional imaging in normal human subjects as well as single neuron recording studies in rodents and monkeys have examined the distinct roles of components of the medial temporal lobe damaged in H.M. These studies have largely converged on the view that the hippocampus makes a unique contribution to memory and that the surrounding cortical areas also make distinct contributions, as will be discussed below.

DAMAGE TO THE HIPPOCAMPAL REGION SPARES REMOTELY ACQUIRED MEMORIES

The early findings on amnesia in H.M. were characterised as a severe and selective impairment in 'recent memory', as contrasted with spared memory experiences that occurred remotely prior to the surgery, and formal tests on H.M.'s memory for public and personal events subsequent to the Scoville and Milner paper showed that his retrograde amnesia extended back a limited number of years (Corkin, 1984). Many other studies of patients with damage limited to the hippocampal region also report temporally graded retrograde amnesia for factual knowledge and news events over a period extending several years (Manns et al., 2003; Bayley, Hopkins, & Squire, 2006). In addition, several 'prospective' studies on amnesia in animals, where hippocampal damage occurs at different time points after learning, have demonstrated temporally graded amnesia across multiple species and memory tasks (reviewed in Milner, Squire, & Kandel, 1998). These studies have been interpreted as showing that the hippocampus plays a critical role in the consolidation of memories across species.

However, there remains debate about whether the hippocampus always remains involved in episodic memory, suggesting that the hippocampus may play a role in retrieval of specific events that occurred even remotely before the onset of amnesia (Nadel & Moscovitch, 1997). In support of this view are reports, including recent work with H.M. (Steinvorth et al., 2005), that present evidence of temporally *ungraded* retrograde impairments for episodic memories, although there are also findings of spared remote autobiographical memories in patients with hippocampal region damage. In addition, functional imaging studies have consistently reported that the hippocampus is activated when associated with both recently and remotely acquired episodic and autobiographical memories. These findings contrast with observations showing that hippocampal activation during retrieval of famous faces, names, and news events (i.e., memories of facts and not personal events) declines over years after the periods in which these events occurred. A possible reconciliation of this mixture of observations on remote memory is that the hippocampus remains engaged whenever detailed associative or contextual information must be recalled.

Notably, as described above, the hippocampus is also involved even when people imagine detailed events that have never occurred. This suggests that the hippocampus may become engaged by cues that generate an extensive memory search and reconstruction of a complex memory, regardless of the age of the memory. Consistent with this suggestion, recent studies have suggested that the hippocampus may support memory consolidation by integrating new memories into previously established semantic networks, or 'schemas', that contain memories of related world and personal knowledge (reviewed in McKensie & Eichenbaum, 2011). In support of this suggestion are recent studies in animals showing rapid, hippocampal-dependent memory consolidation for newly acquired memories that are embodied within a schema of existing memories. Additional studies on animals and humans have shown that the hippocampus is engaged in and essential for interleaving memories that have common elements into schematised networks of knowledge. Possibly, the process of memory consolidation continues as long as additional memories demand interleaving new information with old in a restructuring of existing knowledge to incorporate new memories.

HOW DOES THE HIPPOCAMPAL REGION SUPPORT MEMORY?

The discoveries about H.M. by Scoville and Milner were a major landmark in our understanding of how memories are made. They showed an essential role for the hippocampal region that has remained a guide for studies ever since. Further discoveries on H.M., and those that have followed this pioneering work, have generated multiple hypotheses about the fundamental information-processing function of the hippocampus and the medial temporal lobe more generally. A major direction of subsequent discoveries has been to expand and incorporate our knowledge about the anatomy and physiology of the hippocampal region into accounts of the mechanisms by which the hippocampus plays its critical role.

Anatomical, physiological, and behavioural evidence, from studies on both humans and animals, indicates that the functional organisation of the medial temporal lobe involves a convergence of major processing streams in the cortex that carry information about perceptual events and the spatial-temporal context in which they occur (Eichenbaum, Yonelinas, & Ranganath, 2007; Figure 7.3). Thus, the ventral visual steam and other cortical areas that process information about perceptual objects and events ('what' information) project to the perirhinal cortex, which in turn projects primarily to the lateral entorhinal cortex. In parallel, the dorsal visual stream and other areas that process information about spatial (and perhaps temporal) contextual information projects to the parahippocampal cortex, which projects in turn primarily to the medial entorhinal cortex. Based on these anatomical observations, a

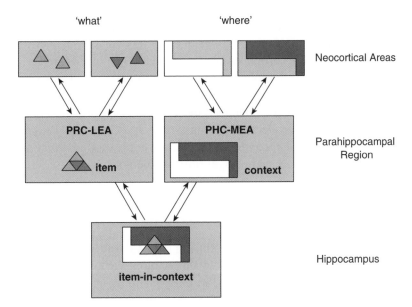

Figure 7.3 Pathways of information flow between the hippocampus and cortical areas. PRC: perirhinal cortex; LEA: lateral entorhinal area; PHC: parahippocampal cortex; MEA: medial entorhinal area. Revised from Eichenbaum et al., 2007.

major current view is that the perirhinal cortex and lateral entorhinal cortex represent important objects, people, actions, and other specific events that compose the *contents* of memories. In contrast, the parahippocampal cortex and medial entorhinal cortex may represent the spatial and temporal *organisation* in which these important events occur (Eichenbaum, 2013). Subsequently, the hippocampus *binds* the contents of memories within the organisation of their spatial and temporal context, a prototypical feature of episodic memory.

Substantial experimental evidence supports these characterisations of distinct roles for separate components of the medial temporal region. Several studies have shown that damage limited to the hippocampus itself results in an impairment that is selective to memory for associations between events and the context of unique experiences (episodic memory), leaving intact a sense of familiarity with recently experienced stimuli without associations or context. In contrast, damage that includes the parahippocampal cortical areas surrounding the hippocampus, particularly the perirhinal cortex, results in deficits in familiarity. Consistent with these observations, many functional imaging studies have dissociated activation of the hippocampus associated with recall of associative and episodic memory versus activation of the perirhinal cortex associated with familiarity. Notably, these dissociations have been questioned and it remains debated whether the hippocampus and neighbouring cortical areas play distinct roles in memory. Ongoing research is likely to provide a deeper understanding of the basic information-processing mechanisms behind these functional dissociations (Eichenbaum, 2012).

In addition to associating events with one another and with the spatial-temporal context of experience, other evidence indicates that the hippocampus also encodes sequences of events into representations of temporally extended experiences (episodes). Furthermore, the hippocampus may additionally integrate multiple related event and episode representations to create networks of memories (schemas). As additional new experiences occur, the overall memory organisation may be modified according to the relevant relations between new memories and the structure of the established memory organisation, as a basis for memory consolidation. The processing of this information by the full circuit, including the hippocampus, supports our ability for recollection of events, their associates, and the context in which they occurred. The combination of these processing functions may comprise fundamental mechanisms of declarative memory.

CONCLUSIONS

In the 50+ years since Scoville and Milner (1957), cognitive neuroscience has amassed hundreds of studies guided by this seminal work, identifying the main long-term memory systems, providing an understanding of neural mechanisms behind the distinctions perception and memory, between short-term and long-term memory, and between declarative and non-declarative memory. We now have a preliminary understanding of the flow of information in the hippocampal system, including how the hippocampus binds events in memory within a framework of spatial and temporal context and integrates new memories with existing knowledge in support of the consolidation of long-term memories. The classic paper provided a framework for key questions about how memory works, and the answers are now unfolding in current investigations that combine the findings in human and animal research.

FURTHER READING

Andersen, P., Morris, R., Amaral, D., Bliss, T., & O'Keefe, J. (2007). *The hippocampus book*. New York: Oxford University Press.

Corkin, S. (2013). *Permanent present tense: The unforgettable life of the amnesic patient H.M.* New York: Basic Books.

Eichenbaum, H. (2012). What H.M. taught us. *Journal of Cognitive Neuroscience*, 25, 14–21.

Eichenbaum, H. (2013). Memory on time. *Trends in Cognitive Sciences*, 17, 81–88.

Eichenbaum, H., & Cohen, N. J. (2001). *From conditioning to conscious recollection: Memory systems of the brain.* New York: Oxford University Press.

Scoville, W. B., & Milner, B. (1957). Loss of recent memory after bilateral hippocampal lesions. *Journal of Neurology, Neurosurgery, and Psychiatry*, 20, 11–21.

REFERENCES

Andersen, P., Morris, R., Amaral, D., Bliss, T., & O'Keefe, J. (2007). *The hippocampus book*. New York: Oxford University Press.

Bartsch, T., Schonfed, R., Muller, F. J., Alfke, K., Leplow, B., Aldenhoff, J., Deuschl, G., & Koch, J. M. (2010). Focal lesions of human hippocampal CA1 neurons in transient global amnesia impair place memory. *Science*, 328, 1412–1415.

Bayley, P. J., Hopkins, R. O., & Squire, L. R. (2006). The fate of old memories after medial temporal lobe damage. *Journal of Neuroscience*, 26, 13311–13317.

Brewer, J. B., Zhao, Z., Desmond, J. E., Glover, G. H., & Gabrieli, J. D. (1998). Making memories: Brain activity that predicts how well visual experience will be remembered. *Science*, 281, 1185–1187.

Cabeza, R., & Moscovitch, M. (2013). Memory systems, processing modes, and components: Functional neuroimaging evidence. *Perspectives on Psychological Science*, 8, 49–55.

Corkin, S. (1984). Lasting consequences of bilateral medial temporal lobectomy: Clinical course and experimental findings in H.M. *Seminars in Neurology*, 4, 249–259.

Corkin, S. (2013). *Permanent present tense: The unforgettable life of the amnesic patient H.M.* New York: Basic Books.

Eichenbaum, H. (2004). Hippocampus: Cognitive processes and neural representations that underlie declarative memory. *Neuron*, 44, 109–120.

Eichenbaum, H. (2012). What H.M. taught us. *Journal of Cognitive Neuroscience*, 25, 14–21.

Eichenbaum, H. (2013). Memory on time. *Trends in Cognitive Sciences*, 17, 81–88.

Eichenbaum, H., & Cohen, N. J. (2001). *From conditioning to conscious recollection: Memory systems of the brain*. New York: Oxford University Press.

Eichenbaum, H., Yonelinas, A. R., & Ranganath, C. (2007). The medial temporal lobe and recognition memory. *Annual Review of Neuroscience*, 30, 123–152.

Graham, K. S., Scahill, V. L., Hornberger, M., Barense, M. D., Lee, A. C. H., Bussey, T. J., & Saksida, L. M. (2006). Abnormal categorization and perceptual learning in patients with hippocampal damage. *Journal of Neuroscience*, 26, 7547–7554.

Hannula, D. E., Tranel, D., & Cohen, N. J. (2006). The long and short of it: Relational memory impairments in amnesia, even as short lags. *Journal of Neuroscience*, 26, 8352–8359.

Hassabis, D., Kumaran, D., Vann, S. D., & Maguire, E. A. (2007). Patients with hippocampal amnesia cannot imagine new experiences. *Proceedings of the National Academy of Science of the United States of America*, 104, 1726–1731.

Komorowski, R. W., Manns, J. R., & Eichenbaum, H. (2009). Robust conjunctive item-place coding by hippocampal neurons parallels learning what happens. *Journal of Neuroscience*, 29, 9918–9929.

Lashley, K. S. (1950). In search of the engram. *Symposium of the Society of Experimental Biology*, 4, 454–482.

Manns, J. R., Hopkins, R. O., Reed, J. M., Kitchener, E. G., & Squire, L. R. (2003). Recognition memory and the human hippocampus. *Neuron*, 37, 171–180.

McKensie, S., & Eichenbaum, H. (2011). Consolidation and reconsolidation: Two lives of memories? *Neuron*, 71, 224–233.

Milner, B., Squire, L. R., & Kandel, E. R. (1998). Cognitive neuroscience and the study of memory. *Neuron*, 20, 445–468.

Mishkin, M. (1978). Memory in monkeys severely impaired by combined but not by separate removal of amygdale and hippocampus. *Nature*, 273, 297–298.

Murray, E. A., & Mishkin, M. (1998). Object recognition and location memory in monkeys with excitotoxic lesions of the amygdale and hippocampus. *Journal of Neuroscience*, 18, 6568–6582.

Nadel, L., & Moscovitch, M. (1997). Memory consolidation, retrograde amnesia and the hippocampal complex. *Current Opinion in Neurobiology*, 7, 217–227.

O'Keefe, J. A. (1976). Place units in the hippocampus of the freely moving rat. *Experimental Neurology*, 51, 78–109.

O'Keefe, J., & Nadel, L. (1978). *The hippocampus as a cognitive map*. New York: Oxford University Press.

Scoville, W. B., & Milner, B. (1957). Loss of recent memory after bilateral hippocampal lesions. *Journal of Neurology, Neurosurgery, and Psychiatry*, 20, 11–21.

Steinvorth, S., Levine, B., & Corkin, S. (2005). Medial temporal lobe structures are needed to re-experience remote autobiographical memories: Evidence from two MTL amnesic patients, H.M. and W.R. *Neuropsychologia*, 43, 479–496.

Voss, J. L., Gonsalves, B. D., Federmeier, K. D., Tranel, D., & Cohen, N. J. (2011). Hippocampal brain-network coordination during volitional exploratory behavior enhances learning. *Nature Neuroscience*, 14, 115–120.

Voss, J. L., Warren, D. E., Gonsalves, B. D., Federmeier, K. D., Tranel, D., & Cohen, N. J. (2011). Spontaneous revisitation during visual exploration as a link among strategic behavior, learning, and the hippocampus. *Proceedings of the National Academy of Sciences*, 108, E402–409.

Wagner, A. D., Schacter, D. L., Rotte, M., Koutstaal, W., Maril, A., Dale, A. M., Rosen, B. R., & Buckner, R. L. (1998). Building memories: Remembering and forgetting of verbal experiences as predicted by brain activity. *Science*, 281, 1188 –1191.

Zola-Morgan, S., Squire, L. R., & Amaral, D. G. (1986). Human amnesia and the medial temporal region: Enduring memory impairment following a bilateral lesion limited to field CA1 of the hippocampus. *Journal of Neuroscience*, 6, 2950–2967.

Zola, S. M., Squire, L. R., Teng, E., Stefanacci, L., Buffalo, E. A., & Clark, R. (2000). Impaired recognition memory in monkeys after damage limited to the hippocampal region. *Journal of Neuroscience*, 20, 451–463.

8

Working memory: Beyond Baddeley and Hitch's (1974) working memory

Robert H. Logie (University of Edinburgh)

BACKGROUND TO THE CLASSIC STUDY

Crucial for every day functioning is the human ability to retain information on a temporary basis and to keep track of what we are doing moment to moment, allowing completion of a current task or to function in a novel environment. Information is held for only a few seconds and continually updated, so forgetting of details is almost immediate. For example, in order to understand the text you are reading now, it is important to remember the text that you have just read, and the most recently read text is continually being updated as you progress through the document. Likewise, successful driving on the motorway requires continual monitoring of the position of nearby traffic and this is continually updated in memory with rapidly changing traffic patterns. Normally, there is no requirement to retain precise details such as the exact wording and font of the text read 10 minutes ago, or the precise position, model and colour of the car that was overtaking 15 minutes ago. Those details are important at the time, but not subsequently, and so are held for just a few seconds and then are forgotten as the information is updated.

This ability to retain, manipulate, and update information on a moment-to-moment basis is often referred to as working memory, a concept that was first explored in depth by two UK-based researchers, Alan Baddeley and Graham Hitch, working in the early 1970s in the United Kingdom at the Universities of Sussex and Stirling, then at the Medical Research Council Applied Psychology Research Unit in Cambridge (now known as the Cognition and Brain Sciences Unit). Working memory is used for almost every daily activity; mental operations during mental arithmetic, navigating around unfamiliar environments, keeping track of current intentions and the flow of a conversation, making a meal, creative thinking, or keying a telephone number. A joint publication in 1974 by Baddeley and Hitch broke away from traditional experiments at the time on the much narrower concept of short-term memory, and laid the foundations for what is now over 40 years of research on working memory. In the two decades prior to their 1974 paper, research on short-term memory worldwide had focused on immediate memory for sequences of verbal material such as letters, numbers, and words. Baddeley and Hitch put their heads above the scientific parapet by asking what a short-term memory system would be for. They asked why humans would have a need for a system that had previously been studied by asking people to remember lists of words, letters, and digits. It seemed unlikely that evolution had resulted in a system that helps us remember telephone numbers and shopping lists. Their 1974 paper explored in detail the extent to which a verbal short-term memory might be important for everyday tasks that should be supported by working memory, such as understanding language and logical reasoning.

The concept of a temporary memory system that supports moment-to-moment human cognition has been around since the work of the British philosopher John Locke, writing in 1690, who referred to 'contemplation' as 'keeping an idea actually in view' in contrast to the 'storehouse of ideas', which is now referred to as long-term memory. Two centuries later, the American psychologist William James (1890/1905) referred to temporary memory as 'Primary Memory', and long-term memory as 'Secondary Memory'. In 1958, the British researcher Donald Broadbent referred to a short-term store that acted as a limited-capacity temporary memory buffer between sensory input and longer term memory. Broadbent proposed that this temporary memory system was also closely involved in controlling attention to some of the incoming information, while acting to filter out information that was not needed. During the 1960s, two American researchers, Waugh and Norman (1965), adopted the terms Primary Memory and Secondary Memory, specifying that Primary Memory for sequences of words, letters, and numbers was a system that was limited in capacity, and that information it held could be displaced by new material unless the items were rehearsed by repeating the sequence mentally or aloud. For Waugh and Norman, rehearsal was also the means by which information was copied into Secondary Memory to be retained over longer time periods.

The term 'working memory' was first given a passing mention in 1960 in a book by Miller, Galanter, and Pribram, but they did not elaborate or test the concept. A much more detailed exploration appeared in a 1968 research report by Atkinson and Shiffrin, who developed Broadbent's (1958) ideas regarding the need to include control processes for selection of material to be retained, and proposed that these would also include encoding, rehearsing, manipulating, and retrieving as well as storing information on a temporary basis. They focused again on memory for verbal material and suggested that people could strategically focus on the control processes with a consequent reduction in memory capacity, or could store more verbal material but reduce their capacity to undertake control processing. Like Broadbent ten years earlier, Atkinson and Shiffrin viewed their concept of working memory as a temporary workspace that received information directly from sensory input (primarily vision and hearing), processed that information, and transferred some of the information into a long-term store. Their view is illustrated in Figure 8.1a.

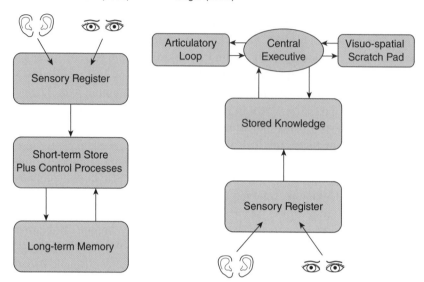

Figure 8.1 Alternative proposals for information flow in human memory, with working memory as (a) a single flexible system supporting control processes and short-term memory that sits between sensory input and long-term memory, or (b) as a set of executive control processes plus temporary, limited-capacity memory systems for verbal (articulatory loop) and non-verbal (visuo-spatial scratch pad) material (right diagram) that deals with material activated from long-term memory

DETAILED DESCRIPTION OF THE CLASSIC STUDY

In their seminal 1974 paper, Baddeley and Hitch noted that there was remarkably little experimental evidence for the idea that a working memory included control processes involved in storage (learning) and retrieval from long-term memory or other abilities such as understanding language or logical reasoning. Of the evidence that was available, several previous research findings could not easily be explained by the Atkinson and Shiffrin (1968) proposed theory of working memory. For example, studies by Patterson in 1971 had shown that remembering a plan for retrieving information from long-term memory was unaffected by asking people to count backwards. Other studies by Brown in the UK in 1958, and by Peterson and Peterson in the USA in 1959, showed that the number of letters and words that can be remembered is greatly reduced if participants in the experiments are asked to count backwards after they have been given a verbal sequence to recall, but before they are asked to retrieve the sequence. So, backwards counting affects short-term verbal memory but not working memory for a control process.

Even more problematic for the Atkinson and Shiffrin theory was evidence from studies of people who suffered from very specific short-term memory impairments following localised brain damage. Baddeley and Hitch referred to one individual known by the initials 'KF', who was studied by Warrington and Shallice in the early 1970s in London. KF had a very severe short-term verbal memory deficit that was specific for word sequences. For example, After hearing a random sequence of numbers, such as 4–9–6–3–5–1, KF had great difficulty in remembering more than one or two of the numbers (e.g. 4–9). A healthy adult typically can remember more than five random numbers. However, despite this problem, KF had no difficulty in understanding language and holding conversations, in learning new information, and in retrieving information from long-term memory. In addition, KF could remember more numbers if he could read them rather than listen to them. When he made errors, these tended to be based on what the words and numbers looked like, rather than what they sounded like. This suggested the use of some form of visual short-term memory. So, KF had a specific problem with verbal short-term memory, while the remainder of his working memory was intact (Warrington & Shallice, 1972).

The pattern of impairments and sparing of memory and cognitive ability in patient KF raised several problems for the Atkinson and Shiffrin theory. First, if there is a general-purpose short-term memory system that supports processing and temporary storage of information, then damage to this system should be associated with impairments of the processing abilities and memory, and for non-verbal as well as verbal material. Yet, KF had no difficulty with processing for language understanding, and his ability to remember material presented visually appeared to be largely intact. Only his ability to repeat back verbal sequences that he had heard was severely impaired. Over the subsequent decades, largely inspired by the Baddeley and Hitch (1974) paper, multiple studies of other patients with specific short-term verbal memory deficits have been reported. This evidence demonstrated clearly that short-term memory for words could be damaged independently of short-term memory for visually presented material, and independently of other important aspects of human cognition. That is, contrary to Atkinson and Shiffrin's view, the control processes could be separated from short-term memory rather than memory and processing both relying on the same cognitive system. This led Baddeley and Hitch to suggest that control processes might be part of executive processes (central executive in Figure 8.1b) which interact with, but are separate from, a verbal short-term memory, and possibly also from a visual short-term memory.

A second problem for the Atkinson and Shiffrin theory that was not specifically addressed by Baddeley and Hitch, but was later noted by Logie in 1995, and subsequently in a joint paper by Baddeley and Logie in 1999, is that if working memory acts as a form of workspace or gateway between sensory input and long-term memory, then damage to the working memory system should prevent access to long-term memory for interpreting sensory input. It is also clear that the contents of working memory are not raw sensory images, but that sensory input accesses and activates (makes available) stored knowledge in long-term memory about sounds or combinations of lines and shapes, and the words, letters or numbers that are represented by those sounds and shapes *before* any information is available in working memory. If this was not the case, then the contents of working memory would be meaningless. We only know that particular sounds and shapes represent words, letters, and numbers because we have learned, and have in our store of knowledge that, for example, the shape 'A' is the first letter in the alphabet with a particular combination of lines on the page and particular ways in which that letter should sound when pronounced. In other words, working memory cannot be placed between sensory input and long-term memory, but rather deals with information that is activated from long-term memory. This alternative route to working memory is illustrated in Figure 8.1b. Note that working memory is seen here not simply as the currently activated material in long-term memory (referred to as 'stored knowledge' in Figure 8.1b). Evidence from studying patients such as KF, but also from experimental studies with healthy adults (reviewed in Baddeley & Logie, 1999; Logie, 1995, 2011a, 2011b), point to the idea shown in Figure 8.1b that working memory is a set of systems that is separate from long-term memory (the store of knowledge, skills, and experiences accumulated over the lifetime), and receives the information currently activated from the knowledge store, retains that information on a temporary basis, and processes it according to current task demands.

The primary focus for the 1974 classic paper was a series of experiments to investigate in much greater depth than in previous studies whether short-term memory, which had been shown to be important for retaining short verbal sequences, might also be important for reasoning and understanding language. One set of their experiments used a simple reasoning task in which experimental participants had to decide whether or not a sentence was a true description of the order of a pair of letters. For example 'B follows A – AB' would be true, whereas 'A follows B – AB' would be false. Some of the sentences were more difficult than others, for example, 'A is not followed by B – BA' is both passive and negative, whereas the first two examples are somewhat easier because they are both active and affirmative. This reasoning task shows modest correlations with general intelligence, suggesting that it does assess some complex cognitive processes. Participants were first given one or two digits as a preload (e.g., 9–4) that they had to remember. They were then given 32 of the 'AB reasoning' sentences to verify, after which they had to recall the previously presented numbers. This was compared to a condition in which the reasoning task was performed with no memory preload. Participants could recall the preload numbers perfectly and reasoning time was the same whether or not people had a memory preload. Only when the preload was increased to six items, and participants were asked to focus mainly on the reasoning task, was there a drop in recall of the preload, but reasoning time was unaffected. When participants were asked instead to focus on remembering the six memory items, there was an increase in the amount of time to complete the reasoning task, but memory performance was unaffected. Similar results were obtained when combining a preload with a test of language comprehension: there was no effect on memory or comprehension with a memory load of three items, but there was an effect with six items. Results for reasoning time, with and without a preload of six items are illustrated in Figure 8.2. Note that as the difficulty of the

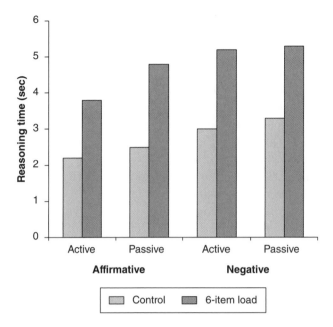

Figure 8.2 Mean reasoning time for different forms of reasoning problem without (control) and with a preload of six digits (figure redrawn from Baddeley & Hitch (1974), Figure 1, with permission)

sentences increased (from active-affirmative to passive-negative), the overall reasoning time increased. Crucially, the effect of a concurrent memory load of six items was exactly the same, regardless of the difficulty of the reasoning problem.

Baddeley and Hitch argued that there is a short-term verbal memory system, with a capacity of perhaps three or four items, which can function in parallel with the more complex processes of reasoning and language comprehension. However, when the capacity of that short-term verbal memory system is exceeded, then other control processes, such as verbal rehearsal, are required, and this draws on the system in working memory that is also important for reasoning and comprehension. However, the effect of overloading the memory system was the same regardless of the difficulty of the reasoning task. This suggested that the reasoning task perhaps overlapped with rehearsal of the letters or consolidation of the letters in memory, but did not overlap with short-term storage unless the memory load exceeded the capacity of the short-term storage system.

In contrast, if participants are prevented from rehearsing a verbal sequence, then there is a substantial reduction in memory performance. So, in follow-up experiments, Baddeley and Hitch (1974) asked volunteer participants to repeat aloud the same irrelevant word, for example, 'the–the–the' while they were trying to store random sequences of six visually presented digits. This requirement, known as articulatory suppression, resulted in much poorer recall of the digits than when digit sequences were presented in silence. This suggests an important role for verbal rehearsal in short-term verbal memory, and led to the proposal in a paper (Baddeley, 1983), and then book on working memory (Baddeley, 1986), that short-term memory for verbal sequences might be held in what he referred to as an 'articulatory loop' (see Figure 8.1b). Related findings were that sequences of words which are phonologically similar, such as 'bat–mat–cat–sat–rat–fat' are more difficult to repeat back in the correct order than are sequences of words that are phonologically different, such as 'cup–tree–bread–chair–head–watch'. This is true, even when people are reading the words, and not only when they are listening to them. This suggested that the short-term memory system retains the words on the basis of their sound, thereby leading to confusions among words that are similar in sound, known as the phonological similarity effect. Experiments reported by Baddeley, Thomson, and Buchanan in 1975 demonstrated that sequences of words that take a long time to say, such as 'typhoon, Friday, harpoon, cyclone, nitrate, tycoon' are more difficult to repeat back in the correct order than are sequences of words that take less time to say, such as 'cricket, bishop, hackle, decor, wiggle, pewter'. This suggested a further link between spoken rehearsal and verbal short-term memory, and came to be known as the word length effect. Later experiments demonstrated that the faster people can speak, then the longer are the verbal sequences they can remember. Together, these findings led to a more detailed proposal in Baddeley's 1986 book that verbal short-term memory comprises a phonological store that can retain around two seconds worth of speech, and material can be retained in that store as long as it is rehearsed mentally or aloud. Together, the phonological store and the rehearsal process were referred to as the articulatory loop, although, subsequently, Baddeley changed the name of this component of working memory to the 'phonological loop'.

IMPACT OF THE CLASSIC STUDY

The concept of an articulatory or phonological loop dominated the development of Baddeley's ideas on working memory for two decades following the original 1974 paper. In experiments carried out during the 1980s and summarised in his 1986 book, he demonstrated that if words are presented visually, and people are undertaking articulatory suppression, then both the word length effect and the phonological similarity effect disappear. Typically, participants are asked to write down the sequence for recall to allow articulatory suppression to continue, or, if articulatory suppression stops before recall, to avoid the possibility that spoken recall might involve the articulatory loop. However, if people hear the word sequence while undertaking articulatory suppression, then long and short words are remembered equally well, but the phonological similarity effect remains. Baddeley interpreted this by suggesting that when items are presented visually, there is automatic activation of the associated phonological codes stored in long-term memory. The articulatory rehearsal process is then important for transferring those phonological codes into the phonological store. If articulatory suppression prevents the rehearsal process, then the phonological codes are lost, and so there is no effect of phonological similarity when the verbal sequence is recalled in writing by participants. When the items are heard, Baddeley suggested that the phonological codes from long-term memory are made available immediately to the phonological store, so the stored phonological codes generate a phonological similarity effect, even if articulatory rehearsal is prevented. However, the word length effect arises from the use of articulatory rehearsal, and because rehearsal is prevented by articulatory suppression, the word length effect cannot occur.

Articulatory suppression disrupts verbal short-term memory, but does not wipe it out, particularly when items are presented visually. This suggests that there are other systems that support short-term memory that do not overlap with concurrent articulation. One suggestion was that this might be a visual short-term memory. This same visual short-term memory system could have been used by patient KF to retain visually presented verbal sequences.

The possibility of a visual short-term memory system was mentioned only briefly in the 1974 paper, and the concept developed much more slowly than did the articulatory loop. Two studies by Baddeley, Grant, Wight, and Thomson (1975), and by Baddeley and Lieberman (1980) demonstrated that the ability to retain in memory a random path around an imagined pattern of squares was disrupted by carrying out concurrent arm movement. This then linked the control of arm movement with the memory system that could retain a sequence of movements. A series of experiments published by Logie in 1986 demonstrated that retaining visual mental images was disrupted by presentation of irrelevant, random pictures of objects, but was not disrupted by presenting streams of irrelevant random spoken words. In contrast, remembering a set of visually presented words was disrupted by irrelevant spoken words but not by irrelevant pictures. This complemented other studies carried out by Salamé and Baddeley (1982), which had shown that retaining a sequence of visually presented digits was disrupted by presenting recordings of random spoken words. These sets of results pointed towards a short-term memory system for remembering movement sequences, visual images, and possibly also the visual appearance of letters and numbers, that was separate from a short-term memory system for retaining phonological codes for words. Baddeley (1983, 1986) referred to this as a visuo-spatial scratch pad, shown in Figure 8.1b. However, it was not until a book by Logie in 1995 that the concept of visuo-spatial aspects of working memory was explored in detail. The evidence collated at that time led to the proposed change in the direction of the information flow shown in the lower half of Figure 8.1b, and led to the development of ideas about how visual and spatial information might be supported within working memory, illustrated in Figure 8.3. Logie (1995, 2003, 2011b) proposed that mental imagery was more likely to be an executive or control process coupled with activated long-term memory, and linked to conscious experience of mental images. Visual short-term memory was thought to function in an analogous way to the phonological loop, but comprised a passive and non-conscious store, the visual cache, with capacity for a single visual pattern or array of shapes limited by complexity or amount of detail, and an inner scribe that supported the retention of sequences of movements, and possibly acted as a control process to help rehearse or refresh the contents of the visual cache. Some recent evidence for this general view of visuo-spatial working memory is reported in van der Meulen, Logie, and Della Sala (2009) and Borst, Niven, and Logie (2012).

The influence of the 1974 paper on the broader research community over the following two decades was largely restricted to researchers and research groups within the UK and in some countries in the rest of Europe, notably Italy. Here, the interest was on developing an understanding of what is referred to as the architecture of working memory; the general principles governing how working memory is structured, organised, and how it functions in all healthy adults. In the late 1980s, Hitch and colleagues explored how working memory develops in young children, demonstrating a tendency to rely on visual short-term memory for objects they have seen (Hitch, Halliday, Schaafstal, & Schragen, 1988). It is only around 8 or 9 years of age that they spontaneously rely on the names of objects and show evidence of the effects of phonological similarity or word length. Another British researcher, Susan Gathercole, worked with Baddeley (Gathercole & Baddeley, 1989, 1993) on the relationship between the phonological loop and the

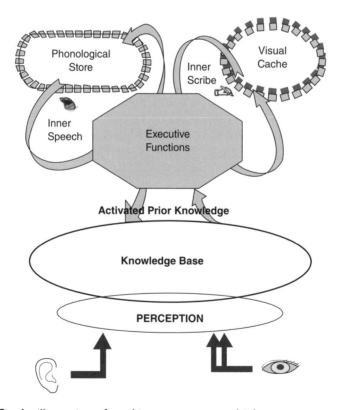

Figure 8.3 An illustration of working memory as multiple components originally proposed by Logie (1995) (figure reproduced from Logie, 2003)

development of language in young children. This work demonstrated that children around the age of 3 or 4, who were good at repeating a nonsense word, were also the children who had better language skills both at the time they were first tested and also when they were re-tested four years later at ages 7 or 8. This led to the idea that the ability of the phonological loop to store a completely new verbal sound sequence and repeat it back in the correct order is important for learning new vocabulary. That is, the phonological loop appeared to be one of the essential ingredients for humans to acquire language in childhood, thereby answering part of Baddeley and Hitch's original question as to why having a verbal short-term memory might be useful.

During the same period of the 1980s and 1990s, there was a rapidly growing interest in the UK in understanding the nature of memory and other cognitive impairments in adults who had suffered brain damage. There was a similar rapidly growing interest among Italian neurologists in developing cognitive tests to assess their brain-damaged patients who appeared to have very specific cognitive impairments. For example, in 1975, two Italian neurologists, De Renzi and Nichelli, described patients who had very specific impairments in remembering visual patterns and pathways, but had intact verbal short-term memory. Baddeley worked with another Italian neurologist (Vallar & Baddeley, 1984) in a detailed study of a patient known as 'PV', who, like patient KF mentioned above, had a very specific verbal short-term memory deficit. PV also had difficulty learning vocabulary from an unfamiliar foreign language, supporting the idea that efficient functioning of the phonological loop is important for learning new vocabulary. These results could be interpreted by suggesting that the De Renzi and Nichelli patient had a deficit in the visuo-spatial scratch pad, whereas both KF and PV had deficits in the operation of the phonological store. These dissociations between patients are very difficult to explain within an Atkinson- and Shiffrin-type model, which would predict that an impairment of short-term verbal memory should be associated with impairments of visual short-term memory and of control processes because they all rely on the same part of the cognitive system. The results are also incompatible with the idea that working memory is simply the activated information from long-term memory, because if this were the case, then KF, PV, and the De Renzi and Nichelli patient should also have problems in accessing long-term memory. But in all these, and many similar cases of short-term memory impairment, long-term memory access is intact. A review of studies of patients with short-term verbal memory impairments is given by Vallar and Shallice (1990). A review of studies with patients who have short-term visual memory impairments is given by Logie and Della Sala (2005).

The common interest across Europe led to other very successful collaborations between British cognitive psychologists and Italian neurologists, and some of the collaborations formed in the 1980s continue in 2014. For example, in 1986, Baddeley and Logie, working with Italian neurologists Spinnler, Bressi, and Della Sala, compared healthy younger and older adults with patients suffering from Alzheimer's disease on their ability to perform two tasks at the same time.

The tasks were chosen to rely respectively on the phonological loop and the visuo-spatial scratch pad, and to avoid input and output conflicts (heard input with spoken output for digits and visual presentation for input with arm movement for output). They found that healthy adults, old or young, could listen to and repeat back sequences of random digits (phonological loop) at the same time as using a stylus to follow a randomly moving target around a computer screen (scratch pad), with very little reduction in verbal memory or tracking performance compared with doing each task separately. The Alzheimer patients could perform each task on its own, but had very considerable difficulty performing the two tasks together. Della Sala and Logie continued the collaboration, demonstrating the same and similar findings across multiple experiments (e.g., Della Sala, Foley, Parra, & Logie, 2011; Logie, Cocchini, Della Sala, & Baddeley, 2004) and recently have been developing versions of the original laboratory tasks as formal clinical tests to help diagnosis of Alzheimer's disease.

In 2000, Baddeley proposed the addition of another component of working memory, the 'episodic buffer', which was thought to be a temporary memory system for integrated representations that, for example, maintains the meaning of an ongoing conversation, but also holds combinations (or temporary bindings) of colours and shapes, such as remembering that you just saw a red circle and a green triangle rather than a green circle and a red triangle. Subsequent studies on the concept of the episodic buffer have shown that it can function automatically without reliance on control processes. Information in the buffer also appears to be fragile and is easily overwritten by new information (e.g. Allen, Baddeley, & Hitch, 2006; Logie, Brockmole, & Vandenbroucke, 2009). A recent brain imaging study (Parra, Della Sala, Logie, & Morcom, 2014) suggested that areas in the frontal areas of the brain may be recruited for undertaking the temporary binding, whereas more posterior areas of the parietal cortex are involved in temporary memory for single features, such as shape only. However, it remains an open question as to whether temporary memory for these kind of bindings requires the concept of an episodic buffer rather than being a function of, for example, a visual short-term memory system as part of the working memory system coupled with activated long-term memory.

CRITIQUE OF THE CLASSIC STUDY

The Baddeley and Hitch (1974) paper has been, and continues to be, frequently cited by researchers worldwide as the primary source for the working memory concept. So it remains highly influential. However, even after the accumulation of four decades of evidence, there has been and remains considerable reluctance among most North American researchers and some European researchers to accept the Baddeley and Hitch's (1974) core proposal that short-term memory functions separately from control processes, or that there might be separate verbal and visual short-term memory systems. Indeed, there are now multiple research groups whose work is focused on exploring how the Baddeley and Hitch proposal might be wrong. Here, the research has been heavily influenced by the view of working memory as a combination of memory and control processes sharing a common resource, which were largely ideas proposed by Broadbent (1958) and by Atkinson and Shiffrin (1968), and shown to be problematic by Baddeley and Hitch (1974).

There has been less interest in North America in using cognitive theories to help understand the impact of specific forms of brain damage, or to understand how different systems in the brain work together to support everyday activities. As a result, working memory in North America has come to be viewed as a general mental capacity for holding information on a temporary basis in the presence of ongoing processing and other distracters. One major influence came from a paper published in 1980 by two North American researchers, Daneman and Carpenter. They developed a sentence span test in which participants were asked to read a series of sentences and for each sentence they had to remember the final word. After all the sentences had been read, participants were asked to recall all of the final words in the order in which they had been presented. The number of sentences, and hence the number of words to be remembered, increased as this process was repeated until the participant was unable to recall the final words correctly. The maximum number of words that people can recall in the task varies from person to person, and Daneman and Carpenter showed that people who were good at this task also were good at a wide range of other complex tasks, such as language comprehension. Likewise, people who were poor at the sentence span task also were poor at language comprehension. The researchers argued that their sentence span task was measuring a fundamental human mental ability and they referred to this as working memory.

Subsequent studies developed different variations of the task. Most notably, US researcher Randall Engle and colleagues (e.g., Engle, Kane, & Tuholski, 1999; Turner & Engle, 1989) developed a version that they called 'operation span', in which people were given simple arithmetic sums, instead of sentences, followed in each case by an unrelated word. Variation in how many words people could remember when interspersed by arithmetic showed good correlations with performance on language comprehension, but also on a wide range of other tests of cognitive ability, including general intelligence and performance in exams. This approach of using individual differences in memory performance in the presence of a distraction continues to dominate working memory research in North America, where the focus is on understanding why it is that people vary in their capacity for these tasks, and what that variation tells us about the underlying factors which determine that capacity. There is less interest in the underlying range of resources that might be deployed to perform these tasks. In terms of the Baddeley and Hitch view of working memory, the individual differences measures are reflecting the operation of both control processes and short-term memory, or in other words, the executive resources and the phonological loop. This was recognised in passing by Engle and Conway (1998). More recent research on the operation span has shown that it correlates highly with measures of access to long-term episodic memory (e.g., Unsworth & Engle, 2007). Other research has shown that operation span measures do not correlate highly with another widely used measure of working memory, known as the n-back task (Kane, Conway, Miura, & Colflesh, 2007), in which participants have to continually update their working memory for recently presented items. These findings suggest that operation span and sentence span are measuring a general capacity of the whole cognitive system, and in particular the ability to encode and retrieve information in long-term memory. This would explain why these measures correlate with general intelligence and a wide range of other complex abilities. However, the findings also suggest that although these are referred to as working memory capacity measures, they might not actually be measuring working memory. This argument is explored in detail by Logie and Niven (2012).

A further difficulty with the individual differences approach noted by Logie (2011a) is that it relies on the maximum score that participants can achieve on the test they are given, and how these scores vary from one person to another. However, this means that any cognitive abilities that are required for task performance at less than their maximum capacity will be completely invisible. For example, reading sentences and remembering the final word from each sentence requires our ability to see and our knowledge of the language in which the sentences are shown. However, the task is well within the visual and language abilities of most people. Only the ability to remember and repeat back the words will vary from one person to another. This would tell us nothing about the contribution from other abilities that are required to do the task. There could also be modest contributions from a visual short-term memory system as people move their eyes across the words of the sentences, but this too would not be evident from the memory scores. In other words, measuring individual differences does not tell us about the range of working memory and other cognitive abilities that are available for performing a task, and developing a theory of working memory based on individual differences in maximum test scores is a blunt instrument for exploring the nature of working memory. This approach does allow us to predict who will do well or who will do poorly when they perform other very demanding tasks, but might have little to say about how we perform daily activities that are well within our working memory capacities. A related problem is illustrated by considering how human biology is assessed. We could have a measure of our general health and fitness, and this might predict how quickly we might run 100 metres. However, this would tell us nothing about the specific functioning of the heart, the liver, the kidneys, or the lungs. Nor would it reveal what is required for us to walk 100 metres at a leisurely pace. So too, a general measure of working memory might predict how well we will perform in university exams, but will tell us nothing about how different aspects of working memory function, or how they support our thinking and memory when chatting to our friends, reading a newspaper, driving to work, or typing numbers on a cash machine.

Another prominent North American working memory researcher, Nelson Cowan, was more directly influenced by the earlier work of Broadbent (1958) and, in 1997, Cowan proposed a theory linking working memory closely with the control of attention (see also Cowan, 2005). His view was that working memory comprised the currently activated information from long-term memory, coupled with a limited capacity focus of attention on a small subset of that activated information. This was a hybrid of both theories in Figure 8.1, in that it retained the idea from Broadbent that working memory relies on a single limited-capacity resource (the focus of attention), but it also incorporated an important feature of the lower half of Figure 8.1b, by suggesting that the contents of working memory are activated from long-term memory, not directly from sensory input. However, like Atkinson and Shiffrin (1968), Cowan's approach does not incorporate any clear distinction between control processes and temporary memory, and does not readily explain the specific verbal or visual short-term memory impairments in patients. Also, Cowan does not view working memory as clearly separate from the activated contents of long-term memory.

The actual theoretical proposal in Baddeley and Hitch (1974) continues to be influential for groups in the UK and in other countries of Europe, and to a certain extent in Asia and in Australia, as well as for some groups in North America. In 2013, Alan Baddeley had twice as many citations worldwide than he did in 2003, so the influence is growing, not waning, and the 1974 paper alone has been cited over 9,000 times since its first publication. However, it is not clear that authors who reference the 1974 classic paper have looked at the detail of the original paper, and many appear to include this reference in their papers because other researchers do so. For example, the 1974 paper is very commonly referenced as the source for the top part Figure 8.1b, but that figure did not appear anywhere until it was included in a paper published by Baddeley in 1983. Also, rarely do contemporary papers on working memory refer to experimental findings in the 1974 paper that are still highly relevant to contemporary debates, such as whether or not control processes and short-term memory share a common resource.

CONCLUSIONS

A major motivation for the original Baddeley and Hitch (1974) paper was a lack of agreement among researchers as to precisely what is meant by short-term memory, and what short-term memory might be used for. Over the 40 years since its publication, many thousands of experiments have been carried out and published, including numerous brain imaging studies. So there is no shortage of empirical evidence available. However, it is striking that 40 years later, such a wide range of different theoretical conceptions are in use, and different groups refer to rather different concepts when using the term 'working memory', even if they refer to the Baddeley and Hitch (1974) paper as the original source of the concept. So, this classic paper inspired several generations of researchers to use the concept of working memory to answer different questions, and the kinds of questions they ask tend to determine the nature of the theoretical perspective that they develop or adopt. In a recent conference, Baddeley referred to the plethora of theories as being like toothbrushes. Everyone needs one, but each person is reluctant to use one that belongs to someone else. This approach of different researchers developing their own theoretical perspective and experimental paradigms might help develop understanding of specific aspects of working memory, such as why people differ in their working memory capacity, or why we forget what we have just seen when we are distracted. Multiple papers have explored possible alternative explanations for phenomena such as the phonological similarity effect or the word length effect, suggesting that the original interpretations of these phenomena might be misleading. In some sense, this is how science progresses, by refining a problem or research question and then focusing efforts on that question. However, there is a danger of missing the broader picture, and while an alternative theory might offer an alternative explanation for the specific phenomena studied, that alternative theory might not be so successful at explaining other phenomena that have been explained by the multiple component approach to understanding working memory illustrated in Figures 8.1b and 8.3, such as the specific impairments in brain-damaged patients.

A major strength of the multiple-component working memory approach is that it is relatively simple. A further strength is that it has been shown to be useful in explaining research results from a very wide range of research topics, for example, aspects of children's language development, aspects of counting and mental arithmetic, reasoning and problem solving, dividing and switching attention, navigating unfamiliar environments, the cognitive impairments resulting from healthy ageing and from specific forms of brain damage, the ways in which people vary in their mental abilities, as well as how we keep track of our every waking moment. The longevity of a theory attests to its scientific value. The fortieth anniversary of the publication of the Baddeley and Hitch 1974 paper was recently celebrated in 2014 in Cambridge, UK, at a conference that was grossly oversubscribed and had a waiting list of delegates hoping for 'standby' places. This demonstrates the continuing popularity of the topic among researchers, and the continuing substantial influence of an important scientific milestone.

AFTERTHOUGHT: COMMENT FROM ALAN BADDELEY

We asked Alan Baddeley for his comments on this chapter, and he responded by sending us an account of his memories of the origins of the working memory model. Here is Alan's response:

> I began my research career working at the MRC Applied Psychology Unit in Cambridge on long-term memory as part of a project concerned with designing postal codes. My interest in short-term memory came through attempting to use it as an indirect means of assessing the quality of telephone lines, arguing that recall of acoustically similar lists might be more sensitive than a listening test. It wasn't. I compared acoustic with semantic similarity. I found clear effects of phonologically similarity on STM but not LTM, unlike semantic similarity which showed the opposite

pattern. These results seemed to fit nicely into the then current controversy as to whether it was necessary to assume more than one kind of memory, suggesting two stores, STM based on a phonological and LTM on a semantic code. This proved far too simple. There must also be phonological LTM, or how could we ever learn new word forms, while STM tasks such as memory span could be shown to reflect semantic factors in sentence recall.

By this time I had moved from Cambridge to Sussex and after a sabbatical year in San Diego, my head of department, Stuart Sutherland, suggested it was about time I got a research grant. It supported a postdoc, Graham Hitch, originally a physicist, who had done the one-year psychology masters course in Sussex and was just completing a PhD under Donald Broadbent at the APU. Together we put forward a proposal to investigate the link between STM and LTM.

It seemed an inauspicious time, given that the dominant theory of STM proposed by Atkinson and Shiffrin was under attack and many people were leaving the field to focus on Levels of Processing and on semantic memory. We decided to focus on the question of what *function* was served by STM. If, as commonly assumed, it served as a working memory, why did patients who had grossly impaired digit span and hence reduced STM not show either LTM or general cognitive deficits? Not having access to such patients we decided to simulate them. We did so by loading up our participants with strings of digits of varying lengths, on the assumption that if STM functioned as a working memory, a greater load should lead to more impairment. We tested reasoning comprehension and learning and, as you will see in the next chapter, we struck lucky, coming up with complex results that were, however, interpretable provided we divided the old unitary model into three components.

Finally, we were also fortunate in receiving an invitation from the editor, Gordon Bower, to contribute to an influential annual volume *Recent Advances in Learning and Motivation*. We were a little doubtful about accepting, given that our model was not entirely worked out (as, of course, is still the case!), but decided to go ahead. The paper's initial impact was modest; STM was yesterday's question. However, the concept of a working memory, that went beyond STM by assuming a functionally important system involving both storage and processing, proved a fruitful one and has, I am happy to say, continued to do so.

FURTHER READING

Baddeley, A. D. (2007). *Working memory, thought and action*. Oxford: Oxford University Press.

Baddeley, A. D. (2012). Working memory, theories, models and controversy. *The Annual Review of Psychology, 63*, 12.1–12.29.

Logie, R. H. (2011a). The functional organisation and the capacity limits of working memory. *Current Directions in Psychological Science, 20* (4), 240–245.

Logie, R. H., & Morris, R. G. (Eds.) (2015). *Working memory and ageing*. Hove, UK: Psychology Press.

Miyake, A., & Shah, P. (Eds.) (1999). *Models of working memory*. New York: Cambridge University Press.

REFERENCES

Allen, R. J., Baddeley, A. D., & Hitch, G. J. (2006). Is the binding of visual features in working memory resource-demanding? *Journal of Experimental Psychology: General*, 135, 298–313.

Atkinson, R. C., & Shiffrin, R. M. (1968). Human memory: A proposed system and its control processes. In K. W. Spence & J. T. Spence (Eds.), *The psychology of learning and motivation: Advances in research and theory* (Vol. 2). New York: Academic Press.

Baddeley, A. D. (1983). Working memory. *Philosophical Transactions of the Royal Society of London*, B302, 311–324.

Baddeley, A. D. (1986). *Working memory*. Oxford: Oxford University Press.

Baddeley, A. D. (2000). The episodic buffer: A new component of working memory? *Trends in Cognitive Sciences*, 4, 417–423.

Baddeley, A. D., & Hitch, G. J. (1974). Working memory. In G. H. Bower (Ed.), *Recent advances in learning and motivation* (Vol. 8, pp. 47–89). New York: Academic Press.

Baddeley, A. D., & Lieberman, K. (1980). Spatial working memory. In R. S. Nickerson (Ed.), *Attention and performance* (Vol. VIII, pp. 521–539). Hillsdale, NJ: Lawrence Erlbaum Association.

Baddeley, A. D., & Logie, R. H. (1999). Working memory: The multiple component model. In A. Miyake & P. Shah (Eds.), *Models of working memory* (pp. 28–61). New York: Cambridge University Press.

Baddeley, A. D., Grant, W., Wight, E., & Thomson, N. (1975). Imagery and visual working memory. In P. M. A. Rabbitt & S. Dornic (Eds.), *Attention and performance* (Vol. V, pp. 205–217). London: Academic Press.

Baddeley, A. D., Logie, R., Bressi, S., Della Sala, S., & Spinnler, H. (1986). Senile dementia and working memory. *Quarterly Journal of Experimental Psychology*, 38A, 603–618.

Baddeley, A. D., Thomson, N., & Buchanan, M. (1975). Word length and the structure of short-term memory. *Journal of Verbal Learning and Verbal Behavior*, 14, 575–589.

Borst, G., Niven, E. H., & Logie, R. H. (2012). Visual mental image generation does not overlap with visual short-term memory: A dual task interference study. *Memory and Cognition*, 40, 360–372.

Broadbent, D. (1958). *Perception and communication*. Oxford: Pergamon Press.

Brown, J. (1958). Some tests of decay of immediate memory. *Quarterly Journal of Experimental Psychology*, 10, 12–21.

Cowan, N. (1997). *Attention and memory: An integrated framework*. Oxford: Oxford University Press.

Cowan, N. (2005). *Working memory capacity*. Hove, UK: Psychology Press.

Daneman, M., & Carpenter, P. A. (1980). Individual differences in working memory and reading. *Journal of Verbal Learning and Verbal Behavior*, 19, 450–466.

Della Sala, S., Foley, J. A., Parra, M. A., & Logie, R. H. (2011). Dual tasking and memory binding in Alzheimer's. *Journal of Alzheimer Disease*, S23, 22–24.

De Renzi, E., & Nichelli, P. (1975). Verbal and nonverbal short term memory impairment following hemispheric damage. *Cortex*, 11, 341–353.

Engle, R. W., & Conway, A. R. A. (1998). Working memory and comprehension. In R. H. Logie & K. J. Gilhooly (Eds.), *Working memory and thinking* (pp. 67–91). Hove, UK: Psychology Press.

Engle, R. W., Kane, M. J., & Tuholski, A. W. (1999). Individual differences in working memory capacity and what they tell us about controlled attention, general fluid intelligence, and functions of the prefrontal cortex. In A. Miyake & P. Shah (Eds.), *Models of working memory* (pp. 102–134). New York: Cambridge University Press.

Gathercole, S., & Baddeley, A. D. (1989). Evaluation of the role of phonological STM in the development of vocabulary in children: A longitudinal study. *Journal of Memory and Language*, 28, 200–213.

Gathercole, S., & Baddeley, A. D. (1993). *Working memory and language*. Hove, UK: Lawrence Erlbaum.

Hitch, G. J., Halliday, M. S., Schaafstal, A. M., & Schraagen, J. M. C. (1988). Visual working memory in young children. *Memory and Cognition*, 16, 120–132.

James, W. (1890/1905). *Principles of psychology* (Vol. 1). London: Methuen & Co.

Kane, M. J., Conway, A. R. A., Miura, T. K., & Colflesh, J. H. (2007). Working memory, attention control, and the n-back task: A question of construct validity. *Journal of Experimental Psychology: Learning, Memory, and Cognition*, 33, 615–622.

Locke, J. (1690). *An essay concerning humane understanding*, Book II, Chapter X, paragraphs 1–2.

Logie, R. H. (1986). Visuo-spatial processing in working memory. *Quarterly Journal of Experimental Psychology*, 38A (2), 229–247.

Logie, R. H. (1995). *Visuo-spatial working memory*. Hove, UK: Lawrence Erlbaum Associates.

Logie, R. H. (2003). Spatial and visual working memory: A mental workspace. In D. Irwin & B. Ross (Eds.), *Cognitive vision: The psychology of learning and motivation* (Vol. 42, pp. 37–78). San Diego: Academic Press.

Logie, R. H. (2011a). The functional organisation and the capacity limits of working memory. *Current Directions in Psychological Science*, 20 (4), 240–245.

Logie, R. H. (2011b). The visual and the spatial of a multicomponent working memory. In A. Vandierendonck & A. Szmalec (Eds.), *Spatial working memory* (pp. 19–45). Hove, UK: Psychology Press.

Logie, R. H., & Della Sala, S. (2005). Disorders of visuo-spatial working memory. In A. Miyake & P. Shah (Eds.), *Handbook of visuospatial thinking* (pp. 81–120). New York: Cambridge University Press.

Logie, R. H., & Niven, E. H. (2012). Working memory: An ensemble of functions in on-line cognition. In V. Gyselinck & F. Pazzaglia (Eds.), *From mental imagery to spatial cognition and language: Essays in honour of Michel Denis* (pp. 77–105). Hove, UK: Psychology Press.

Logie, R. H., Brockmole, J. R., & Vandenbroucke, A. (2009). Bound feature combinations in visual short-term memory are fragile but influence long-term learning. *Visual Cognition*, 17, 160–179.

Logie, R. H., Cocchini, G., Della Sala, S., & Baddeley, A. D. (2004). Is there a specific executive capacity for dual task co-ordination? Evidence from Alzheimer's disease. *Neuropsychology*, 18, 504–513.

Miller, G. A., Galanter, E., & Pribram, K. H. (1960). *Plans and the structure of behavior*. New York: Holt, Rinehart and Winston.

Parra, M. A., Della Sala, S., Logie, R. H., & Morcom, A. (2014). Neural correlates of shape-color binding in visual working memory. *Neuropsychologia*, 52C, 27–36.

Patterson, K.A. (1971). Limitations on retrieval from long-term memory. Unpublished doctoral dissertation, University of California, San Diego.

Peterson, L. R., & Peterson, M. J. (1959). Short-term retention of individual verbal items. *Journal of Experimental Psychology*, 58, 193–198.

Salamé, P., & Baddeley, A. D. (1982). Disruption of short-term memory by unattended speech: Implications for the structure of working memory. *Journal of Verbal Learning and Verbal Behavior*, 21, 150–164.

Turner, M. L., & Engle, R. W. (1989). Is working memory capacity task dependent? *Journal of Memory and Language*, 28, 127–154.

Unsworth, N., & Engle, R. W. (2007) The nature of individual differences in working memory capacity: Active maintenance in primary memory and controlled search from secondary memory. *Psychological Review*, 114 (1), 104–132.

Vallar, G., & Baddeley, A. D. (1984). Fractionation of working memory: Neuropsychological evidence for a phonological short-term store. *Journal of Verbal Learning and Verbal Behavior*, 23, 151–161.

Vallar, G., & Shallice, T. (Eds.) (1990). *Neuropsychological impairments of short-term memory*. Cambridge, UK: Cambridge University Press.

Van der Meulen, M., Logie, R. H., & Della Sala, S. (2009). Selective interference with image retention and generation: Evidence for the workspace model. *Quarterly Journal of Experimental Psychology*, 62, 1568–1580.

Warrington, E. K., & Shallice, T. (1972). Neuropsychological evidence of visual storage in short-term memory tasks. *Quarterly Journal of Experimental Psychology*, 24, 30–40.

Waugh, N. C., & Norman, D. A. (1965) Primary memory. *Psychological Review*, 72, 89–104.

9 | Memory systems: Beyond Tulving's (1972) episodic and semantic memory

Michael W. Eysenck (Roehampton University and Royal Holloway University of London) and David Groome (University of Westminster)

BACKGROUND TO THE CLASSIC STUDY

Suppose you were asked to recall the last time you rode a bicycle. You would need to search for a memory of an actual event or episode in your life, occurring in a particular time and place. On the other hand, if someone asked you to tell them what a bicycle is, you would require a different kind of memory retrieval, one that involved the recall of a piece of knowledge and with no need to retrieve an actual experience or context. These two types of memory retrieval seem to be fundamentally different from one another, and they provide the basis of Tulving's distinction between 'episodic' and 'semantic' memory, respectively.

Long-term memory plays an absolutely central role in our lives. Without long-term memory, we would be unable to learn anything, we would have no knowledge of our own past, and everyone we met would appear to be a stranger. In view of its importance, it is unsurprising that numerous attempts have been made over the past 2,000 years or more to understand its workings. Many theorists have made use of the spatial metaphor to describe long-term memory (Roediger, 1980). According to the spatial metaphor, memories are stored in specific locations in the mind and we retrieve these memories by searching through the mind. For example, Plato compared the mind to an aviary with the individual memories represented by birds. Subsequent theorists compared the long-term memory system to switchboards, tape recorders, conveyor belts, and the stores found in computers (Roediger, 1980).

One of the major limitations of most theories based on the spatial metaphor is that they failed to distinguish among different types of long-term memory. That limitation was also present in the extremely influential multi-store model proposed by Atkinson and Shiffrin (1968). They identified a single long-term store that holds information over very long periods of time.

If you think about it, it is not very plausible to assume that we possess only a single long-term memory system. Our long-term memory contains knowledge about the world (e.g., that Rome is the capital of Italy) and about our personal experiences over the years (e.g., an actual visit we made to Rome), as well as information about how to ride a bicycle and perhaps how to play tennis.

With the benefit of hindsight, it is strange that so few memory researchers prior to Tulving (1972) had attempted to investigate different forms of long-term memory. This was so in spite of the fact that several theorists had drawn rather similar distinctions between two forms of long-term memory (see Tulving, 1983, for a review). For example, Reiff and Scheerer (1959, p. 25) distinguished between memories '*with* the experience of the autobiographical index, to be called *remembrances*, and those *without* the experience of an autobiographic index to be called *memoria* ... remembrances are always accompanied by the experience of personal continuity through time, while in memoria this experience is absent'.

DETAILED DESCRIPTION OF THE CLASSIC STUDY

Tulving's (1972) starting point was that the distinction between two forms of long-term memory proposed by theorists such as Reiff and Scheerer (1959) was of enormous potential importance. What he set out to achieve was to provide a more detailed theoretical account comparing these two forms of memory. This would make it easier for researchers to investigate the similarities and differences between them.

Tulving (1972) used the terms 'episodic memory' and 'semantic memory' to describe the two forms of long-term memory. Episodic memory 'receives and stores information about temporally dated episodes or events, and temporal-spatial relations among these events. A perceptual event ... is always stored in terms of its autobiographical reference to the already existing contents of the episodic memory store' (pp. 385–386). Episodic memory closely resembles what Reiff and Scheerer (1959) had called 'remembrances'.

In contrast, semantic memory 'is the memory necessary for the use of language. It is a mental thesaurus, organized knowledge a person possesses about words and other verbal symbols, their meaning and referents, about relations among them, and about rules, formulas, and algorithms for the manipulation of these symbols, concepts, and relations' (p. 386). Semantic memory is very similar to what Reiff and Scheerer (1959) called 'memoria'.

Tulving (1972) argued that nearly all laboratory research on human memory had focused on episodic memory. There had been a few studies on semantic memory (e.g., asking participants to free associate to specific words), but none at all comparing episodic and semantic memory. As we will see, he changed his mind on this issue later on (Tulving, 1983).

It is sometimes erroneously assumed that Tulving (1972) argued that episodic memory and semantic memory are completely separate from each other. In fact, Tulving actually claimed that 'the specific form in which perceptual input is registered into the episodic memory can at times be strongly influenced by information in semantic memory' (p. 386).

One of Tulving's (1972) most valuable contributions was to make four assumptions about the nature of episodic and semantic memory. First, perceptual events are stored in episodic memory, whereas semantic memory registers the 'cognitive referents of input signals' (p. 386). Episodic memories are formed *directly* following the experience of an event. In contrast, semantic memories can be formed *indirectly* by combining different items of knowledge already contained in semantic memory. Thus, for example, your semantic memory might have stored in it information that A is taller than B and that B is taller than C. You could then use inferential reasoning to work out that A is taller than C without having specifically learned that piece of information.

Second, and most obviously, episodic and semantic memory differ in terms of the nature of the stored information. Episodic memories have an autobiographical quality whereas semantic memories are based on organised knowledge and so have a 'cognitive' quality.

Third, episodic memory and semantic memory differ in terms of the consequences of retrieval. Retrieval of information from episodic memory acts as an input into episodic memory and so changes the information stored in episodic memory. In contrast, retrieval of information from semantic memory does not affect the information stored within that system.

Fourth, and related to the third point, episodic memories are vulnerable to interference and loss of stored information. In contrast, semantic memories are much less vulnerable to interference and loss of information.

IMPACT OF THE CLASSIC STUDY

Tulving's (1972) classic study has had an enormous impact over the years. We can obtain an approximate measure of this impact with reference to *Web of Science*. There were 2,230 articles with 'episodic memory' in their title and 1,606 with 'semantic memory' in their title published by the middle of 2014. Of interest, the number of articles with one or other term in their title has shown a dramatic increase over the years. The term 'episodic memory' appeared in the title of approximately 20 articles a year up to 1995 but an average of approximately 150 per year in the past decade. The respective figures for 'semantic memory' are approximately 25 per year up to 1995 but approximately 65 a year in the past decade.

Tulving's (1972) theory led researchers to carry out studies in which episodic and semantic memory were compared. One major line of research involved considering the effects of brain damage on episodic and semantic memory and the consequent pattern of amnesic symptoms (see Greenberg & Verfaellie, 2010, for a review). One very important contribution made by Tulving's distinction between episodic and semantic memory was that it enabled researchers to reveal aspects of memory and amnesia which were previously obscured by the confounding of these two types of memory measure. Early studies of amnesia failed to distinguish between episodic and semantic measures of memory performance, so research findings often reflected a mixture of the two. Even worse, researchers would often confound measures of these two types of memory with other task comparisons. For example, the early studies of amnesia typically used episodic questions to test recent memory (e.g., what did you do yesterday morning?) while using semantic questions to test the more distant past (e.g., who was Winston Churchill?). This confounding of two different types of memory test caused a serious misunderstanding of the relative severity of anterograde amnesia (which means loss of memory for the time period since the onset of amnesia) and retrograde amnesia (loss of memory for the time period preceding onset). A good example of the above was the classic study of the amnesic patient Henry Molaison (HM) (Scoville and Milner, 1957; see Chapter 7). Scoville and Milner reported that Henry suffered very severe anterograde amnesia but virtually no retrograde amnesia. However, later studies of Henry, using separate episodic and semantic measures of remote memory, revealed that he actually suffered a very extensive episodic retrograde impairment (Steinvorth, Levine, & Corkin, 2005).

Studies of anterograde amnesia have established that episodic memory performance and semantic memory performance frequently show different degrees of impairment. Since Tulving argued that episodic memory is more vulnerable than semantic memory, we might assume that brain damage should have a greater adverse effect on episodic than semantic memories. Most of the early amnesia research, focusing on patients with damage to the hippocampus, tended to confirm that episodic memory does indeed tend to be more severely impaired than semantic memory. Spiers, Maguire, and Burgess (2001) carried out a meta-analysis of 147 amnesic patients. They discovered that episodic memory was impaired (often severely) in all 147 cases. In contrast, many patients had relatively mild impairment of semantic memory.

More recent research has suggested a more complex picture. Certainly there are some brain-damaged amnesic patients whose impairment is largely restricted to their episodic memory. One clear example is the patient 'KC', who displays a specific episodic impairment with almost no detectable semantic deficit (Tulving, 2001; Rosenbaum, Kohler, Schacter, Moscovitch, Westmacott, Black, Gao, & Tulving, 2005). KC sustained bilateral hippocampal lesions as a result of a motorcycle accident, and Rosenbaum et al. (2005, p. 994) described his condition as follows:

> His store of semantic facts about himself and the world, procedural skills that were acquired in the first 30 years of his life, and his effortless functioning in his everyday environment are comparable to most of his age mates. What makes him different, even from many amnesic cases, is his inability to recollect any specific event in which he himself participated or any happening that he himself witnessed.

Another similar case involving a focal episodic impairment is the patient 'Jon' (Gardiner, Brandt, Baddeley, Vargha-Khadem, & Mishkin, 2008), who developed amnesia as a consequence of suffering hippocampal damage due to hypoxic-ischemia shortly after birth. Gardiner et al. (2008, p. 2865) reported that 'The results further support the hypothesis that despite a severely compromised episodic memory and hippocampal system, there is nevertheless the capacity to accrue semantic knowledge available to recall'. These individuals show a relatively intact semantic memory but they are unable to recall any specific events from their lives since the onset of their amnesia. This pattern of amnesia has been called 'episodic amnesia' (Rosenbaum et al., 2005), and it is usually associated with lesions that are restricted to the hippocampus.

Patients have also been studied who show a specific impairment of semantic memory without any significant episodic deficit. This condition is known as 'semantic amnesia' or more often 'semantic dementia' since it tends to be accompanied by a more general impairment of cognitive function, and it is usually found in patients who have damage to the anterior temporal lobe. Such patients have severe loss of concept knowledge from semantic memory (Mayberry, Sage, & Lambon Ralph, 2011). However, they have reasonably intact episodic memory, at least during the early stages of the disease. In one study (Adlam, Patterson, & Hodges, 2009), patients with semantic dementia recalled which tasks they had performed the previous day, where they had performed those tasks, and when they had occurred in the course of the experimental session. The key finding was that the overall performance of the patients was comparable to that of healthy controls.

In general terms, the overall findings from amnesic patients and patients with semantic dementia support the notion that episodic and semantic memory can each be separately impaired, and thus probably depend on somewhat separate brain systems. More specifically, we have a double dissociation in which amnesic patients have very poor episodic memory but reasonable semantic memory, whereas patients with semantic dementia have very poor semantic memory but reasonable episodic memory.

The amnesia studies described above mostly focus on anterograde amnesia, but many amnesic patients also suffer from retrograde amnesia. A number of studies of retrograde amnesia have revealed a very extensive episodic impairment which stretches back over a very long period, often extending back to childhood and involving as much as 20 or 30 years of lost memories. In contrast, these patients show a far shorter period of semantic retrograde impairment, which is typically limited to a period only about two or three years before onset. This pattern of retrograde impairment has been reported in Alzheimer's patients (Addis & Tippett, 2004), patients with Herpes Simplex Encephalitis (McCarthy, Kopelman, & Warrington, 2005), and the temporal lobe surgery patient 'Henry M' (Steinvorth, et al., 2005).

A possible explanation for the above finding of extensive episodic but limited semantic retrograde amnesia is provided by the Multiple Trace Theory (Moscovitch, Yaschyshyn, Ziegler, & Nadel, 1999). This theory proposes that each time a memory is retrieved it acquires new neural connections and creates new memory traces. A newly acquired episodic memory will thus acquire connections with other related memory traces over the next few years, which eventually allow a series of episodic memories to combine together to create a more general semantic memory. For example, a number of specific experiences of meeting dogs may combine to form a general semantic memory of what dogs are like. Moscovitch et al. suggest that once these semantic memories are formed, they become fairly robust and invulnerable to disruption, and more specifically they are no longer dependent on the hippocampus to maintain and retrieve them. Damage to the hippocampus is known to cause impairment mainly to episodic memories, so it would be expected that hippocampal lesions would impair all of the individual's episodic memories but only the most recent of their semantic memories, because they are the ones which are still in the process of being constructed from episodic memories. The Multiple Trace Theory thus provides a possible explanation for the findings of the retrograde amnesia studies described above, and these findings are also consistent with the view that semantic memories are created by the binding together of a number of episodic memories.

Tulving (1972) assumed that episodic memory and semantic memory are often interdependent in their functioning and there is accumulating support for that assumption. Kan, Alexander, and Verfaellie (2009) gave participants an episodic memory task involving learning the prices of grocery items. Semantic memory was also relevant because the prices of some items were congruent with participants' existing knowledge of those prices whereas others were incongruent. Healthy controls had better memory performance for grocery prices congruent with their prior knowledge than for incongruent prices, indicating that their performance on the episodic memory task was influenced by semantic memory. Amnesic patients with reasonably intact semantic memory had similar findings, but amnesic patients with severely impaired semantic memory showed no congruency effect at all.

Greenberg, Keane, Ryan, and Verfaillie (2009) used the semantic memory task of generating as many category members as possible from various semantic categories. The categories were selected so that performance on some of them (e.g., things given as birthday presents) would benefit from the use of episodic memory whereas episodic memory would be much less useful for other categories (e.g., objects that are typically red). Amnesic patients performed much worse overall than healthy controls. This was especially the case with categories benefitting from episodic memory, because the amnesic patients were less likely than the controls to use episodic memory to organise the retrieval of category members.

One of the greatest influences of Tulving's (1972) article on the development of memory research was to encourage theorists to identify memory systems in addition to episodic and semantic memory. For example, Schacter and Tulving (1994) argued for the existence of four memory systems, including episodic and semantic memory. The other two memory systems were the perceptual representational system involved in priming and procedural memory involved in the learning of and memory for motor skills. Schacter and Tulving argue that semantic memory can be regarded as a form of implicit memory (i.e., involving unconscious and automatic retrieval processes), whereas episodic recall involves explicit memory (i.e., requiring conscious and effortful retrieval). However, Squire (1992) argues that episodic and semantic memories should both be classified within the same memory system, since they are both impaired in amnesic patients. In the memory classification system proposed by Squire, episodic and semantic memory are both considered to be forms of 'declarative' memory (i.e., memories which are available for conscious retrieval), as opposed to 'non-declarative' (memories which cannot be consciously retrieved).

Consciousness is actually one of the most fundamental issues in the distinction between episodic and semantic memory. Tulving (2002) argued that episodic memory represents the highest form of memory in terms of evolutionary advancement, because it involves a greater degree of conscious awareness than is required for semantic memory. Tulving describes episodic memory as allowing a form of 'mental time travel', whereby we can relive our experiences from the past in a conscious way. Tulving also argued that episodic memory represents the most advanced type of memory and the most recently evolved, and he further speculated that episodic memory may be restricted to humans and other primates, and may not occur in other animal species. This is a theory which is difficult to substantiate, as it is not possible to ask a dog or a cat whether it can consciously retrieve specific events from the past.

Since the introduction of brain-imaging techniques, researchers have been able to investigate the regions of the brain which are associated with episodic and semantic memory activity. Functional MRI scanning has shown that the brain areas activated during the retrieval of episodic and semantic memories respectively are largely distinct from one another, but with some areas of overlap. The retrieval of semantic memories mainly activates the left prefrontal cortex and the left temporo-parietal region. Episodic memory retrieval also activates the left prefrontal cortex, but in addition there is activation of the right temporo-parietal cortex and the medial temporal cortex (Levine, Turner, Tisserand, Hevenor, Graham, & McIntosh, 2004). These findings offer some support for the view that episodic and semantic memory depend on different brain systems, but with connections between the two systems.

The finding that semantic memory retrieval activates the left prefrontal cortex and the left temporo-parietal region (Levine et al., 2004) shows some consistency with the lesions found in semantic dementia. Hodges and Patterson (2007) reported that semantic dementia patients showed extensive atrophy of the anterior temporal lobes (which are known to be involved in memory retrieval) and of the perirhinal cortex (which is known to be involved in object recognition and the binding of sensory information).

Episodic memory retrieval has been found to activate the right prefrontal cortex, the medial temporal lobe (including the hippocampus), and the temporo-parietal cortex (Levine et al., 2004; Shimamura, 2014). The medial temporal lobe was already known to be involved in memory encoding and retrieval from the study of individuals with damage to this region (Scoville & Milner, 1957; Steinvorth et al., 2005), and these findings have now been confirmed by brain imaging studies (Buckner, 2000; Ranganath, 2010). These studies have also suggested that the medial temporal lobe plays an important part in both activating and binding together the various different features of an experienced event to encode or retrieve a complete episodic memory. The role of the prefrontal cortex in episodic retrieval appears to be mainly concerned with performing a memory search (Cabeza, Locantore, & Anderson, 2003), as the prefrontal region is known to be important in search activities carried out by the central executive of the working memory. Cabeza, Ciaramelli, and Moscovitch (2012) have reported activation of the ventral posterior parietal cortex (VPPC) during episodic retrieval. The VPPC has been found to play a role in the correct identification of 'hits' in recognition testing, so it may help to make the individual confident that their search has generated a correct response. Consistent with this hypothesis, it is interesting to note that patients with lesions in the VPPC do not normally show severe amnesic symptoms, but they do tend to suffer some impairment of autobiographical memory with a reduced level of confidence in the correctness of their retrieval (Hower, Wixted, Berryhill, & Olsen, 2014).

CRITIQUE OF THE CLASSIC STUDY

Our task in providing a critique of Tulving's (1972) classic study is made easier by the fact that Tulving (1983) explicitly considered its shortcomings! According to Tulving (1983), perhaps the greatest shortcoming of his earlier article was that it assumed that laboratory studies of memory had predominantly focused only on episodic memory, with successful memory performance indicating that participants remembered the context in which a given item had been encountered.

There is considerable empirical evidence showing that the above assumption is oversimplified. For example, consider a study by Harand, Bertran, La Joie, Landeau, Mézange, Desgranges, et al. (2012). They presented their participants with nearly 200 pictures and then assessed their recognition-memory performance for these pictures at two retention intervals: three days and three months. The most relevant findings relate to those pictures that were recognised at both retention intervals. Participants could retrieve specific details about their encoding of some of these pictures (contextual information) at both retention intervals, suggesting the memories were episodic throughout.

With other pictures recognised at both retention intervals, the memories were episodic at the short retention interval (i.e., contextual information was retrieved) but semantic at the long retention interval (i.e., no contextual information was retrieved). This change over time for these latter pictures is known as semanticisation, meaning that what are originally episodic memories can become semantic ones over time.

What other shortcomings did Tulving (1983) identify in his 1972 article? First, he admitted that he had not been as explicit as he might have been about the *similarities* between episodic and semantic memory and their frequent interdependence. Second, he failed to indicate clearly that there might well be forms of memory other than episodic and semantic memory, such as procedural or skill learning. Third, the term 'semantic memory' is somewhat misleading. It leads us to think of the meanings of words and other symbols and so implies that semantic memory is narrower than is actually the case. Tulving (1983) suggested that 'knowledge of the world' would be a more accurate description.

Tulving (1972, 1983) assumed that episodic memory includes autobiographical memory (long-term memory for the events of one's own life). This assumption has proved somewhat controversial, although definitive evidence one way or the other is lacking. For example, there would appear to be important differences between remembering that the word 'chair' was presented in the second list (episodic memory) and a holiday romance (autobiographical memory). Episodic memory typically lacks the direct relevance to the self that is found with autobiographical memory. Gilboa (2004) carried out a meta-analysis of neuroimaging studies. There was much more activation in the right mid-dorsolateral prefrontal cortex in episodic than autobiographical memory because episodic memory requires conscious monitoring to minimise errors. However, there was much more activation in the left ventromedial prefrontal cortex in autobiographical memory than episodic memory perhaps because it involves monitoring retrieved memories with respect to activated knowledge of the self.

A matter of current controversy concerns the value of the entire memory-system approach pioneered by Tulving (1972). In essence, the central criticism of this approach is that it is far too neat and tidy (e.g., task X allegedly involves only episodic memory whereas task Y allegedly involves only semantic memory). An alternative approach that is starting to become more popular is based on the assumption that learning and memory involve numerous processing components that can be combined and re-combined depending on the precise nature of the task (e.g., Dudai & Morris, 2013). This processing-component approach has the advantage over the memory-system approach in that it permits much more flexibility in terms of the specific processes engaged by any given learning/memory task. This approach is supported by neuroimaging research. Cabeza and Moscovitch (2013, p. 49) reviewed such research and concluded that: 'Brain regions attributed to one memory system can contribute to tasks associated with other memory systems.'

At present, the jury is out on whether the memory-system or processing-component approach provides the more adequate explanation of long-term memory. It is perhaps fair to conclude that the processing-component approach is a promising one and has received preliminary support from within cognitive neuroscience. However, the number and nature of the specific processing components remain somewhat unclear and much more needs to be done to specify how processing components combine during learning and memory. In sum, the approach is somewhat 'fuzzy' and often fails to make specific predictions.

CONCLUSIONS

Tulving's (1972) article on the distinction between episodic and semantic memory was of major importance in leading theorists to consider in detail the number and nature of long-term memory systems. This issue remains important now, over 40 years since the article was published.

FURTHER READING

Cabeza, R., & Moscovitch, M. (2013). Memory systems, processing modes, and components: Functional neuroimaging evidence. *Perspectives on Psychological Science*, 8, 49–55.

Greenberg, D. L., & Verfaellie, M. (2010). Interdependence of episodic and semantic memory: Evidence from neuropsychology. *Journal of the*

International Neuropsychology Society, 16, 748–753.

Tulving, E. (1972). Episodic and semantic memory. In E. Tulving & W. Donaldson (Eds.), *Organisation of memory*. London: Academic Press.

Tulving, E. (1983). *Elements of episodic memory*. Oxford: Oxford University Press.

REFERENCES

Addis, D. R., & Tippett, L. J. (2004). Memory of myself: Autobiographical memory and identity in Alzheimer's disease. *Memory*, 12, 56–74.

Adlam, A.-L. R., Patterson, K., & Hodges, J. R. (2009). 'I remember it as if it were yesterday': Memory for recent events in patients with semantic dementia. *Neuropsychologia*, 47, 1344–1351.

Atkinson, R. C., & Shiffrin, R. M. (1968). Human memory: A proposed system and its control processes. In K. W. Spence & J. T. Spence (Eds.), *The psychology of learning and motivation* (Vol. 2). London: Academic Press.

Buckner, R. L. (2000). Neuroimaging of memory. In M. S. Gazzaniga (Ed.), *The new cognitive neurosciences* (2nd edn). Cambridge, MA: The MIT Press.

Cabeza, R., & Moscovitch, M. (2013). Memory systems, processing modes, and components: Functional neuroimaging evidence. *Perspectives on Psychological Science*, 8, 49–55.

Cabeza, R., Ciaramelli, E., & Moscovitch, M. (2012). Cognitive contributions of the ventral parietal cortex: An integrative theoretical account. *Trends in Cognitive Sciences*, 16, 338–352.

Cabeza, R., Locantore, J. K., & Anderson, N. D. (2003). Lateralization of prefrontal activity during episodic memory retrieval: Evidence for the production-monitoring hypothesis. *Journal of Cognitive Neuroscience*, 15, 249–259.

Dudai, Y., & Morris, R. G. M. (2013). Memory trends. *Neuron*, 80, 742–750.

Gardiner, J. M., Brandt, K. R., Baddeley, A. D., Vargha-Khadem, F., & Mishkin, M. (2008). Charting the acquisition of semantic knowledge in a case of developmental amnesia. *Neuropsychologia*, 46, 2865–2868.

Gilboa, A. (2004). Autobiographical and episodic memory – one the same? Evidence from prefrontal activation in neuroimaging studies. *Neuropsychologia*, 42, 1336–1349.

Greenberg, D. L., & Verfaellie, M. (2010). Interdependence of episodic and semantic memory: Evidence from neuropsychology. *Journal of the International Neuropsychology Society*, 16, 748–753.

Greenberg, D. L., Keane, M. M., Ryan, L. R., & Verfaillie, M. (2009). Impaired category fluency in medial temporal lobe amnesia: The role of episodic memory. *Journal of Neuroscience*, 29, 10900–10908.

Harand, C., Bertran, F., La Joie, F., Landeau, B., Mézange, F., Desgranges, B., et al. (2012). The hippocampus remains activated over the long term for the retrieval of truly episodic memories. *PloS One*, 7 (8), e 43495.

Hodges, J. R., & Patterson, K. (2007). Semantic dementia: a unique clinicopathological syndrome. *Lancet Neurology*, 6, 1004–1014.

Hower, K. H., Wixted, J., Berryhill, M. E., & Olson, I. R. (2014). Impaired perception of mnemonic oldness, but not mnemonic newness, after parietal lobe damage. *Neuropsychologia*, 56, 409–417.

Kan, I. P., Alexander, M. P., & Verfaellie, M. (2009). Contribution of prior semantic knowledge to new episodic learning in amnesia. *Journal of Cognitive Neuroscience*, 21, 938–944.

Levine, B., Turner, G. R., Tisserand, D., Hevenor, S. J., Graham, S. J., & McIntosh, A. R. (2004). The functional neuroanatomy of episodic and semantic autobiographical remembering: A prospective functional MRI study. *Journal of Cognitive Neuroscience*, 16, 1633–1646.

Mayberry, E. J., Sage, K., & Lambon Ralph, M. A. (2011). At the edge of semantic space: The breakdown of coherent concepts in semantic dementia is constrained by typicality and severity but not modality. *Journal of Cognitive Neuroscience*, 23, 2240–2251.

McCarthy, R. A., Kopelman, M. D., & Warrington, E. K. (2005). Remembering and forgetting of semantic knowledge in amnesia: A 16-year follow-up investigation of RFR. *Neuropsychologia*, 43, 356–372.

Moscovitch, M., Yaschyshyn, M., Ziegler, M., & Nadel, L. (1999). Remote episodic memory and retrograde amnesia: Was Endel Tulving right all along? In E. Tulving (Ed.), *Memory, consciousness, and the brain: The Tallin conference*. New York: Psychology Press.

Ranganath, C. (2010). Binding items and contexts: The cognitive neuroscience of episodic memory. *Current Directions in Psychological Science*, 19, 131–137.

Reiff, R., & Scheerer, M. (1959). *Memory and hypnotic age regression*. New York: International Universities Press.

Roediger, H. L. (1980). Memory metaphors in cognitive psychology. *Memory & Cognition*, 8, 231–246.

Rosenbaum, R. S., Kohler, S., Schacter, D. L., Moscovitch, M., Westmacott, R., Black, S. E., Gao, F., & Tulving, E. (2005). The case of K.C.: Contributions of a memory-impaired person to memory. *Neuropsychologia*, 43, 989–1021.

Schacter, D. L., & Tulving, E. (1994). What are the memory systems of 1994? In D. L. Schacter & E. Tulving (Eds.), *Memory systems*. Cambridge, MA: The MIT Press.

Scoville, W. B., & Milner, B. (1957). Loss of recent memory after bilateral hippocampal lesions. *Journal of Neurology, Neurosurgery & Psychiatry*, 20, 11–21.

Shimamura, A. P. (2014). Remembering the past: Neural substrates underlying episodic encoding and retrieval. *Current Directions in Psychological Science*, 23, 4257–4263.

Spiers, H. J., Maguire, E. A., & Burgess, N. (2001). Hippocampal amnesia. *Neurocase*, 7, 357–382.

Squire, L. R. (1992). Declarative and nondeclarative memory: Multiple brain systems supporting learning and memory. *Journal of Cognitive Neuroscience*, 4, 232–243.

Steinvorth, S., Levine, B., & Corkin, S. (2005). Medial temporal lobe structures are needed to re-experience remote autobiographical memories: Evidence from H.M. and W.R. *Neuropsychologia*, 43, 479–496.

Tulving, E. (1972). Episodic and semantic memory. In E. Tulving & W. Donaldson (Eds.), *Organisation of memory*. London: Academic Press.

Tulving, E. (1983). *Elements of episodic memory*. Oxford: Oxford University Press.

Tulving, E. (2001). The origin of autonoesis in episodic memory. In H. L. Roediger & J. S. Nairne (Eds.), *The nature of remembering: Essays in honour of Robert G. Crowder*. Washington, DC: American Psychological Association.

Tulving, E. (2002). Episodic memory: From mind to brain. *Annual Review of Psychology*, 53, 1–25.

10 Encoding and retrieval: Beyond Tulving and Thomson's (1973) encoding specificity principle

James S. Nairne (Purdue University)

BACKGROUND TO THE CLASSIC STUDY

Tulving and Thomson's (1973) landmark treatise on the encoding specificity principle marked the end of a decade-long investigation into the effectiveness of retrieval cues. Today, all memory scholars accept that the recovery of stored memories depends on an appropriate retrieval cue. More importantly, few would question that the effectiveness of any given cue is determined by the conditions of study. Retrieval cues do not acquire their eliciting properties in a vacuum – the way a target item is encoded, or processed at the time of its presentation, sets the occasion for a retrieval cue to be effective. This is settled science in the second decade of the twenty-first century, but in 1973 such notions were far more controversial.

In the decade or so preceding the Tulving and Thomson (1973) paper, the ideational framework for studying memory was still largely dominated by interference theory (Postman, 1961). To interference theorists, heavily influenced by classical learning theory (e.g., Melton & Irwin, 1940), remembering was mainly determined by competition among associations. Most of the research effort focused on acquisition – or, more specifically, on how learning strengthened associations between stimuli and responses. Interference theorists recognised that successful retrieval required a proper eliciting stimulus, and that a difference existed between learning and performance, but these distinctions shaped neither experiment nor theory (Thomson & Tulving, 1973, p. 352). Retrieval success was interpreted mainly as evidence about the strength of existing associations.

Acquisition was important to Tulving and his colleagues as well, but they considered it only one part of the story of remembering. Instead, they claimed, remembering is better regarded as a 'joint product of information stored in the past and information present in the immediate cognitive environment of the rememberer' (Tulving & Thomson, 1973, p. 352). In other words, what happens at the point of retrieval is just as important as what happens during original learning. Throughout the 1960s, Tulving's lab conducted 'retrieval experiments' designed to show that the accessibility of information could be manipulated while holding constant the conditions of storage. Tulving and Pearlstone (1966) is a seminal example. People were asked to study word lists of differing lengths (12, 24, or 48 words) comprised of categories of different sizes (1, 2, or 4 examples per category). At test everyone was asked to recall the studied words, but in one condition the category names were given as extralist cues (e.g., *fruit*). Tulving and Pearlstone (1966) found that: (1) cued recall was much higher than non-cued (free) recall; and (2) cuing affected only the number of categories represented in recall and had no effect on the proportion of words recalled within the recalled categories.

Given that 'storage' was held constant across the two retrieval conditions, the performance differences could be tied directly to the presence or absence of an appropriate retrieval cue. Forgetting was not simply a function of competition among responses; it depended as well on an interaction between stored information and certain features of the retrieval environment. As we shall see shortly, this relatively benign notion that remembering depends on the presence of an appropriate retrieval cue was eventually to develop into a much more radical idea – that the effectiveness of any retrieval cue is entirely dependent on what has been stored. This conclusion, embodied in the encoding specificity principle, shook the foundations of virtually all existing memory theories.

DETAILED DESCRIPTION OF THE CLASSIC STUDY

THE EFFECTIVENESS OF EXTRALIST CUES

The main focus of Tulving and Thomson's (1973) seminal article was on the effectiveness of extralist retrieval cues, that is, cues that were not physically presented during the study episode. In the Tulving and Pearlstone (1966) experiment, people never actually saw the category name during study – it was not presented – yet it facilitated recall nonetheless. Why does providing the category name make it easier to retrieve the category exemplars from the list? More generally, what are the necessary and sufficient conditions for a cue to be effective in aiding recall? In their paper, Tulving and Thomson (1973) set out to answer these questions, first by characterising current theory, then by reporting empirical evidence that seemed to falsify these views, and finally by promoting the concept of encoding specificity.

Tulving and Thomson (1973) were mainly interested in a particular class of associative retrieval models called generate-recognise models (e.g., Bahrick, 1970). Generate-recognise models conceptualise retrieval as a kind of search process, wherein one combs through existing associative networks in an effort to 'find' previously studied items. Retrieval cues help because they enable one to *generate* candidate responses, by virtue of the pre-existing associative connections, which can then be *recognised* as having occurred in the experimental context. Compared to free recall, where no retrieval cue is presented, cued-recall performance improves because of a narrowing of the target search process.

Importantly, there was a key assumption embodied in all generate-recognise models of the time, namely, that words have single representations or 'senses' in memory – those that roughly correspond to their dictionary meanings. Tulving and Thomson (1973) called this assumption trans-situational identity: words have fixed representations that are activated whenever they are seen, heard, spoken, written, thought about, or remembered. Any external event that subsequently provides access to the target representation, such as an extralist retrieval cue, should therefore improve one's ability to remember the target's prior occurrence. The coding of actual occurrence – the fact that an item occurred on the memory list – was assumed to involve some kind of activation or modification of this fixed internal representation during the study episode (e.g., Anderson & Bower, 1972).

Generate-recognise theories of memory also made a clear empirical prediction – it should always be easier to recognise an item than to recall it. The act of recall requires two separate processes: the fixed representation of the item needs to be accessed, presumably as a consequence of a generation phase, and then recognised as having occurred in the experiment. Once the item is located and recognised, it can be recalled. Given that recognition requires only one process – you are given the item and asked merely to decide whether it occurred previously – it cannot yield performance levels lower than those found when two processes are required. As described in the next section, this assumption of generate-recognise theory turns out to be wrong.

RECOGNITION FAILURE OF RECALLABLE WORDS

Empirically, Tulving and Thomson's (1973) paper is best known for its introduction of the recognition-failure paradigm, a procedure designed to test the assumptions and predictions of generate-recognise theories. The recognition-failure paradigm consists of three essential steps: (1) presentation of target words for study in the context of other material; (2) a recognition test for the targets in the absence of the study context; and (3) recall of the target words in the presence of cues related to the list context (see Tulving, 1983). The important finding is that recall of the target words is better in the study context than recognition of the target words in the absence of the study context. As noted above, such a pattern essentially falsifies standard generate-recognise models of memory.

Experiment 1 of Tulving and Thomson (1973) introduces the general proce-dure. Participants were asked initially to study 24 cue-target pairs. The 'cues' in this case, representing the study context, were words that were only weakly asso-ciated to the targets – for example, *glue*–CHAIR. Half of the words from the study list were then tested using strong extralist cues – for example, *table*. Participants were told that each of the cue words was related to one of the target words from the study list and they should use the cues to help remember the studied words. Performance was poor – only about 15% of the targets were recalled successfully. By itself, this finding is noteworthy because the strong extralist cue *table* should have provided good access to the representation of the target CHAIR.

In the next phase of the experiment, participants were given strong extralist cues for the remaining 12 targets and were asked to produce free associates to each cue mentally, checking to see if any generated associate was a word from the study list; if so, they were to recall the word by writing it down. Note that this test procedure directly mimics the generate-recognise process. Once again, performance was relatively poor (30%), but better than the first test procedure.

In the third test phase of the experiment, the strong extralist cues were supplied once again and people were instructed to write down all the words that they could generate as free associations to the words. Up to six responses were allowed for each of the cue words. The point of this procedure was to determine whether people would actually generate the studied words to the strong extralist cues – that is, would they produce CHAIR to *table*? They did – 74% of the studied words were produced as associates to the strong extralist cues, a value that closely matches what is found in standard word association norms. Finally, everyone was instructed to look over all of the generated words and to circle the words that they recognised as studied words from the first part of the experiment. Surprisingly, people circled only 24% of the studied target words that had been generated. Recognition performance was poor. As a final check, participants were given the 24 input cues from the initial study list (e.g., *glue*) and asked to recall the associated target words from the original study list. Performance on this test averaged 63% correct.

The procedure is a little complicated, but here are the main findings of interest. First, a strong extralist cue (*table*) can be a poor retrieval cue for a highly-associated target (CHAIR) if the target has been studied in a 'unique' context (e.g., paired with a weak associate such as *glue*). Second, if people are explicitly instructed to engage in the two processes proposed by generate-recognise theories – generation of associates followed by recognition of list members – performance remains relatively poor. Third, recall of targets in the original list context (with the weak associate) is much better than recognition, even though in the latter people are making an occurrence decision about the target (CHAIR) itself. Put differently, the weak associate *glue* is a better retrieval cue for remembering CHAIR than the presentation of CHAIR itself. Suffice to say, these findings were difficult to reconcile with existing forms of generate-recognise theory.

THE ENCODING SPECIFICITY PRINCIPLE

The important lesson of the recognition-failure paradigm, as well as earlier studies such as Tulving and Pearlsone (1966), is that the effectiveness of a retrieval cue depends on the conditions of study. Obviously, a category name is apt to be a more effective retrieval cue when people are asked to study a categorised list. If only one member of a category is presented in an otherwise unrelated word list, then the category name is going to be a less useful cue. To take a more extreme case, 'river' will not be an effective cue for 'bank' if during study 'bank' was thought about as a place to store money. Once again, the conditions of study set the occasion for cues to be effective. Remembering, then, will always be a 'joint product of information stored in the past and information present in the immediate cognitive environment of the rememberer' (Tulving & Thomson, 1973, p. 352).

These sentiments were formalised by Tulving and his colleagues into what they called the *encoding specificity principle* (see also Thomson & Tulving, 1970). In its mild form, the principle merely restates the conclusions noted above – how an item is studied or encoded determines what retrieval cues will be effective in providing access to what has been stored. In its more radical form, arguably demanded by the results of the recognition-failure paradigm, the principle asserts that specific retrieval cues will facilitate recall *if and only if* information about them and their relation to the studied items is established at the time of study or encoding. Consequently *table*, despite its well-established associative connection with CHAIR, will enhance the recall of CHAIR if and only if a connection between *table* and CHAIR is established during encoding. If no connection is made – that is, *table* is not part of the encoded trace complex – then *table* will be useless as a retrieval cue for CHAIR. Retrieval cues, as processed at the point of test, need to overlap or *match* the contents of the stored trace in order to be effective.

To appreciate the encoding specificity principle, even in its strictest form, it is important to recognise that episodic memory experiments test occurrence information. What needs to be remembered is not the concept of a chair, or knowledge about chairs, but the fact that the word CHAIR occurred in a particular temporal-spatial context – the experimental session. Similarly, presenting the target word CHAIR and asking the participant if it occurred before is called a recognition test, but it requires the participant to recover occurrence information rather than knowledge *per se*. If you forget that CHAIR occurred in the list-learning experiment, you are not forgetting the concept of a 'chair' – you are simply forgetting that the word CHAIR occurred at a particular time in a particular place. Knowing things about chairs – they are for sitting, have legs, and so on – tells you nothing about when the word CHAIR might have occurred in a memory experiment.

A visual search analogy makes the concept somewhat easier to understand. Imagine you were asked to search through a list of printed words and find every word with double letters embedded in the middle (e.g., COTTON). This would be an easy task because the discriminative stimulus (e.g., the presence or absence double letters) is part of the visual array. In memory, however, what is 'present' in the episodic record depends entirely on the experience. If the word COTTON was presented aloud on the memory list, there will be no orthographic record to search because orthography was not part of the original experience. You may know that COTTON has double letters in the middle, but this knowledge will not be helpful during retrieval because it does not match anything in the episodic record itself. At best, you could attempt to generate every instance of a word with double letters in the middle – SUMMER, LADDER, KETTLE, COTTON, etc. – and then 'check' to see whether any of the generated words matches something in the episodic record. However, as the data from the recognition-failure paradigm reveal, this kind of generate-recognise strategy is no guarantee of good performance.

To Tulving and Thomson (1973), the results of the recognition-failure paradigm illustrate the encoding specificity principle at work. A retrieval cue that merely accesses a word's permanent representation in memory, the place where conceptual knowledge about 'chairs' is stored, provides no information about whether CHAIR occurred on the memory list. Occurrence information is stored in a separate episodic record. For *table* to be an effective cue, then, it needs to tap the episodic record – that is, table and its relationship to CHAIR need to be processed at the time of encoding, at the point in which the episodic record is established. To Tulving and Thomson (1973), presenting CHAIR in the context of a weak associate (*glue*) lowers this probability. Even the copy cue *chair* can fail as a retrieval cue for CHAIR if the cue is interpreted conceptually – the *chair* stored in permanent memory is not the same CHAIR that occurred on the memory list.

To explain recognition failure, one needs to assume that the copy cue *chair* produces less overlap with the true episodic record than the list cue *glue*.

IMPACT OF THE CLASSIC STUDY

The publication of Tulving and Thomson (1973) led to a flurry of studies supporting and critiquing both the encoding specificity principle and the recognition-failure paradigm. The phenomenon of recognition failure of recallable words was subsequently replicated numerous times (see Tulving, 1983, for a review), although some important exceptions and boundary conditions were reported (see Nilsson & Gardiner, 1993). Today, recognition failure remains a core memory phenomenon, one afforded coverage in virtually all general memory textbooks. It is also grist for anyone interested in developing formal models of memory. In the decade and a half that followed Tulving and Thomson (1973) virtually all formal mathematical models of memory incorporated mechanisms for explaining recognition failure of recallable words (see Ratcliff & McKoon, 1989).

Empirically, the recognition-failure paradigm also led to widespread interest in the statistical relationship between recognition and cued recall. From the perspective of traditional generate-recognise theory, recall is completely dependent on successful recognition ($p(Rn|Rc) = 1.0$). However, subsequent research revealed only a moderate degree of dependency between the two. As Flexser and Tulving (1978, p. 156) noted, the pattern of data 'describes a state of affairs in which recognition and recall are neither stochastically independent nor completely dependent'. Moreover, the magnitude of recognition failure in any given experimental condition, or its complement, the probability of recognition given successful recall, turns out to be highly predictable from the overall recognition level. The function relating the conditional probability of recognition given recall to the probability of recognition overall can be expressed mathematically and is known as the Tulving-Wiseman law (Tulving & Wiseman, 1975). A remarkable range of data, collected across diverse experimental paradigms, is consistent with this 'law' (e.g., Nilsson, Law, & Tulving, 1988). Some critics, though, have suggested that mathematical constraints may importantly influence the range of outcomes that can be expected with this analysis (see Hintzman, 1992).

Generate-recognise models underwent needed revisions as well. For example, one can salvage generate-recognise theory by assuming that the output or decision criteria are different for recognition and recall. If the decision criterion for recognition ('Did this item occur in the list?') is higher than for recall, then it is possible to account for recognition failure (Kintsch, 1978). One can also reject the assumption of trans-situational identity and assume that items have many different 'senses' or meanings in memory (e.g., Reder, Anderson, & Bjork, 1974; Martin, 1975). When CHAIR is encoded in the context of the weak associate *glue*, perhaps meanings and images related to the construction of a chair are activated whereas encoding CHAIR in the context of *table* activates knowledge tied to sitting. The generate-recognise processes could remain intact, but for recognition to occur the candidates generated by the retrieval cue need to include the 'senses' of the target established during encoding. As Tulving (1983) cogently remarked, however, this resurrection of generation-recognise theory co-opts the main premise of the encoding specificity principle: how an item is encoded determines what retrieval cues will be effective in providing access to what has been stored. In addition, recognition failure remains robust when words containing only a single meaning in the dictionary are used as study targets or even when famous people or unique city names are used (Nilsson et al., 1988; Tulving & Watkins, 1977).

A more radical change was offered by Jacoby and Hollingshead (1990), who proposed that the generation process is based on recent episodic experiences rather than on some abstract semantic or associative network. As they pointed out, target generation in an indirect memory test, such as word fragment completion, is strongly influenced by specific prior experiences. In an indirect test, people are not trying to explicitly remember anything; they are simply trying to complete a word fragment. Yet their completion performance is enhanced by a matching prior experience. If the generation process used in cued-recall is driven by immediate prior experiences, rather than fixed associative networks, then generate-recognise models can be easily reconciled with the encoding specificity principle. Presentation of CHAIR in the context of a weak or strong associate (*glue* versus *table*) will dramatically shape the target candidates that are ultimately generated to different retrieval cues.

Jacoby and Hollingshead (1990) also suggested that the recognition stage can be bypassed in some situations, leading to the recall of items that cannot be recognised. To prevent false recall, we need some kind of recognition stage because recall candidates can come to mind for a variety of reasons. However, the ease with which a candidate comes to mind – its retrieval fluency – can also be a marker for prior occurrence. If the generation of a word is sufficiently fluent at test, Jacoby and Hollingshead (1990) argued, it may not be subjected to the final recognition check – people simply assume that the item occurred recently on the memory list. The combination of episode-based generation and fluency-based recall easily accounts for recognition failure of recallable words.

Today, most memory researchers accept generate-recognise theory in some form because, as just noted, monitoring or evaluation of recall candidates is necessary to prevent false recall. In fact, in recent years researchers have become increasingly interested in how people monitor and control their memories for past experiences (e.g., Dunlosky & Metcalfe, 2009). But the idea that the generation process is guided by a context-free search of an abstract semantic network, as typified by the early generate-recognise models discussed by Tulving and Thomson (1973), is no longer taken seriously. Instead, prior experiences or instances are thought to play the key role in the candidate generation process, along with other biases that may be induced by the experimental setting (see Higham & Tam, 2005).

CRITIQUE OF THE CLASSIC STUDY

The encoding specificity principle, as noted throughout, is a statement about the effectiveness of retrieval cues. Given that remembering is deemed retrieval-cue dependent, it is not surprising that considerable scrutiny was given to assessing its merits as an empirical principle. The claim that remembering is context-dependent, and that pre-existing cue–target associations can fail to promote recall, has received substantial support over the years. For example, Godden and Baddeley (1975) showed that when deep-sea divers listened to lists of words either on land or underwater, the 'match' between the conditions of study and test determined performance. If the divers learned the words originally underwater, then recall was significantly better when they were tested underwater, a result that proved to have significant practical applications for diver training. There is substantial support for state-dependent learning as well. If material is learned while under the influence of alcohol or a drug, recall is enhanced when the person is tested in a similar state (see Eich, 1980, for a review). Our ability to remember depends on recovering or 'matching' the original context in which the information was encoded.

However, the 'if and only if' clause in the encoding specificity principle has remained controversial, partly because there is no obvious way of determining exactly what has been processed and stored at the time of an original encoding. Whether 'unencoded' cues can be effective in eliciting a target response can never be proved conclusively without knowing the true content of the encoded episode. It also remains a mystery why presenting the copy cue CHAIR in the recognition failure paradigm does not elicit some 'senses' of the target as encoded during its original presentation. Indeed, one of the strongest empirical arguments against the strict separation of episodic and semantic memory is the persistent presence of episodic 'priming' on semantic tasks. Presenting the word ELEPHANT on a memory list increases the chances that one will later complete the word fragment E_ _P_AN_ correctly on an implicit test, even when no conscious contact is made between the fragment test and the earlier occurrence of the word (see Roediger, 1990). It is difficult to reconcile episodic priming, where the cue fragment is clearly contacting the prior episode, with the poor recognition performance seen in the recognition failure paradigm.

But even if we reject the strict form of the encoding specificity principle, or consider it ultimately untestable, it continues to color the way memory theorists think. As a case in point, the principle is responsible for two widely-accepted postulates of modern memory theory: (1) the stability and robustness of episodic retention is a function of elaboration, or the number of connections that are formed during encoding between the to-be-remembered target and other information in memory; and (2) successful retrieval is monotonically related to the match or overlap between the conditions of encoding and test. Both of these ideas are reasonable inferences from the encoding specificity principle, as I briefly outline below.

Elaboration. If retrieval cues are effective mainly to the extent that they are 'part' of the episodic record, then richer or more elaborate memory traces seem likely to be better remembered. If connections are drawn between the target item and lots of other things in memory, then the study experience will afford more potential retrieval cues (e.g., Bradshaw & Anderson, 1982). Researchers regularly appeal to the concept of elaboration or 'richness of encoding' to explain mnemonic phenomena. For example, the mnemonic benefits of retrieval practice (Karpicke & Roediger, 2007) and survival processing (Nairne, Thompson, & Pandeirada, 2007) have recently been interpreted as examples of enhanced elaboration (see Carpenter, 2009; Kroneisen & Erdfelder, 2011).

The concept of elaboration gained traction initially from work conducted by Craik and Tulving (1975) on the levels-of-processing framework (Craik & Lockhart, 1972). In the original levels framework, memory was seen as a byproduct of processing depth, with deep (semantic) levels producing the best retention. However, as Craik and Tulving (1975) showed, large retention differences are sometimes found for items processed to a similar depth. For example, when people are asked to decide whether target words fit into sentence frames (e.g., He met a ___ in the street), targets given a 'yes' response (FRIEND) are remembered better than targets given a 'no' response (CLOUD). Because both responses require deep semantic processing, this 'congruity effect' proved troubling for the original levels framework. Craik and Tulving (1975) suggested that 'spread of encoding' was a better metaphor than depth – 'yes' responses, because the target can be integrated seamlessly into the sentence frame, produce more elaborate traces than 'no' responses. Deeper levels of processing are effective, they argued, primarily because they lead to richer, more elaborate episodic records.

If the encoding specificity principle is true, and the episodic record is the ultimate source of retrieval cues, then the reasoning of Craik and Tulving (1975) makes sense. But conceptual problems remain. In fact, pragmatically, 'elaboration is a rather slender reed to lean on' (Postman, Thompkins, & Gray, 1978, p. 684). First, there is no generally accepted method for measuring it. We can induce elaboration in the laboratory (e.g., by requiring participants to generate connections to target items), but no magic window into the structure of a memory trace yet exists.

This invites circularity in reasoning: if a target item is remembered well, then it must have an elaborate trace. Second, elaborations create the potential for interference. Although a rich trace may produce more usable retrieval cues, increasing trace complexity should make it more difficult to access any particular component to the exclusion of others. It is well established that increasing the number of targets connected to a cue lowers the accessibility of any given target – a condition known as cue overload (Watkins & Watkins, 1975) – and a similar process should result from elaborative processing. Every potential retrieval cue is also a potential source of interference.

Finally, it is difficult to judge the merits of elaboration without a well-specified theory of retrieval cue generation. What determines the operative retrieval cue in any particular retrieval environment? In cued-recall, we are given the retrieval cue (*glue*) and the task is to supply the associated target (CHAIR). It is not obvious why increasing the number of retrieval cues should help in this case, although the generation of mediators between the cue and the target can help in some circumstances (e.g., Carpenter, 2009). In free recall, no overt cues are supplied other than the general context in which the learning occurred. Recent models of free recall rely heavily on contextual encodings, and to some extent on meaningful relationships among to-be-remembered items, but fail to specify how increasing the number of potential retrieval cues aids recovery (e.g., Polyn, Norman, & Kahana, 2009). Whether elaboration should help or hinder retention, then, depends on the assumptions that are made about the generation and use of retrieval cues.

The encoding-retrieval match. A second implication of the encoding specificity principle is that retention depends directly on the match between the retrieval cue and the encoded trace. After all, retrieval cues are effective only to the extent that they represented in the relevant episodic record, so match is a requisite of good performance. As we have seen, there is considerable evidence for context-dependent memory which, in turn, validates the importance of the encoding-retrieval match. Considerable evidence exists as well for the usefulness of transfer-appropriate processing at encoding: to ensure good retention, one should process material in a way that is 'appropriate' for the conditions likely to be present at retrieval (e.g., Morris, Bransford, & Franks, 1977; Kolers & Roediger, 1984).

However, stipulating that retrieval cues must be a part of the original encoding complex does not imply that *increasing* the encoding-retrieval match is necessarily good for retention. Memory researchers commonly assume that maximising the similarity between study and test benefits retention, but this assumption is almost certainly wrong. First, any matching retrieval cue needs to provide information that is not already available to the rememberer. For example, Tulving and Pearlstone (1966) found that presenting category cues at test had little effect if the number of categories represented in the studied list was small. When there are only a few salient categories, those categories are presumably already available to the participant at test. Thus, presenting category name 'cues' is redundant and unlikely to improve performance. Second, as I have discussed in detail elsewhere (Nairne, 2002), it is not really the match that drives retention, but the extent to which a retrieval cue is diagnostic of a particular episodic record (see also Mantyla, 1986). Any given retrieval cue is likely to match many incorrect episodic records as well as the correct one. Even within an episodic record, especially if elaboration has occurred, the target needs to be distinguished from other connections that have been formed. It is CHAIR that needs to be remembered, not the elaborations that have been produced to CHAIR during study. Again, every new retrieval cue that has been generated as a consequence of elaboration is itself a potential source of interference.

A simple thought experiment is sufficient to make the point. Imagine that we present people with a list of eight words and later ask them to remember the item that occurred in a particular serial position. Here, the task is not only to remember the words, but to discriminate among them on the basis of position. Further, suppose that each word is presented in red during its initial presentation. According to the encoding specificity principle, red is a potential retrieval cue – it was encoded along with the target word during presentation – but it is a completely irrelevant cue in this context. Red matches every single item on the list. Supplying red as a retrieval cue at test, along with the serial position prompt, increases the encoding-retrieval match (compared to when red is not presented), but it will not increase correct recall. Such a result was recently confirmed empirically by Goh and Lu (2012). They found that performance on a cued-recall test did not improve when a second matching cue was added during testing, as long as the additional cue also matched alternative responses. In fact, it is easy to envision how increasing the encoding-retrieval match might impair performance if the added feature matches other incorrect information in the episodic record.

What matters to retrieval is not the absolute encoding-retrieval match but the relative match. The situation is somewhat akin to the relationship between intensity and brightness perception. Brightness perception is determined primarily by relative intensity information – how many photons of light are falling in the centre relative to the surround. Although in most cases increasing the absolute amount of intensity makes something look brighter, it is easy to decouple the two. If intensity increases or decreases by the same amount in both the centre and the surround, brightness perception remains constant (brightness constancy); if intensity increases more in the surround than in the centre, the centre spot can appear darker even though more absolute light is falling in the area. Similarly, it is not the absolute match between encoding and retrieval that is critical, but the extent to which any given matching cue is diagnostic of a particular target. Put differently, effective cues need to be distinctive, that is, they need to specify a particular stored event to the exclusion of others (Eysenck, 1979; Nairne, 2006).

CONCLUSIONS

It has now been over 40 years since the appearance of Tulving and Thomson (1973), clearly a landmark paper in the history of memory research. The paper itself has been cited over 3,000 times (according to *Google Scholar*) and its conclusions about the effectiveness of retrieval cues remain largely intact. In many respects, modern memory researchers continue to view episodic retrieval through the 'lens' crafted and polished by Tulving and his associates. The memory field's reliance on concepts such as elaboration, the encoding-retrieval match, and context-dependent retrieval can be traced directly to the empirical and theoretical insights offered in Tulving and Thomson (1973).

At the same time, considerable challenges remain as the memory field struggles to move beyond encoding specificity. Although much has been learned about the conditions that promote effective retrieval cues, little is known about the generation of the cues themselves. Throughout the day, each of us regularly encounters events that 'match' prior episodes in our lives – think about the 'matches' engendered by a daily encounter with your neighbour or even your coffee cup – but few of these events yield instances of conscious recollection. When is a coffee cup just a cup, and when does it acquire properties as a potential retrieval cue? Put differently, what drives the engagement of a 'retrieval mode' wherein one begins to interpret events in the environment as 'cues' to remember the past (Tulving, 1983)? To truly understand how people remember and forget, it will be necessary to develop effective theories about how retrieval cues are generated and used in the world (see Berntsen, 2009).

It will also be necessary for the field to come to grips with the reconstructive nature of remembering. Although the encoding specificity principle champions the relativity of retrieval cues, and rejects the notion of a fixed and abstract memory store, it still characterises remembering as a process of accessing an episodic 'record'. Experience establishes a memory trace which is then accessed by an appropriate – a.k.a. 'matching' – retrieval cue. Yet the act of remembering is almost always coloured by reconstructions, additions, and deletions that were not part of the original encoding experience. Many instances of remembering, particularly autobiographical memories of our distant past, are strategically driven, relying on cultural scripts and norms rather than on matching cues. There is a growing recognition as well that remembering is not about recovering the veridical past, primarily because the past can never occur again in exactly the same form. Rather, our memory systems must be engineered to use the past in the service of the present, or to promote future adaptive behaviour (Nairne & Pandeirada, 2008). For all its value as a mnemonic insight, the encoding specificity principle has little, if anything, to say about such matters.

AFTERTHOUGHT: COMMENT FROM ENDEL TULVING

We asked Endel Tulving to comment on this chapter, and he sent us a reply (see below), which refers mainly to Tulving's findings on recognition failure. Previously, it had been assumed that any items that could be recalled would also be recognised. In other words, recognition failure for recallable words should never be found. In contrast, Tulving, with his emphasis on the notion that contextual information is of crucial importance in retrieval, claimed that recognition failure for recallable words should often be the case. For example, you might not recognise 'Doyle' as a famous writer, but might be able to recall the word 'Doyle' if asked to fill in the blank from 'Sir Arthur Conan --------'. The Tulving-Wiseman function provided a detailed account of how much recognition failure of recallable words would be expected in various conditions. The finding of recognition failure for recallable words was regarded in the 1970s and 1980s as crucial evidence in support of the encoding specificity principle. In the following commentary, Tulving is discussing an experiment of his on recognition failure for recallable words designed to see whether this effect was general or only obtainable with certain materials.

Endel Tulving's comments were as follows:

[In the experiment] we found that the Tulving-Wiseman function holds for TARGET items representing unique names of famous people and unique city names as well as it does for any other material. Examples of the names we used are 'Florence Nightingale' and 'George Washington', examples of city names are 'Stockholm' and 'Toronto'. BTW, this paper was prompted by a comment made by my buddy Gordon Bower, who, like most other august members of the establishment, did not fancy (euphemism!) some of the things I said in those years. He said, 'Well, you can show that you get the recognition failure effect with words such as 'handshake' or 'adultery' (as we had done), but they came out for the same reason that explain the earlier findings – multiple senses of words. There are different kinds of handshakes and different kinds of adultery. You'd never get it with the names of US presidents'.

Hence, unique names of people and cities. For Gordon's benefit, I separated from the rest of the data two subsets that we obtained with 'George Washington' and 'Abraham Lincoln'. Putting the two sets together, we got a data point that sat RIGHT ON the T-W function. 'Right on' means that the deviation of the data from the function was ZERO. The zero deviation, of course, is just a fluke; the fact that the data point was indistinguishable from all the others we had from all those previous experiments was the telling finding. Gordon never responded to my letter in which I sent him the graph, and I never pressed him. He is a friend, and a good man. Our paper in JEP [*Journal of Experimental Psychology*] has not been cited. Ignoring of the T-W function became a norm after we published the paper. Yet another demonstration that scientists are human.

FURTHER READING

Nairne, J. S. (2002). The myth of the encoding-retrieval match. *Memory*, 10, 389–395.

Roediger, H. L. (2000). Why retrieval is the key process to understanding human memory. In E. Tulving (Ed.), *Memory, consciousness and the brain: The Tallinn conference* (pp. 52–75). Philadelphia, PA: Psychology Press.

Surprenant, A. M., & Neath, I. (2009). *Principles of memory*. New York: Psychology Press.

Tulving, E. (1983). *Elements of episodic memory*. New York: Oxford University Press.

REFERENCES

Anderson, J. R., & Bower, G. H. (1972). Recognition and retrieval processes in free recall. _Psychological Review_, 79, 97–123.

Bahrick, H. P. (1970). A two-phase model for prompted recall. _Psychological Review_, 77, 215–222.

Berntsen, D. (2009). _Involuntary autobiographical memories: An introduction to the unbidden past_. Cambridge, UK: Cambridge University Press.

Bradshaw, G. L., & Anderson, J. R. (1982). Elaborative encoding as an explanation of levels of processing. _Journal of Verbal Learning and Verbal Behavior_, 21, 165–174.

Carpenter, S. K. (2009). Cue strength as a moderator of the test effect: The benefits of elaborative retrieval. _Journal of Experimental Psychology: Learning, Memory, & Cognition_, 35, 1563–1569.

Craik, F. I. M., & Lockhart, R. S. (1972). Levels of processing: A framework for memory research. _Journal of Verbal Learning and Verbal Behavior_, 11, 671–684.

Craik, F. I. M., & Tulving, E. (1975). Depth of processing and the retention of words in episodic memory. _Journal of Experimental Psychology: General_, 104, 268–294.

Dunlosky, J., & Metcalfe, J. (2009). _Metacognition_. Beverly Hills, CA: Sage.

Eich, J. E. (1980). The cue-dependent nature of state-dependent retrieval. _Memory & Cognition_, 8, 157–173.

Eysenck, M. W. (1979). Depth, elaboration, and distinctiveness. In L. S. Cermak & F. I. M. Craik (Eds.), _Levels of processing in human memory_ (pp. 89–118). Hillsdale, NJ: Lawrence Erlbaum Associates.

Flexser, A. J., & Tulving, E. (1978). Retrieval independence in recognition and recall. _Psychological Review_, 85, 153–171.

Godden, D. R., & Baddeley, A. (1975). Context-dependent memory in two natural environments: On land and underwater. _British Journal of Psychology_, 66, 325–331.

Goh, W. D., & Lu, S. H. X. (2012). Testing the myth of the encoding-retrieval match. _Memory & Cognition_, 40, 28–39.

Higham, P. A., & Tam, H. (2005). Generation failure: Estimating metacognition in cued recall. _Journal of Memory and Language_, 52, 595–617.

Hintzman, D. L. (1992). Mathematical constraints on the Tulving-Wiseman law. _Psychological Review_, 99, 536–542.

Jacoby, L. L., & Hollingshead, A. (1990). Toward a generate/recognize model of performance in direct and indirect tests of memory. _Journal of Memory and Language_, 29, 433–454.

Karpicke, J. D., & Roediger, H. L., III (2007). Repeated retrieval during learning is the key to long-term retention. _Journal of Memory and Language_, 57, 151–162.

Kintsch, W. (1978). More on recognition failure of recallable words: Implications for generation-recognition models. _Psychological Review_, 85, 470–473.

Kolers, P. A., & Roediger, H. L., III (1984). Procedures of mind. _Journal of Verbal Learning and Verbal Behavior_, 23, 425–449.

Kroneisen, M., & Erdfelder, E. (2011). On the plasticity of the survival processing effect. *Journal of Experimental Psychology: Learning, Memory, & Cognition*, 37, 1553–1562.

Mantyla, T. (1986). Optimizing cue effectiveness: Recall of 500 and 600 incidentally recalled words. *Journal of Experimental Psychology: Learning, Memory, and Cognition*, 12, 66–71.

Martin, E. A. (1975). Theoretical notes: Generation-recognition theory and the encoding specificity principle. *Psychological Review*, 82, 150–153.

Melton, A. W., & Irwin, J. M. (1940). The influence of degree of interpolated learning on retroactive inhibition and the overt transfer of specific responses. *American Journal of Psychology*, 53, 173–203.

Morris, C. D., Bransford, J. D., & Franks, J. J. (1977). Levels of processing versus transfer appropriate processing. *Journal of Verbal Learning and Verbal Behavior*, 16, 519–533.

Nairne, J. S. (2002). The myth of the encoding-retrieval match. *Memory*, 10, 389–395.

Nairne, J. S. (2006). Modeling distinctiveness: Implications for general memory theory. In R. R. Hunt & J. B. Worthen (Eds.), *Distinctiveness and memory* (pp. 27–46.) New York: Oxford University Press.

Nairne, J. S., & Pandeirada, J. N. S. (2008). Adaptive memory: Remembering with a stone-age brain. *Current Directions in Psychological Science*, 17, 239–243.

Nairne, J. S., Thompson, S. R., & Pandeirada, J. N. S. (2007). Adaptive memory: Survival processing enhances retention. *Journal of Experimental Psychology: Learning, Memory, & Cognition*, 33, 263–273.

Nilsson, L.-G., & Gardiner, J. (1993). Identifying exceptions in a database of recognition failure studies from 1973 to 1992. *Memory & Cognition*, 21, 397–410.

Nilsson, L.-G., Law, J., & Tulving, E. (1988). Recognition failure of recallable unique names: Evidence for an empirical law of memory and learning. *Journal of Experimental Psychology: Learning, Memory, & Cognition*, 14, 266–277.

Polyn, S. M., Norman, K. A., & Kahana, M. J. (2009). A context maintenance and retrieval model of organizational processes in free recall. *Psychological Review*, 116, 129–156.

Postman, L. (1961). The present status of interference theory. In C. N. Cofer (Ed.), *Verbal learning and Verbal behavior*. New York: McGraw-Hill.

Postman, L., Thompkins, B. A., & Gray, W. D. (1978). The interpretation of encoding effects in retention. *Journal of Verbal Learning and Verbal Behavior*, 17, 681–705.

Ratcliff, R., & McKoon, G. (1989). Memory models, text processing, and cue-dependent retrieval. In H. L. Roediger, III & F. I. M. Craik (Eds.), *Varieties of memory and consciousness: Essays in honour of Endel Tulving* (pp. 73–92). Hillsdale, NJ: Lawrence Erlbaum Associates.

Reder, L. M., Anderson, J. R., & Bjork, R. A. (1974). A semantic interpretation of encoding specificity. *Journal of Experimental Psychology*, 102, 648–656.

Roediger, H. L., III (1990). Implicit memory: Retention without remembering. *American Psychologist*, 45, 1043–1056.

Thomson, D. M., & Tulving, E. (1970). Associative encoding and retrieval: Weak and strong cues. *Journal of Experimental Psychology*, 86, 255–262.

Tulving, E. (1983). *Elements of episodic memory*. New York: Oxford University Press.

Tulving, E., & Pearlstone, Z. (1966). Availability versus accessibility of information in memory. *Journal of Verbal Learning and Verbal Behavior*, 5, 381–391.

Tulving, E., & Thomson, D. M. (1973). Encoding specificity and retrieval processes in episodic memory. *Psychological Review*, 80, 352–373.

Tulving, E., & Watkins, O. C. (1977). Recognition failure of words with a single meaning. *Memory & Cognition*, 5, 513–522.

Tulving, E., & Wiseman, S. (1975). Relation between recognition and recognition failure of recallable words. *Bulletin of the Psychonomic Society,* 92, 257–276.

Watkins, O. C., & Watkins, M. J. (1975). Buildup of proactive inhibition as a cue-overload effect. *Journal of Experimental Psychology: Human Learning and Memory*, 1, 442–452.

11 Human problem solving: Beyond Newell, Shaw, and Simon's (1958) theory of human problem solving

Fernand Gobet (University of Liverpool) and Peter Lane (University of Hertfordshire)

BACKGROUND TO THE CLASSIC STUDY

What are the cognitive mechanisms involved when people make decisions and solve problems? Are there commonalities in the mechanisms involved in solving puzzles, proving a theorem in logic, and choosing a move in chess? Are these mechanisms similar to those involved in more lofty achievements, such as making a major discovery in science?

At first blush, the 1950s were not a good time to answer these questions if you were a psychologist living in the USA. The first part of twentieth century had been dominated by behaviourism. Advocating a strong empiricism, behaviourism shunned theoretical terms and speculative theorising. Under this influence, most experiments in psychology were concerned with conditioning (often with animals as subjects) and the learning of nonsense syllables. The closest psychology had been to studying cognitive processes was the research into intelligence and the development of tests to measure faculties such as mechanical reasoning and verbal fluency.

In this world, narrowly focused on stimulus–response bonds, there was little research on problem solving in psychology. (The state of the field is well reflected in Johnson (1955), a book published three years before the target article.) The little activity there was in the USA was due to the efforts of European Gestalt psychologists who had fled Nazism. Their research was characterised by clever, and sometimes spectacular, experiments (e.g., those on insight), but also by weak attempts to build theories. There was also a weaker influence from the Würzburg School of psychology, which was interested in complex problem solving, such as understanding a philosophical idea, and from Otto Selz, who developed an overarching theory of thinking. This theory, expressed in an opaque legalistic style that few could understand (Selz was trained as a lawyer), was one of the very few detailed theories on problem solving.

It is in this rather barren environment that Allen Newell, John C. Shaw, and Herbert A. Simon set out in the early 1950s to develop computer models of problem solving.

Newell was a dropout graduate student in mathematics, employed by the RAND Corporation, a think-tank carrying out research for the American armed forces. Shaw, who had a background in mathematics, was systems programmer at RAND. Simon was a well-respected social scientist, specialising in understanding decision making in organisations (March & Simon, 1958). He had also published several important papers using mathematical models in the social sciences (Simon, 1957) and had done technical work in econometrics (Holt, Modigliani, Muth, & Simon, 1960).

The trio first dabbled with geometry, but the difficulty in capturing perceptual processes in the computer led them to use more abstract tasks. They then worked on developing a computer program playing chess, but the task turned out to be too difficult given the limited computer resources of the time. (They finally managed to write a program playing (weak) chess; see Newell, Shaw, & Simon, 1958a). Elementary symbolic logic was their final choice, and the specific aim was to write a program that would prove theorems starting with axioms and rules of inference.

Progress was rapid, and by 1957 they had written together several conference papers (Newell & Shaw, 1957; Newell, Shaw, & Simon, 1957; Newell & Simon, 1956) describing the Logic Theorist (LT), the program that had achieved their goal. However, the target audience of these publications was the nascent field of computer science and related disciplines in engineering. Newell, Shaw, and Simon (1958b) – the target article of this chapter – was the first publication intended for psychologists and the first paper to present what was later known as information-processing psychology.

DETAILED DESCRIPTION OF THE CLASSIC STUDY

At the outset, Newell et al. (1958b) make it clear that their theory was not originally developed as a theory of human problem solving, but as an 'artificial intelligence' program (although they did not use this term). They first present an overview of their new *information-processing system* approach, then describe the Logic Theorist and describe several experiments carried out with it. This leads to a discussion of how LT's behaviour captures key features of human problem solving. Finally, they draw broad comparisons with alternative approaches in psychology. We follow the same order in our description of the article.

The theory

Information-processing psychology, which will be further developed in several publications and fully presented in Newell and Simon (1972), proposes that the cognitive system consists of different components, similar at some level of abstraction to those of a computer: receptors, effectors, memories, and a control system. The focus of the theory is on the last component. It is assumed that memories contain symbols and primitive information processes. Critically, both symbols and processes are fully implemented in a physical substrate (the computer). Memories also contain a set of rules that make it possible to combine processes into full programs. Such programs enable one to deduce unambiguously the external behaviour generated by the theory. This behaviour can be compared to actual human behaviour, which provides a test of the theory.

A program, used as a theory of behaviour, is extremely specific as it accounts for a specific organism facing a distinct class of problems. Different organisms, different amounts of knowledge and different problems will require different programs as explanations. Newell et al. (1958b) note that a program can be used as a theory in two different ways. First, one can use it as a means of testing specific predictions of the program (e.g., the number and kind of errors that will be made). Second, it is possible to examine the similarities between programs developed to explain behaviour in different situations (e.g., playing chess, solving cryparithmetic problems and proving theorems in logic) or to compare the programs used by different individuals in the same task. In both cases, broad theoretical generalisations can be made. We note that there is an interesting paradox here: programs written to explain behaviour with a high level of detail lead to a general theory of human problem solving. The second approach, which is more qualitative than the first, is the one that Newell et al. use in their paper.

A key idea of the paper is that programs provide an explanation of behaviour *by generating this behaviour*. Thus, a theory of the way humans think when selecting a move in chess should be able to play chess. This test of sufficiency is an extremely strong feature of the approach proposed by Newell et al. How sequences of elementary operations could lead to the solution of complex problems had often been seen as a mystery, but, as Newell et al. (1958b, p. 152) put it, '[our] theory dissolves the mystery by showing that nothing more need to be added to the constitution of a successful problem solver'. Another key contribution of their theory, according to Newell et al., is that it explains how human problem solving can be decomposed into elementary processes and thus can be explained mechanistically.

Newell et al. repeatedly emphasise that the analogy between the computer and the human mind is at a functional level, through the concept of a program, not at a physical level: 'these programs describe both human and machine problem solving at the level of information processes' (1958b, p. 153). In particular, they are not interested in the neural implementation of the symbols and the components of the information-processing system (receptors, effectors, memories, and control system), although such an implementation obviously exists in the human brain. Computers offer an efficient way to carry out the simulations, but are not necessary for Newell et al.'s theory. In fact, the simulations of the first version of the theory were carried out by hand or by Simon's children being assigned and carrying out the elementary operations (McCorduck, 1979; Simon, 1991). Thus, the authors argue, the relation between a program and an organism's behaviour is the same as the relation between a system of differential equations and the behaviour of planets.

THE LOGIC THEORIST

The program tries to find proofs in elementary logic (more precisely, in propositional logic, also known as symbolic logic). The task is similar to finding proofs in elementary geometry. Put simply, the task consists in identifying and generating possible (partial) solutions and evaluating them.

At the beginning of a simulation, LT stores in its memory a list of axioms, the list of admissible operations and the logical expression that needs to be proved. For example, one of the axioms used is 'p implies (q or p)'. The task is thus to derive, starting from the axioms, a proof establishing the validity of the target expression. As an example, theorem 2.01 is '(p implies not-p) implies not-p'. When intermediary expressions ('theorems') are generated during this process, they are 'learned' (i.e., stored in LT's memory), so that they can be used later in the proof of the target expression and of different expressions. Intermediate expressions that have been proved during search are also stored in LTM. When a proof is found, it is printed so that the details can be examined and possibly compared to human behaviour, for example, by using verbal protocols.

When attempting to find a proof, LT uses four *rules of inference. Substitution* allows a variable to be substituted by a new variable or expression, as long as all instances of the variable are substituted. For example, from '[p or p] implies p' one can derive '[[a or b] or [a or b]] implies [a or b]' by substituting [a or b] for p. With *replacement*, it is possible to replace a connective (e.g., 'implies') by its definition in terms of other connectives. For example, 'a implies b' can be replaced by 'not-a or b'. *Detachment* concerns expressions such as 'a implies b'. If a is a true expression, then b is a true expression as well. Finally, *syllogism* (or *chaining*) works as follows: if 'a implies b' and 'b implies c', then 'a implies c' is a true expression.

The fact that these inference rules can be used does not mean that their use is necessarily useful – the situation is just like chess, where the legality of a move does not imply its quality. In addition to rules of inference, LT is given several *proof methods*, which are essentially *strategies* aimed at making search efficient.

The *substitution method* tries to substitute variables and replace connectives. The *detachment method* uses the inference rule of detachment. If we need to prove b, and we know a theorem of the form 'a implies b', then we need only prove a. *Forward chaining* uses the rules of syllogism. Thus, if 'a implies b' is known and one wants to show that 'a implies c', then one needs only show 'b implies c'. *Backward chaining* does the same backwards: if 'b implies c' is known and one wants to show that 'a implies c', then one needs only show 'a implies b'.

In addition to these methods, an executive process carries out a number of functions: coordination of the use of methods, selection of theorems to which methods will be used, and learning. Two important processes common to all methods are the *matching process*, which tries to remove the differences between two sub-expressions, and the *similarity test*, which decides whether two expressions are similar.

Surprisingly for an article published in the leading theoretical journal in psychology, as noted above, Newell et al. explicitly state that LT was not developed as a theory of human problem solving. Rather, the aim was to develop a program that would be able to find proofs in logic. While Newell et al. thought that trying to understand the way humans think would provide important cues to develop machines that think, this was not a necessary assumption. Indeed, in the very domain studied by Newell et al. – symbolic logic – more powerful programs have been developed since that use techniques wholly different from those used by humans (Wang, 1960).

THE EXPERIMENTS

In their paper, Newell et al. (1958b) report three experiments. These experiments might seem a bit odd to psychologists, as there are no animal or human subjects. In addition, LT is run only once in each experiment. However, the term 'experiment' is justified, as an agent is put in a given situation and its behaviour observed. In addition, amount of training is manipulated across the three experiments, so we do have a kind of independent variable.

Experiment 1

LT receives as input the axioms of *Principia Mathematica* (Whitehead & Russell, 1910), a colossal work that aimed to establish the foundations of mathematics by starting from axioms in logic. The task is to prove the 52 theorems of Chapter 2 of that book. The theorems are given in the same sequence as in *Principia*. As noted above, if a theorem is proved, it is stored in memory so that it can be used for proving further theorems. LT successfully proved 38 of the 52 theorems (a 73% success rate). The time to find proofs increased considerably with each additional step in the proof, which could be expected given that the number of possible derivations increases exponentially with the length of a proof.

This first experiment showed that LT was able, at least in most cases, to find correct proofs for the theorems it was presented with. This establishes that the postulated elementary processes and the way they are organised in a strategy offer a *sufficient* explanation for the task at hand. Newell et al. are cautious to point out that their explanation is *not necessary*, as other theories could in principle be implemented as computer programs and be able to find similar proofs. However, they also note that 'specification of a set of mechanisms sufficient to produce observed behavior is strong confirmatory evidence for the theory embodying these mechanisms, especially when it is contrasted with theories that cannot establish their sufficiency' (Newell et al., 1958b, pp. 155–156).

Finding such proofs is no trivial matter, as the search space is huge. Even restricting the length of a proof to 20 logic expressions and limiting the length of each expression to 23 symbols, there are 10^{235} proofs (10 followed by 235 zeroes) (Newell & Simon, 1972). Brute force, where all possible proofs are enumerated and checked in a systematic way, would fail to find proofs except for the simplest theorems. A key feature of LT is its ability to be selective by carrying out *heuristic* search. Unlike algorithms, which are guaranteed to find a solution if there is one, heuristics are rules of thumb that simplify search, work most of the time, but might fail.

It is also interesting to note that, although the task environment is elementary logic, some of the proofs found by LT were shorter and more elegant than those found by Whitehead and Russell, two of the leading mathematicians of the twentieth century. In a letter to Simon (2 November 1956), Russell found these results remarkable: 'I'm delighted to know that *Principia Mathematica* can now be done by machinery. I wish Whitehead and I had known of this possibility before we both wasted ten years doing it by hand' (Simon, 1991, p. 208).

Experiment 2

In this experiment, LT tries to solve one later theorem (Theorem 2.12) without first attempting the theorems that precede it, and possibly storing them in memory if a successful proof was found. Although it was able to find a proof in the first experiment, it fails in the second.

This experiment shows that LT is sensitive to the order with which theorems are presented to it. In the first experiment, it can use the theorems it had proved earlier to find a solution to problem 2.12. This additional knowledge allows it to skip steps and thus to reduce the search space.

Experiment 3

This experiment is similar to Experiment 2, except that one specific theorem (Theorem 2.03) preceding Theorem 2.12 is stored in memory. LT is able to find a proof, but it is longer (3 steps versus 1 step) and takes considerably more time than in Experiment 1 (15 minutes versus less than 1 minute).

This experiment shows that providing a 'hint' (Theorem 2.03) to LT allows it to solve the problem. Newell et al. mention that humans can take advantage of hints as well, although they do not provide specific data on the use of hints with symbolic logic.

CHARACTERISTICS OF THE PROBLEM-SOLVING PROCESS

Newell et al. (1958b) devote a long section to problem-solving characteristics. The analysis uses data from tasks different from logic, and compares LT's characteristics with those of humans.

Set phenomena

A *set*, according to Johnson (1955, p. 65), is 'a readiness to make a specific response to a specified stimulus'. Newell et al. argue that LT exhibits set due, first, to the application of solving methods in a fixed order (first substitution, then detachment, then chaining forward, and finally chaining backward). Second, the 'hint' provided in Experiment 3 directs LT to a different subspace of the search space.

Referring to Luchins's (1942) classical study on the set effect, Newell et al. also note that this hint is possible because of the specific learning that has taken place. Crucially, they note that any problem solver searching a large search space and using a strategy will show set effects, as the strategy implies that the problem solver will examine the possible solutions in some order and not by random trial and error.

Insight

The paper starts the discussion of insight by mentioning the debate between trial-and-error learning and insight, and argues that 'the performance of LT ... shows that this controversy, as it is usually phrased, rests on ambiguity and confusion' (Newell et al., 1958b, p. 160). LT clarifies this issue by displaying insight both by trial-and-error search, leading to a sudden solution, and with heuristics, which keep random search reasonably low.

Concepts

LT is a performance program and has nothing to say about concept formation, which is the central topic of psychological research on concepts. However, it does shed some light on the use of concepts during problem solving, in the sense that they facilitate search. Theorems sharing a similar description are searched for attempting to employ substitutions, detachments, or chaining; thus, theorems sharing a similar description can be considered to belong to the same concept.

Hierarchies of processes

Hierarchies are essential in the way LT works. By breaking problems into sub-problems, the program builds complex hierarchies. This decomposition is similar to what de Groot (1946) had found in his study of chess players.

Learning

LT also sheds some light on learning. The basic learning is done in a rather unin-teresting way, psychologically-proved theorems are simply stored in LTM. More interesting is that sub-problems are also stored and that, in some versions of LT, useful theorems are remembered for each specific proof method. Among the kinds of learning that are lacking in LT, Newell et al. (1958b) mention the acquisition of new methods and being able to modify the definition used to measure the degree of similarity between problems.

COMPARISON WITH OTHER THEORIES

A clever aspect of the paper is that it argues that the presented ideas, while not fully consistent with alternative accounts, share important similarities with them.

Newell et al. (1958b) focus on two main approaches: associationism, in which they include behaviourism, and Gestalt theories, in which they include Selz's (1922) and de Groot's (1946) theory of directed thinking.[1]

Associationism

In common with associationism, LT proposes elementary, mental processes, and provides a mechanical explanation for behaviour. Unlike these theories, Newell et al. emphasise the *functional equivalence* between computers and brains; the underlying implementation of information-processing mechanisms lies at a different theoretical level. Further, associationism depicts a relatively *passive* system upon which stimuli impinge, whereas LT actively responds to stimuli, selecting and possibly using complex behaviours.

Newell et al. conclude their criticism of the 'switching networks' used by associationism by noting that 'the real importance of the digital computer for the theory of higher mental processes lies not merely in allowing us to realize such processes "in the metal" and outside the brain, but in providing us with a much profounder idea than we have hitherto had of the characteristics a mechanism must possess if it is to carry out complex information-processing tasks' (Newell et al., 1958b, p. 163).

Gestalt theories

Newell et al. (1958b) do not say much about classic Gestalt theories, considering instead Selz's theory of 'directed thinking', as presented in de Groot (1946). Several similarities are noted, such as the concept of 'operation', and how operations are used together as strategies. A major difference is that LT is expressed formally, while Selz's theory is stated verbally, and thus is ambiguous and vague.

IMPACT OF THE CLASSIC STUDY

The impact of this paper and of the technical reports that preceded it is simply extraordinary: the creation of three scientific fields. First, it introduced a new form of theory for explaining cognitive processes that went beyond anything that had been proposed in psychology. As such, it was one of the catalysts of the cognitive revolution in psychology.

The information-processing framework, as it came to be known, totally dominated cognitive psychology until the mid-1980s, when connectionism became popular. While some of the ideas were anticipated by psychologists in the Gestalt and Würzburg Schools, and by Selz and, arguably most strongly, de Groot in his

---

[1]This inclusion of Selz and de Groot into Gestalt theorists is surprising, as both are normally considered as outsiders not belonging to any 'official' school. In addition, Selz explicitly criticised the views of Gestalt theorists.

study of chess players, the use of the digital computer allowed a qualitative difference in the extent to which theories can be expressed precisely. The paper also presents the first computer experiment in which one aspect of a simulation (in this case, the amount of training) is manipulated in order to see whether the resulting behaviour can replicate phenomena observed with humans.

The ideas presented in this work were further developed by Newell, Shaw, and Simon to explain human problem solving (e.g., Newell, Shaw, & Simon, 1962; Newell & Simon, 1961; 1972). A central concept, already apparent in the 1958 paper, is that of a *problem space*, which describes a discrete state in the solution of a problem. Problem states are linked by *operators* (e.g., the rules of inference in logic). Finding a solution to a problem can thus be rephrased as finding how to move from an *initial state* to a *goal state*. The *external problem space*, which is achieved by an objective and exhaustive analysis of a problem, lists all the possible states. It makes it possible to find the optimal solution and provides a normative means to analyse a problem solver's behaviour, for example by identifying the places where they diverge from the optimal solution and thus commit errors. A full external problem space can be provided only for relatively simple problems. For problems with larger search spaces (e.g., chess, logic), only statistical regularities can be identified. The *internal problem space*, which typically is a very small subset of the external problem space, describes the space that a problem solver has constructed by her search through the problem space. Just like LT, in most problems it is necessary to carry out a *selective search* or *heuristic search*, where most of the problem states are ignored and only the promising paths are visited. Heuristics are rules of thumb that suggest actions that are good most of the time, but not necessarily all the time.

The problem space theory has been successfully applied to a large number of simple and more complex problems. Some of these problems, including puzzles such as the tower of Hanoi or games such as chess, are *well defined*, in that the initial state, the final state, and the operators are clearly specified. Other problems, in particular those requiring insight or creativity, such as finding a new theory in science, lack this level of specification and are *ill defined*. Note that the application of problem space theory has not been limited to puzzles but has had an impact on the study of expertise as well, such as medical diagnosis and scientific discovery (Gobet, 2015). In total, it is fair to say that Newell, Shaw, and Simon's theory has defined the field of human problem-solving research for nearly half a century. It is for this work that Newell and Simon (Shaw was not that lucky in this respect) received several psychology awards, including the Award for Distinguished Scientific Contributions from the American Psychological Association.

With respect to the second scientific field, LT was one of the very first artificial-intelligence programs and bestowed Newell and Simon the title of founding fathers of artificial intelligence. The paper introduced the 'physical symbol hypothesis', the idea that the manipulation of symbols realised in a physical substrate is a necessary and sufficient condition for intelligence. When developing LT, Newell and his two colleagues created a new form of programming technique, known as list-processing, and devised a specific language (called IPL – Information

Processing Language) to implement it. While IPL was soon replaced by LISP (LISt Processing), which had a simpler syntax while being more flexible, it introduced several key programming ideas, such as list processing, dynamic memory, symbolic computation, and the use of the computer as a virtual machine. These ideas are now central in most programming languages. The paper also anticipates the idea that the sub-problems solved during search can be stored in LTM to be used with future problems; this idea will, for example, play a central role in the Soar cognitive architecture (Newell, 1990). Together, these contributions earned Newell and Simon the A. M. Turing Award in 1975, the highest distinction in computer science.

The third field is at the intersection of the previous two, but can be seen as a distinct methodological contribution: computer modelling or computational modelling. It allows psychologists not only to develop theories with a level of precision never seen before, but also to carry out simulations of complex phenomena. The impact is not as strong as predicted by Simon in 1957, who thought that within ten years 'most theories in psychology would take the form of computer programs or of qualitative statements about computer programs' (McCorduck, 1979, p. 167). But it is clearly the case that a substantial number of theories, either symbolic (e.g., CHREST, Gobet et al., 2001; Soar, Laird, 2012), non-symbolic (e.g., PDP models, McClelland & Rumelhart, 1986), or hybrid (e.g., ACT-R, Anderson et al., 1997; DUAL, Kokinov, 1997) are implemented as computer programs. Several of these theories use a production-system architecture, where knowledge is represented as *productions* or IF-THEN rules. Using productions for modelling human behaviour was proposed by Newell and Simon (1972).

CRITIQUE OF THE CLASSIC STUDY

Although the breadth of Newell et al.'s (1958b) theoretical claims is breathtaking, the study does suffer from several weaknesses. There is a large gap between the actual results with LT and theoretical statements about psychological mechanisms, although these do sound reasonable. The paper alternates between precise descriptions of LT and sometimes rather unsubstantiated theoretical claims. In addition, the paper contains only few simulations, and the methodology used to vary the amount of training and thus knowledge is weak by today's standards. A more serious weakness is that as soon as verbal protocols were collected from human subjects solving logic problems, it became clear that LT was making wrong predictions (Simon, 1991). This was the impetus to the discovery of a new mechanism (means-ends analysis) which was implemented by Newell, Shaw, and Simon in the General Problem Solver (GPS) (Newell, Shaw, & Simon, 1959). A final, perhaps minor, point is that the paper provides few and indeed vague references to previous work on problem solving and alternative theoretical views. This was typical of the style of the day, but is nonetheless irritating for today's reader.

ALTERNATIVE INTERPRETATIONS

As the information-processing framework gained in popularity, the ideas presented in Newell et al. (1958b) and in further publications (e.g., those describing GPS) led to considerable criticism. Dreyfus (1972) criticised the disembodied nature of the kind of theories developed by the information-processing approach and the choice of abstract tasks. Searle (1980) attacked the physical symbol hypothesis. Proponents of connectionism (e.g., Bechtel & Abrahamsen, 1991; McClelland & Rumelhart, 1986) argued that the emphasis on serial processing was implausible. Finally, theorists using the mathematics of dynamic systems (e.g., Beer, 2000) propounded that the hypothesis of discrete entities (symbols) as the basis of human cognition was wrong-headed.

On the experimental side, research into decision making has dominated research into problem solving in recent years, since the influential work of Kahneman and Tversky (Kahneman, Slovic, & Tversky, 1982). The distinction between decision making and problem solving is strange, as both are instances of thinking. It is real, nonetheless, as reflected by a key difference in the methodology typically used in the two fields. In decision-making research, potential solutions are provided and the task is to choose between them. The interest is whether humans behave in a rational or a non-rational way. In problem-solving research, solutions must be generated by the participants, and the central interest relates to the way these solutions are generated and evaluated. It seems to us that eschewing the study of the generation of solutions deprives the psychology of thinking of one of its most interesting questions – precisely that studied with LT.

CONCLUSIONS

Newell et al. (1958b) was one of the main causes behind the creation of information-processing psychology, artificial intelligence, and the methodology of computer modelling in psychology. In addition, it put the study of problem solving back in fashion. This is not bad for a single, admittedly imperfect, piece of research. The study and the work that was later carried out by Newell and Simon, and to a lesser extent Shaw, reinforced these contributions. Unsurprisingly, this work led to considerable criticism. But even today, where cognitive neuroscience is dominating cognitive psychology, the concepts of heuristic search, decomposition into elementary processes, and hierarchy of processes are central in the study of problem solving. Brain imaging studies of high-level functions such as problem solving have led to ambiguous results, not the least because the theories used are expressed verbally and are vague (Uttal, 2012). As a reaction to these shortcomings, we predict that, within ten years, most neuroscience theories will be expressed as computer programs.

FURTHER READING

(Complete citations are in the References section.)

Newell and Simon (1972) provide a full description of LT and of the information-processing approach in general. The book contains large amounts of protocols of participants trying to solve problems in logic, cryptarithmetic (problems in the style of SEND + MORE = MONEY) and chess, all analysed in painstaking detail.

McCorduck (1979) is a history of the beginning of artificial intelligence and information-processing psychology. It provides a personal account, with many interviews of the key players, including Newell, Shaw, and Simon. The development and impact of LT is covered in some detail.

Gardner (1987) offers a history not only of the developments preceeding and surrounding LT, but also of those following it. It provides a detailed discussion of the strengths and weaknesses of information-processing psychology.

Herbert Simon's autobiography (Simon, 1991) contains a detailed account of the development of LT and information-processing psychology.

Bechtel and Abrahamsen (1991) discuss connectionist approaches developed in direct opposition to information-processing psychology. Not only does it provide a clear introduction to the topic, but it also addresses the theoretical and philosophical implications.

REFERENCES

Anderson, J. R., Matessa, M., & Lebiere, C. (1997). ACT-R: A theory of higher level cognition and its relation to visual attention. *Human-Computer Interaction*, 12, 439–462.

Bechtel, W., & Abrahamsen, A. (1991). *Connectionism and the mind: An introduction to parallel processing in networks*. Cambridge, MA: Blackwell.

Beer, R. D. (2000). Dynamical approaches to cognitive science. *Trends in Cognitive Sciences*, 4, 91–99.

De Groot, A. D. (1946). *Het denken van den schaker*. Amsterdam: Noord Hollandsche.

Dreyfus, H. L. (1972). *What computers can't do: A critique of artificial reason*. New York: Harper & Row.

Gardner, H. (1987). *The mind's new science: A history of the cognitive revolution*. New York: Basic Books.

Gobet, F. (2015). *Understanding expertise*. London: Palgrave.

Gobet, F., Lane, P. C. R., Croker, S., Cheng, P. C. H., Jones, G., Oliver, I., et al. (2001). Chunking mechanisms in human learning. *Trends in Cognitive Sciences*, 5, 236–243.

Holt, C., Modigliani, F., Muth, J., & Simon, H. (1960). *Planning production, inventories, and work force*. Englewood Cliffs, NJ: Prentice-Hall.

Johnson, D. M. (1955). *The psychology of thought and judgment*. New York: Harper & Brothers.

Kahneman, D., Slovic, P., & Tversky, A. (Eds.) (1982). *Judgments under uncertainty: Heuristics and biases*. Cambridge, UK: Cambridge University Press.

Kokinov, B. (1997). Micro-level hybridization in the cognitive architecture DUAL. In R. Sun & F. Alexander (Eds.), *Connectionist-symbolic integration: From unified to hybrid architectures*. Hilsdale, NJ: Lawrence Erlbaum Associates.

Laird, J. E. (2012). *The Soar cognitive architecture*. Boston, MA: The MIT Press.

Luchins, A. S. (1942). Mechanization in problem solving: The effect of Einstellung. *Psychological Monographs*, 54.

March, J. G., & Simon, H. A. (1958). *Organizations*. New York: Wiley & Sons.

McClelland, J. L., & Rumelhart, D. E. (Eds.) (1986). *Parallel distributed processing: Explorations in the microstructure of cognition*. Cambridge, MA: The MIT Press.

McCorduck, P. (1979). *Machines who think*. San Francisco, CA: W. H. Freeman.

Newell, A. (1990). *Unified theories of cognition*. Cambridge, MA: Harvard University Press.

Newell, A., & Shaw, J. C. (1957). Programming the logic theory machine. *Proceedings of the Western Joint Computer Conference* (pp. 230–240). New York: Institute of Radio Engineers.

Newell, A., & Simon, H. A. (1956). The logic theory machine. *Transactions of information theory* (Vol. IT-2, pp. 61–79). New York: Institute of Radio Engineers.

Newell, A., & Simon, H. A. (1961). Computer simulation of human thinking. *Science*, 134, 2011–2017.

Newell, A., & Simon, H. A. (1972). *Human problem solving*. Englewood Cliffs, NJ: Prentice-Hall.

Newell, A., Shaw, J. C., & Simon, H. A. (1957). Empirical explorations with the logic theory machine. *Proceedings of the Western Joint Computer Conference* (pp. 218–230). New York: Institute of Radio Engineers.

Newell, A., Shaw, J. C., & Simon, H. A. (1958a). Chess-playing programs and the problem of complexity. *IBM Journal of Research and Development*, 2, 320–335.

Newell, A., Shaw, J. C., & Simon, H. A. (1958b). Elements of a theory of human problem solving. *Psychological Review*, 65, 151–166.

Newell, A., Shaw, J. C., & Simon, H. A. (1959). Report on a general problem-solving program. *Proceedings of the international conference on information processing*, Paris (pp. 256–264).

Newell, A., Shaw, J. C., & Simon, H. A. (1962). The process of creative thinking. In H. E. Gruber, G. Terrell, & M. Werheimer (Eds.), *Contemporary Approaches to Creative Thinking* (Vol. 3, pp. 63–119). New York: Atherton Press.

Searle, J. (1980). Minds, brains and programs. *Behavioral and Brain Sciences*, 3, 417–457.

Selz, O. (1922). *Zur Psychologie des produktiven Denkens und des Irrtums*. Bonn: Friedrich Cohen.

Simon, H. A. (1957). *Models of man: Social and rational*. New York: John Wiley and Sons.

Simon, H. A. (1991). *Models of my life*. New York: Basic Books.

Uttal, W. R. (2012). *Reliability of neuroscience data: A meta-meta-analysis*. Cambridge, MA: The MIT Press.

Wang, H. (1960). Toward mechanical mathematics. *IBM Journal of Research and Development*, 4, 2–22.

Whitehead, A. N., & Russell, B. (1910). *Principia Mathematica* (Vol. 1). Cambridge, UK: Cambridge University Press.

12 | Heuristics and biases: Beyond Tversky and Kahneman's (1974) judgment under uncertainty

Klaus Fiedler and Momme von Sydow
(University of Heidelberg, Germany)

BACKGROUND TO THE CLASSIC STUDY

HEURISTICS AND BIASES FROM A HISTORICAL PERSPECTIVE

It is no exaggeration to say that today's psychology would not be what it is without Daniel Kahneman's and Amos Tversky's seminal work on heuristics and biases, as summarised in a *Science* article (Tversky & Kahneman, 1974) that was cited over 7,000 times – an unbelievable rate for a psychology article. A few years before this word spread like wildfire. The rationalist metaphor of a computer-like human memory and the man-as-scientist analogy conveyed in theories of consistency (Abelson, 1968) and attribution (Jones, Kanouse, Kelley, Nisbett, Valins, & Weiner, 1987) had brought about the so-called cognitive revolution (Dember, 1974). However, this naïvely optimistic view on the human mind turned rapidly into deflating pessimism when statistical tools began to dominate research and theorising came under the dominating influence of Kahneman and Tversky's research programme.

In accordance with Gigerenzer's (1991a) 'tools-as-theories' notion, new methodological tools determined the manner in which the cognitive psychology of the late 1960s and early 1970s now characterised *homo sapiens*. Statistical models now afforded normative benchmarks, to which human judgments and decisions were compared. In this comparison, any deviation between the mind and the normative models had to be interpreted as a failure of the human mind to apply logical and rational rules of thinking and reasoning.

Unlike the old research programme of psychophysics, within which deviations of subjective experience (e.g., loudness) from physical stimulus intensity (e.g., sound pressure) would be hardly interpreted as irrational or dysfunctional, the new programme of psycho-statistics was clearly more judgmental. Deviations of subjective from objective probabilities, or subjective value judgments from objective quantities were from the beginning interpreted as reflective of the pitfalls of a fallible and lazy mind (Nisbett & Ross, 1980). Whereas the objective criterion in psychophysics was nothing but a mundane physical quantity, the criterion in the new psycho-statistics approach was treated like normative truth.

DETAILED DESCRIPTION OF THE CLASSIC STUDY

Starting from the premise that the subjective assessment of most real quantities has to rely on incomplete data of limited validity, Tversky and Kahneman (1974) postulated that the mind has to resort to so-called heuristics, or rules-of-thumb, that afford useful proxies most of the time. 'These heuristics are highly economical and usually effective, but they lead to systematic and predictable errors' in certain task situations (Tversky & Kahneman, 1974, p. 1131). Just like the perceptual illusions in Gestalt psychology, such as colour or size constancy, whose adaptive function was always recognised, the cognitive illusions of the new research programme might have been treated functionally, as useful adaptive devices that allow for accurate inferences under appropriate conditions. However, although Kahneman and Tversky themselves did point out the functional value of heuristic inference tools, the empirical research they triggered was almost totally concerned with biases and shortcomings of the human mind (Gilovich, Griffin, & Kahneman, 2002; Nisbett & Ross, 1980; Ross, 1977) rather than with the adaptive value or maybe even the superiority of heuristics over the theorist's 'narrow' normative models (Gigerenzer, 1996, 2006; Gigerenzer & Todd, 1999).

SYNOPSIS OF MOST PROMINENT HEURISTICS

Let us first illustrate this state of affairs with reference to the three most prominent heuristics – representativeness, availability, and anchoring – all expounded in

Table 12.1   Overview and illustrations of most prominent heuristics

Heuristic	Field of application	Illustration/Example
Availability	Memory-based judgments of frequency or probability	Overestimation of risks that are easily available in memory
Representativeness	Judgments of likelihood of instances belonging to a category	Birth order son-daughter-son-daughter more representative of random outcome than son-son-son-son
Anchoring and adjustment	Quantitative estimates on a unidimensional scale	Cost calculations biased towards starting value

the classical paper by Tversky & Kahneman (1974) and summarised in Table 12.1. The scientific impact and the insights gained from the Kahneman–Tversky research programme will then be discussed in the remainder of this chapter.

Representativeness (Kahneman & Tversky, 1972) was introduced as a heuristic for judging the probability that a stimulus sample belongs to a category. For instance, a stimulus sample or description, *D*, may describe a person named Linda as '31 years old, single, outspoken, and very bright, with a major in philosophy; has concerns about discrimination and social justice; and was involved in anti-nuclear demonstrations while a university student'. This person is judged to be more likely to belong to category '*A & B*' (Women who are active in the feminist movement and bank tellers) than to category '*B*' (Women who are bank tellers). But this often-replicated finding violates the conjunction rule, which says that the conjunction of two events (active feminist and bank teller) cannot be more probable than any of the two events alone (bank teller): $P(A \& B) \leq P(B)$. Yet, according to the representativeness heuristic, the description of Linda (*D*) is more representative of, or more similar to, the conjunction (*A & B*) than of the conjunct (*B*). This exemplifies a phenomenon that is commonly known as the conjunction fallacy (Tversky & Kahneman, 1983).

The representativeness heuristic, like some other theories of the conjunction fallacy (e.g., Fisk, 1996; Hertwig & Chase, 1998), involves the prediction of the so-called base-rate neglect. In medical judgments, for instance, having a pain in one's chest (representative of a heart attack) may suggest that one is probably having a heart attack, although – due to many other causes – the base rate of this symptom is relatively high and the probability of a heart attack may actually be lower than supposed.

Another feature of representativeness, besides base-rate neglect, is insensitivity to sample size. Thus, when asked to judge the number of days in a year on which more than 60% of all babies born are boys, most people erroneously believe that the rate of such abnormal days is approximately the same in a large (45 babies born each day) and in a small hospital (15 babies each day). However, while ≤60% is equally representative of the expected 50% in any hospital, outliers (>60%) occur at a higher rate in small than in large samples. Human judges are often insensitive to this law of the large number (Bernoulli, 1713).

The availability heuristic, too, serves to estimate absolute or relative probabilities or frequencies of events. Unlike representativeness, however, availability is a heuristic driven by a meta-cognitive cue. Judgments of the occurrence rate of a class of events *E* are supposed to reflect the ease with which examples of *E* can be retrieved from memory. To the extent that ease of retrieval is a valid cue for predicting frequency of occurrence – because, conversely, what is frequently encountered can also be easily retrieved – the availability heuristic should provide accurate estimates most of the time. However, whenever memory strength is biased towards other causal factors than original occurrence rate, judgments by availability can be misleading. In a frequently cited classical study, for instance, the frequency of words in the English dictionary with a 'k' as initial letter was erroneously judged to be higher than the frequency of words with a 'k' in the third position (Tversky & Kahneman, 1973). Apparently, the first letter is easier to use as retrieval prompt than the third letter of a word.

Third, the anchoring-and-adjustment heuristic (Tversky & Kahneman, 1974) applies to all kinds of estimations on a specified quantitative dimension. As a starting point for such cognitive estimation processes, judges often use an initial anchor, which is then adjusted in the light of further information stemming from memory or from external sources. This adjustment process is typically insufficient so that final judgments tend to be biased towards the initial anchor. That is, depending on whether the process starts with a low or high anchor, the final judgments tend to be under- or overestimations, respectively. In the planning fallacy (Buehler, Griffin, & Peetz, 2010), for instance, the time required for a project is underestimated when the calculation starts from a low anchor (or zero time). An alternative calculation that starts from a high anchor of maximal time required for comparable projects would arrive at much higher estimates. Most impressive experimental demonstrations refer to the impact of completely irrelevant numerical anchors without any diagnostic value for the quantity to be judged. For instance, judgments of the number of African countries in the United Nations were influenced by starting values established randomly by a roulette wheel.

IMPACT OF THE CLASSIC STUDY

HEURISTICS AND BIASES IN COGNITIVE, SOCIAL, AND APPLIED PSYCHOLOGY

As already mentioned, the impact of this research on the development of cognitive, social, and applied psychology was immense. Nowadays, textbooks and curricula in behavioural science are unimaginable without sizeable parts devoted to heuristics and biases. Modern research on judgment and decision making, cognitive psychology, and in social cognitive psychology still relies heavily on Kahneman and Tversky's work, referring to representativeness when explaining stereotypes and causal attributions, to availability when explaining the overestimation of salient risks (Combs & Slovic, 1979) and egocentric overestimations of one's own contributions (Ross & Sicoly, 1979), and to anchoring when explaining biased cost estimations (Buehler et al., 2010) or courtroom decisions (Englich & Mussweiler, 2001). The notion of heuristics has become common sense shared by students of many other disciplines, medical scientists, journalists, practitioners, and even politicians. And last but not least, heuristically biased assessments of probability and utility had a strong impact on prospect theory (Kahneman & Tversky, 1979) – the most prominent behavioural decision theory in economics, for which Daniel Kahneman, after Amos Tversky's death, received the 2002 Nobel Prize in economics. Prospect theory predicts risk-aversive behaviour when decisions are framed in terms of possible gains but risk-seeking when decisions are framed in terms of losses (cf. Chapter 13 on Prospect Theory).

CRITIQUE OF THE CLASSIC STUDY

Nevertheless, despite the overwhelming acceptance and applause for Kahneman and Tversky's heuristic approach to understanding cognitive illusions, the industrious research it elicited was also met with scepticism and serious critique. Several theorists were concerned with the inherently negative lessons gained from research designs that guarantee deviations from normative models that will inevitably be attributed to insufficiencies of the human mind. Krueger and Funder (2004) pointed out that allegedly irrational judgments and decisions can often be re-interpreted in terms of reasonable assumptions about the task and the problem setting. Others (e.g., Lopes & Oden, 1991) have argued that content-blind normative models are often inappropriate and unjustified as benchmarks of rationality.

However, nobody has pronounced the critique as forcefully as Gigerenzer (1991b, 1996). His dissatisfaction is summarised in the following quotation:

> The heuristics in the heuristics-and-biases program are too vague to count as explanations. They are labels with the virtue of Rorschach inkblots: A researcher can read into them what he or she wishes. The reluctance to specify precise and falsifiable process models, to clarify the antecedent conditions that elicit various heuristics, and to work out the relationship between heuristics have been repeatedly pointed out. (Gigerenzer, 1996, pp. 593–594)

Gigerenzer disqualified one-word-labels like 'representativeness' as theory surrogates that fail to place any testable constraints on the cognitive decision process. A similar point was made by Wolford (1991).

To understand this critical appraisal and why it is presumably justified, let us consider some of the most prominent heuristic explanations. For instance, in an often-cited article on biases in risk assessment (Combs & Slovic, 1979), the overestimation of some causes of death (e.g., murder, lightning) and the underestimation of others (suicide, coronary disease) is confidently attributed to the availability heuristic. Because murder and lightning are readily reported in the media, whereas suicide and coronary disease are rarely reported, it is argued that the former are easier to recall than the latter. However, ease of recall is neither measured nor manipulated directly. Moreover, the very explanation in terms of media coverage suggests an external cause, biased media report, which has to be distinguished from the internal cause of biased memory judgment that is the focus of an availability-heuristic account. Granting fully unbiased and comparable recall of all causes of death, the unequal media coverage provides an alternative sampling account that is essentially different from availability.

In another prominent application, the availability heuristic has been used to explain the so-called egocentric bias (Ross & Sicoly, 1979), that is, the belief that oneself has contributed more than partners or other people to joint activities (e.g., in partnerships or work groups). This phenomenon has been ascribed to enhanced memory of one's own deeds relative to other people's deeds. However, this interpretation is exclusively based on correlational evidence; ease of recalling one's own and other's activities was not manipulated experimentally. The correlation may be simply due to self-consistency; frequency judgments may be attuned to match the recall output, or recall efforts may be adjusted to justify frequency judgments.

The lack of cogent evidence for the underlying cognitive process also characterises the empirical research on the anchoring heuristic. Hardly any research has ever attempted to demonstrate a gradual process of insufficient adjustment of an initial anchor value. Thus, when participants whose last four digits in their social security number was higher also accepted higher selling prices (Chapman & Johnson, 1999), this may simply reflect the impact of numerical priming on the elicitation of a response on a numerical judgment scale (Oppenheimer, LeBoeuf, & Brewer, 2008). It need not be the result of an updating or adjustment process that remains incomplete, due to premature truncation. Epley and Gilovich's (2006, 2010) conclusion that anchoring effects may originate in a variety of different cognitive processes is tantamount to giving up the specific process suggested in the heuristic's original account. To be sure, countless experiments testify to the ability of preceding stimuli to affect subsequent judgments. While such ordinary priming effects may be renamed as different types of anchoring effect, they hardly support the mechanism suggested originally by Tversky and Kahneman (1974) and adopted uncritically by behavioural scientists.

In one experiment designed to test the continuous adjustment assumption, Fiedler, Schmid, Kurzenhaeuser, and Schroeter (2000) drew on the notion of anchoring in lie detection (Zuckerman, Koestner, Colella, & Alton, 1984). When a series of communications is judged on two tasks supposed to induce cooperation (do you understand the message?) and suspicion (could it be a lie?), the communications appear less truthful when the suspicious task that precedes the cooperative task sets a negative anchor. Using a mouse-tracking technique to assess online changes in the subjective believability of a video-taped communication presented on the computer, Fiedler et al. (2000) did not find evidence for an insufficiently adjusted initial bias to either trust or distrust the communicator. Rather, the mouse coordinates started in a middling position and then became more polarised as the communication unfolded, thus reflecting a longitudinal process opposite to the insufficient depolarisation process suggested in the anchoring heuristic.

Last but not least, the failure to establish anchoring as a unique cognitive mechanism is apparent in the co-existence of two completely different theoretical accounts, numerical priming and selective accessibility. Whereas the numerical-priming account predicts that even fully irrelevant numerical primes can influence judgments, the selective-accessibility account (Strack & Mussweiler, 1997) is restricted to the impact of anchors that refer to knowledge relevant to the contents of the judgment task. Note that both accounts not only refer to completely independent process stages – the early stage of knowledge activation and the late stage of transforming a judgment onto a numerical scale. Both processes also diverge from the original account of an insufficient adjustment process. This equivocal state of affairs seems to corroborate Gigerenzer's (1996) fundamental critique that there is little evidence for these heuristics as distinct cognitive processes that might afford precise algorithmic explanations of distinct judgment biases.

HEURISTICS IN THE POST-KAHNEMAN–TVERSKY ERA

The adaptive toolbox. What were the reactions to these complaints, and the new development, in what might be called the post-Kahneman–Tversky era? To be sure, Gigerenzer and his co-workers came up with their own theoretical conception, for which they coined the metaphor of a 'heuristic toolbox'. Each tool in this toolbox is described as a fast and frugal heuristic that requires little information to make people (or animals) smart if applied in the appropriate moment and environment. For instance, the Take-the-Best heuristic (Gigerenzer & Goldstein, 1996), which only uses the one ecologically most valid cue to make a prediction or choice, is only applicable in task settings in which one cue is clearly the most valid. In contrast, tallying (i.e., giving the same weight to many different cues) is appropriate when there are many similarly valid cues.

Related to the Take-the-Best is the recognition heuristic (RH) (Goldstein & Gigerenzer, 2002; see also Pachur, Todd, Gigerenzer, Schooler, & Goldstein, 2011), which is ideally suited to illustrate how the adaptive toolbox functions. RH has a clearly defined domain and decision rule. When exposed to a pair of options in a choice task (e.g., Which one of two towns is larger? Which of two shares should be purchased?), the RH first assesses the value of the two options on the recognition cue (i.e., whether it is recognised as experienced before or not). If the recognition cue discriminates between the two options (i.e., if one is recognised but one is not), RH will choose the familiar option. Since heuristics are applied as adaptive or domain-specific tools, the recognition heuristic should only apply if recognition is highly correlated with the criterion value (as in the city example). In this case, however, no further information should be considered (non-compensatory one-reason decision making) (cf. Pohl, 2011). If the recognition cue does not discriminate, however, another heuristic must be applied (e.g., the fluency heuristic that is sensitive to the frequency of prior exposure), or a decision must be based on random guessing (cf. Hilbig, Erdfelder, & Pohl, 2010). As the ecological validity of the recognition cue is amazingly high (Goldstein & Gigerenzer, 2002) – recognised shares are typically more successful than unrecognised ones – this primitive decision rule leads to a high rate of correct decisions in many task settings. Moreover, the RH can explain why less can be more, that is, why laypeople who only rely on a feeling of familiarity due to recognition can sometimes outperform more knowledgeable judges, who try to utilise more cues at the same time and who thereby capitalise on chance (i.e., give unwarranted weight to invalid cues).

Note that unlike the classical heuristics of the original Kahneman–Tversky programme, the heuristics from the adaptive toolbox are based on clearly spelled-out algorithms. Many constitute lexicographic strategies that rely on a single cue rather than trade-offs between multiple, mutually compensatory cues. Note also that the heuristics of the adaptive toolbox are supposed to render people smart in terms of Simon's (1982) criterion of bounded rationality, rather than being illusory and indicative of cognitive illusions and shortcomings.

However, despite the more transparent algorithms used for simulation studies of this new heuristic research programme (Gigerenzer & Todd, 1999), cogent experimental evidence that human participants' cognitive processes generally follow these specific algorithms remains scarce (Hilbig, 2010; Pohl, 2011). On the one hand, little is known about how the subjective discrimination between recognised and unrecognised options is accomplished. Maybe the seemingly unique recognition cue is itself inferred from a more complex repertoire of other (vicarious) cues. In a similar vein, it is unclear how humans and animals can diagnose the validity of different cues and how they select the cues to be utilised for an inference problem in the first place.

On the other hand, a few experimental tests of specific heuristics suggest that they may not describe the cognitive reality. For example, the so-called priority heuristic (Brandstätter, Gigerenzer & Hertwig, 2006) assumes that choices between pairs of lotteries involve a three-stage process: (1) choosing the option with the higher minimal outcome if the minimal outcomes are different enough; (2) choosing the option with the higher winning probability if probabilities are different enough; or else (3) choosing the option with the higher maximal outcome. The implications of this algorithm that probabilities only matter when minimal values do not strongly differ and that maximal values only matter if probabilities are similar were recently found to be disconfirmed (Fiedler, 2010).

DUAL-PROCESS APPROACHES

While the adaptive toolbox approach arose from a fundamental critique of the old heuristics-and-biases programme, the abundance of dual-process approaches starting in the 1980s can be understood as attempts to reconcile the notion of fallible heuristics with the possibility of accurate and rational information processing (Chaiken & Trope, 1999). Despite the notable differences between the almost 30 dual-process theories proposed, for example, by Petty and Cacioppo (1986), Sloman (1996), Evans (2003) or, more recently, by Stanovich & West (2002), Strack and Deutsch (2004), and Kahneman and Frederick (2005), they all converge in assuming two fundamentally different modes of information processing. Only one of these processing modes is supposed to be prone to heuristic shortcuts and intuitive strategies, whereas the other mode is supposed to use systematic and exhaustive strategies deemed to produce normative results under many conditions. Because the moderator conditions that can evoke one or the other mode are manifold, these dual-process theories offer an account for virtually all judgments that disconfirm some heuristic. For example, if judges do not fall prey to the conjunction fallacy, do not ignore base rates and sample sizes, or if they are not misled by an anchor, one only has to assume that the secondary system has been invoked, which enables unbiased thinking.

Given that thousands of empirical studies and hundreds of scientific careers are grounded on dual-process approaches, it would be justified to praise them as extremely fertile and successful (cf. Smith & DeCoster, 2000). However, they have also been the target of harsh critique (Keren & Schul, 2009; Kruglanski & Thompson, 1999; Osman, 2004), raising the question whether they have delayed rather than supported progress in research on judgment and decision making. What renders dual-process theories unrealistic and scientifically weak is that the two systems are presumed to differ in too many attributes at the same time. One system is supposed to involve automatic associative processes, relying on heuristics and intuition, little capacity constraints and low effort expenditure, no conscious awareness, and no meta-cognitive control. The other system, in contrast, is allegedly based on reflective propositional operations, adhering to rule-based and exhaustive processing demanding high cognitive capacity and effort expenditure, conscious awareness, and meta-cognitive monitoring and control. The assumption that all these attributes are perfectly or highly correlated is far from being confirmed empirically. On the contrary, there is ample evidence to show that even effortful, persistent, and highly conscious and controlled attempts to solve logical problems can produce strong biases (Fiedler, 2008; Le Mens & Denrell, 2011) of the same type as the classical heuristics (e.g., conjunction fallacies, sample-size neglect, or anchoring effects). Conversely, even intuitive, low-effort inferences from single cues and incomplete samples can lead to accurate and logically coherent mental structures (Dijksterhuis & Nordgren, 2006). Whereas some prominent biases are associated with low cognitive ability, others are not (cf. Stanovich & West, 2008).

CONCLUSIONS

APPRAISAL OF 40 YEARS OF RESEARCH ON HEURISTICS AND BIASES

So what can we conclude from this sketch of the heuristics and biases programme and its impact on subsequent behavioural research across four decades? We believe that a fair and appropriate answer has to be split into two radically different conclusions. One conclusion is, frankly speaking, disillusioning whereas the other one is enthusiastic.

Theory development. On the one hand, what is disillusioning and disappointing is how little precision, refinement, and progress was obtained at the theoretical level. Very few cleverly designed experiments were conducted that might have provided cogent evidence for the causal dependence of specific judgment biases – like base-rate neglect, conjunction fallacies, or anchoring effects – on the mechanisms depicted in the classical heuristics. The 'judgment of Solomon' that the same biases can originate in many processes (Epley & Gilovich, 2010) amounts to giving up the explanatory value of the original heuristics. A few serious attempts to test heuristics precisely, according to the standards of modern cognitive science, ruthlessly uncover this frustrating state of affairs.

Considering representativeness, Kahneman and Frederick (2002, 2005) have specified a two-step process of a prototype heuristic, in which a category (e.g., 'bank teller') is represented by a prototypical exemplar, and a second process in which 'a (non-extensional) property of the prototype is then used as a heuristic attribute to evaluate an extensional target attribute'. This does go beyond a 'one-word' heuristic.

Still, Nilsson, Olsson, and Juslin's (2005) attempt to investigate the cognitive substrate of the representativeness heuristic had to start from complete uncertainty about what similarity function is used in the representativeness heuristic, whether categories are indeed represented as prototypes or as lists of exemplars, or what metric is used to compare several categories' representativeness. Empirical and theoretical research at the level of sober cognitive research turns out to be hardly available. As long as no comprehensive theory can predict what bias reflects what process under what condition, the theoretical status of a heuristic is little more than a plausible verbal label for a set of seemingly related findings. Maybe the most conspicuous sign of theoretical vacuum is the lack of debates relating the heuristics-and-biases idea to a growing list of demonstrations of biases emerging from non-heuristic processes (Fiedler, 2008; Le Mens & Denrell, 2011).

At the level of applied psychology, too, the lack of clearly spelt-out theories and the failure to specify heuristics as algorithms have prevented systematic attempts to evaluate the costs and benefits of heuristics relative to other strategies supposed to be non-heuristic – whatever this negation might refer to. As a consequence, researchers and practitioners are free to point out either the fallibility and danger or the intuitive wisdom and low opportunity costs of heuristics in such domains as medical diagnosis, investment, consumer choices, risk control, personnel selection, law, and politics. Whereas clearly explicated decision tools, such as signal-detection analysis (Swets, Dawes, & Monahan, 2000) or lexicographic algorithms (Martignon, Katsikopoulos, & Woike, 2008), have been shown to support accurate judgments and decisions in health, law, and other areas of risk assessment, the classical heuristics have been hardly implemented practically.

Inspiration and fertilisation. On the other hand, however, in spite of the stagnation of strict and precise theorising, the fertility and the fascinating impact that Kahneman and Tversky's work had on contemporary research can be hardly overstated. It may be typical of the growth of science that the impact of a theoretical idea can be detached from the ultimate validity of the original idea itself. Like Wittgenstein's metaphor of a ladder that is no longer needed when one has climbed up a wall, the enormous, almost immeasurable fertilisation and inspiration that grew out of Kahneman and Tversky's work is detached from any empirical test of representativeness, availability, and anchoring. Whoever witnessed the verve and excitement that spread like wildfire among scientists exposed to these authors' disarming demonstrations will probably agree that the impact was gigantic. Psychologists recognised a new research potential that would afford motivation and orientation for many young scientists and a challenging new programme of rationality research. This programme entails a significant task for behavioural scientists to educate the public, journalists, politicians, and professionals in a genuinely behavioural domain: (ir)rational judgment and decision making.

Indeed, the message that not only lay people but also professionals and highly educated experts fall prey to cognitive biases and illusions has become an integral part of intellectual culture and common sense. It is included in curricula for graduate students, undergraduates and even high school students, magazines, popular books, radio and TV programmes, and countless internet sites. The number of references to 'heuristics' found in the PsychInfo data bank amounts to almost 10,000. The readiness with which the notion was adopted in multiple areas of research is evident from the number of references obtained for 'heuristic' AND 'health' (1,452), 'clinical' (1,081), 'medical' (607), 'risk' (595), 'consumer' (391), 'economic' (444), 'organizational' (632), and 'law' (289), to list but a few prominent areas.

Nevertheless, this success story reflects a dialectical rather than a confirmatory process. Pertinent research has flourished not because the original thesis received strong support, but because the provocative demonstration of biases and shortcomings instigated a flood of loosely related studies leading to various anti-theses and sub-theses. Gigerenzer and colleagues' (Gigerenzer & Todd, 1999) adaptive toolbox was antithetical, but was nevertheless motivated by the work of Kahneman and Tversky. The state of the art in current research on cognitive illusions is often detached from, or even inconsistent with, the original heuristic accounts, which have nevertheless inspired the whole research programme.

For instance, research on the conjunction fallacy has led to different potential causes like misunderstanding of logical terms (Hertwig, Benz, & Krauss, 2008) and representation format effects (Hertwig & Chase, 1998). Moreover, it has been argued that standard probability judgments may actually be replaced by averaged probabilities (Jenny, Rieskamp, & Nilsson, 2014), inverse probability judgments (Fisk & Slattery, 2005), pattern probability judgments (von Sydow, 2011), or confirmation judgments (Tentori, Crupi, & Russo, 2013). Presumably the conjunction fallacy is caused by more than one process. In any case, great progress in modern research (e.g., Tentori et al., 2013) no longer relies on representativeness, but is nevertheless influenced by the old heuristic idea.

Likewise, research on anchoring effects is detached from the old anchoring heuristic but has led to many new insights about biased planning calculation (Buehler et al., 2010), legal judgments (Englich & Mussweiler, 2001), prices obtained in auctions (Ritov, 1996), nuclear war risks (Plous, 1989), or social comparisons (Mussweiler, 2003).

In a similar vein, new developments in research on meta-cognition, dealing with fluency and ease of retrieval (Unkelbach & Greifeneder, 2013; Winkielman, Schwarz, & Belli, 1998) as determinants of liking and attitudes, grew out of the availability heuristic, which appears to be obsolete as a testable cognitive process assumption.

Apart from the impact of specific heuristics, the resulting research programme as a whole contributed to several exciting new developments, such as the collaboration between psychologists and economists in rationality research, the new role of behavioural scientists as consultants for politicians and administrative decision makers, and new lines of health education (Gigerenzer, Gaissmaier, Kurz-Milcke, Schwartz & Woloshin, 2007; Swets et al., 2000). Resistance to the pessimistic image of a heuristic mind has led to novel theorising about the appropriateness of normative models (Krueger & Funder, 2004). And last but not least, the dissatisfaction with the restricted focus on heuristic processes within the individual's mind has led to a new cognitive-ecological framework, within which biases can be shown to arise in the absence of biased cognitive processes, merely as a side-effect of information sampling in a complex world (Denrell & Le Mens, 2007; Fiedler & Juslin, 2006).

CONCLUDING REMARK

Provided the present perspective on heuristics-and-biases research is not fully inappropriate, the main conclusion is that the huge impact of Kahneman and Tversky's work is not due to the accrual of confirmatory evidence, but, ironically, to its imperfectness and the persistent failure to clearly define and thus perhaps to falsify and discard the original heuristics. Considered from a distance, this may not be too unusual a state of affairs in the history of scientific discovery (Kuhn, 1962). Still, the accumulated empirical evidence on biases in judgments and decisions is impressive, and many incidental side-effects of this research industry are of practical and theoretical value.

Notwithstanding all empirical results, though, the apparent deficits at the theoretical level must not be overlooked but must be tackled as a challenge for future research. The most difficult and ambitious goal for future behavioural science is not so much to enhance empirical output but to develop theoretical frameworks that allow for critical tests of existing data as well as for the theory-driven refinement of raw hypotheses to be tested in cleverly designed studies. However, this situation – characterised by theory lagging behind empirical evidence – may not be peculiar to heuristics and biases but rather typical of current behavioural science.

Author note: Work on the present paper was supported by a Koselleck grant by the Deutsche Forschungsgemeinschaft to Klaus Fiedler (Fi 294/23-1) and by a DFG grant to Momme von Sydow (Sy 111/2-1, within the priority programme New Frameworks of Rationality, SPP 1516). Valuable comments on this chapter by Mandy Hütter are gratefully acknowledged. Correspondence may be sent via electronic mail to kf@psychologie.uni-heidelberg.de

FURTHER READING

Gigerenzer, G. (1996). On narrow norms and vague heuristics: A reply to Kahneman and Tversky. *Psychological Review*, 103 (3), 592–596.

Gigerenzer, G., & Todd, P. M. (1999). *Simple heuristics that make us smart*. New York: Oxford University Press.

Gilovich, T., Griffin, D., & Kahneman, D. (2002). *Heuristics and biases: The psychology of intuitive judgment*. New York: Cambridge University Press.

Kahneman, D., & Frederick, S. (2005). A model of heuristic judgment. In K. J. Holyoak & R. G. Morrison (Eds.), *The Cambridge handbook of thinking and reasoning* (pp. 267–293). New York: Cambridge University Press.

Kahneman, D., & Tversky, A. (1996). On the reality of cognitive illusions: A reply to Gigerenzer's critique. *Psychological Review*, 103, 582–591.

REFERENCES

Abelson, R. L. (1968). *Theories of cognitive consistency: A sourcebook*. Chicago, IL: Rand-McNally.

Bernoulli, J. (1713). *Ars conjectandi* [Probability calculation]. Basel.

Brandstätter, E., Gigerenzer, G., & Hertwig, R. (2006). The Priority Heuristic: Making Choices Without Trade-Offs. *Psychological Review*, 113, 409–432.

Buehler, R., Griffin, D., & Peetz, J. (2010). The planning fallacy: Cognitive, motivational, and social origins. In M. P. Zanna & J. M. Olson (Eds.), *Advances in experimental social psychology* (Vol. 43, pp. 1–62). San Diego, CA: Academic Press. DOI: 10.1016/S0065-2601(10)43001-4.

Chaiken, S., & Trope, Y. (Eds.) (1999). *Dual-process theories in social psychology*. New York: Guilford Press.

Chapman, G. B., & Johnson, E. J. (1999). Anchoring, activation, and the construction of values. *Organizational Behavior and Human Decision Processes*, 79 (2), 115–153. DOI: 10.1006/obhd.1999.2841.

Combs, B., & Slovic, P. (1979). Newspaper coverage of causes of death. *Public Opinion Quarterly*, 56, 837–843.

Dember, W. N. (1974). Motivation and the cognitive revolution. *American Psychologist*, 29 (3), 161–168. DOI: 10.1037/h0035907.

Denrell, J., & Le Mens, G. (2007). Interdependent sampling and social influence. *Psychological Review*, 114 (2), 398–422. DOI: 10.1037/0033-295X.114.2.398.

Dijksterhuis, A., & Nordgren, L. F. (2006). A theory of unconscious thought. *Perspectives on Psychological Science*, 1 (2), 95–109. DOI: 10.1111/j.1745-6916. 2006.00007.x.

Englich, B., & Mussweiler, T. (2001). Sentencing under uncertainty: Anchoring effects in the courtroom. *Journal of Applied Social Psychology*, 31, 1535–1551. *doi*:10.1111/j.1559-1816.2001.tb02687.x

Epley, N., & Gilovich, T. (2006). The anchoring-and-adjustment heuristic: Why the adjustments are insufficient. *Psychological Science*, 17 (4), 311–318. DOI: 10.1111/j.1467-9280.2006.01704.x.

Epley, N., & Gilovich, T. (2010). Anchoring unbound. *Journal of Consumer Psychology*, 20 (1), 20–24. DOI: 10.1016/j.jcps.2009.12.005.

Evans, J. St. B. T. (2003). In two minds: Dual process accounts of reasoning. *Trends in Cognitive Sciences*, 7 (10), 454–459. *DOI*: 10.1016/j.tics.2003.08.012.

Fiedler, K. (2008). The ultimate sampling dilemma in experience-based decision making. *Journal of Experimental Psychology: Learning, Memory, and Cognition*, 34 (1), 186–203. DOI: 10.1037/0278-7393.34.1.186.

Fiedler, K. (2010). How to study cognitive decision algorithms: The case of the priority heuristic. *Judgment and Decision Making*, 5 (1), 21–32.

Fiedler, K., & Juslin, P. (2006). *Information sampling and adaptive cognition*. New York: Cambridge University Press.

Fiedler, K., Schmid, J., Kurzenhaeuser, S., & Schroeter, V. (2000). Lie detection as an attribution process: The anchoring effect revisited. In V. De Pascalis, V. Gheorghiu, P. W. Sheehan, & I. Kirsch (Eds.), *Suggestion and suggestibility: Advances in theory and research* (pp. 113–136). Munich: M. E. G. Stiftung.

Fisk, J. E. (1996). The conjunction effect: Fallacy or Bayesian inference? *Organizational Behavior and Human Decision Processes*, 67, 76–90. *DOI*: 10.1006/obhd.1996.0066.

Fisk, J. E., & Slattery, R. (2005). Reasoning about conjunctive probabilistic concepts in childhood. *Canadian Journal of Experimental Psychology*, 59, 168–178.

Gigerenzer, G. (1991a). From tools to theories: A heuristic of discovery in cognitive psychology. *Psychological Review*, 98 (2), 254–267. DOI: 10.1037/0033-295X .98.2.254.

Gigerenzer, G. (1991b). How to make cognitive illusions disappear: Beyond 'heuristics and biases'. In W. Stroebe & M. Hewstone (Eds.), *European review of social psychology* (Vol. 2, pp. 83–115). Chichester, UK: Wiley.

Gigerenzer, G. (1996). On narrow norms and vague heuristics: A reply to Kahneman and Tversky. *Psychological Review*, 103 (3), 592–596. DOI: 10.1037/0033-295X.103.3.592.

Gigerenzer, G. (2006). Bounded and rational. In R. J. Stainton (Ed.), *Contemporary debates in cognitive science* (pp. 115–133). Oxford, UK: Blackwell.

Gigerenzer, G., & Goldstein, D. G. (1996). Reasoning the fast and frugal way: Models of bounded rationality. *Psychological Review*, 103 (4), 650–669. DOI: 10.1037/0033-295X.103.4.650.

Gigerenzer, G., & Todd, P. M. (1999). *Simple heuristics that make us smart*. New York: Oxford University Press.

Gigerenzer, G., Gaissmaier, W., Kurz-Milcke, E., Schwartz, L. M., & Woloshin, S. (2007). Helping doctors and patients make sense of health statistics. *Psychological Science in the Public Interest*, 8 (2), 53–96. DOI: 10.1111/j.1539-6053.2008.00033.x.

Gilovich, T., Griffin, D., & Kahneman, D. (2002). *Heuristics and biases: The psychology of intuitive judgment*. New York: Cambridge University Press.

Goldstein, D. G., & Gigerenzer, G. (2002). Models of ecological rationality: The recognition heuristic. *Psychological Review*, 109 (1), 75–90. DOI: 10.1037/0033-295X.109.1.75.

Hertwig, R., & Chase, V. M. (1998). Many reasons or just one: How response mode affects reasoning in the conjunction problem. *Thinking and Reasoning*, 4, 319–352. DOI: 10.1080/135467898394102.

Hertwig, R., Benz, B., & Krauss, B. S. (2008). The conjunction fallacy and the many meanings of *and*. *Cognition*, 108, 740–753. DOI: 10.1016/j.cognition.2008.06.008.

Hilbig, B. E. (2010). Reconsidering 'evidence' for fast-and-frugal heuristics. *Psychonomic Bulletin & Review*, 17 (6), 923–930. DOI: 10.3758/PBR.17.6.923.

Hilbig, B. E., Erdfelder, E., & Pohl, R. F. (2010). One-reason decision-making unveiled: A measurement model of the recognition heuristic. *Journal of Experimental Psychology: Learning, Memory, and Cognition*, 36 (1), 123–134. DOI: 10.1037/a0022638.

Jenny, M. A., Rieskamp, J., & Nilsson, H. (2014). Inferring conjunctive probabilities from experienced noisy samples: Evidence from the configural weighted average model. *Journal of Experimental Psychology: Learning, Memory, and Cognition*, 40, 203–217. DOI: 10.1037/a0034261.

Jones, E. E., Kanouse, D. E., Kelley, H. H., Nisbett, R. E., Valins, S., & Weiner, B. (1987). *Attribution: Perceiving the causes of behavior*. Hillsdale, NJ: Lawrence Erlbaum Associates.

Kahneman, D., & Frederick, S. (2002). Representativeness revised: Attribute substitution in intuitive judgment. In T. Gilovich, D. Griffin, & D. Kahneman (Eds.), *Heuristics and biases: The psychology of intuitive judgement* (pp. 49–81). Cambridge, UK: Cambridge University Press.

Kahneman, D., & Frederick, S. (2005). A model of heuristic judgment. In K. J. Holyoak & R. G. Morrison (Eds.), *The Cambridge handbook of thinking and reasoning* (pp. 267–293). New York: Cambridge University Press.

Kahneman, D., & Tversky, A. (1972). Subjective probability: A judgment of represen-tativeness. *Cognitive Psychology*, 3, 430–454. DOI: 1016/0010-0285(72)90016-3.

Kahneman, D., & Tversky, A. (1979). Prospect theory: An analysis of decision under risk. *Econometrica*, 47, 263–291. DOI: 10.2307/1914185.

Keren, G., & Schul, Y. (2009). Two is not always better than one: A critical evaluation of two-system theories. *Perspectives on Psychological Science*, 4, 533–550. DOI: 10.1111/j.1745-6924.2009.01164.x.

Krueger, J. I., & Funder, D. C. (2004). Towards a balanced social psychology: Causes, consequences, and cures for the problem-seeking approach to social behavior and cog-nition. *Behavioral and Brain Sciences*, 27, 313–327. DOI: 10.1017/S0140525X04000081.

Kruglanski, A. W., & Thompson, E. P. (1999). Persuasion by a single route: A view from the unimodel. *Psychological Inquiry*, 10(2), 83–109. DOI: 10.1207/S15327965PL100201.

Kuhn, T. S. (1962). *The structure of scientific revolutions*. Chicago, IL: University of Chicago Press.

Le Mens, G., & Denrell, J. (2011). Rational learning and information sampling: On the 'naivety' assumption in sampling explanations of judgment biases. *Psychological Review*, 118 (2), 379–392. DOI: 10.1037/a0023010.

Lopes, L. L., & Oden, G. C. (1991). The rationality of intelligence. In E. Eells & T. Maruszewski (Eds.), *Rationality and reasoning: Essays in honor of L. J. Cohen* (pp. 199–223). Amsterdam: Rodopi.

Martignon, L., Katsikopoulos, K. V., & Woike, J. K. (2008). Categorization with limited resources: A family of simple heuristics. *Journal of Mathematical Psychology*, 52 (6), 352–361. DOI: 10.1016/j.jmp.2008.04.003.

Mussweiler, T. (2003). Comparison processes in social judgment: Mechanisms and con-sequences. *Psychological Review*, 110, 472–489. DOI: 10.1037/0033-295X.110.3.472.

Nilsson, H., Olsson, H., & Juslin, P. (2005). The cognitive substrate of subjective prob-ability. *Journal of Experimental Psychology: Learning, Memory, and Cognition*, 31 (4), 600–620. DOI:10.1037/0278-7393.31.4.600.

Nisbett, R. E., & Ross, L. (1980). *Human inference: Strategies and shortcomings of social judgment*. Englewood Cliffs, NJ: Prentice-Hall.

Oppenheimer, D. M., LeBoeuf, R. A., & Brewer, N. T. (2008). Anchors aweigh: A demon-stration of cross-modality anchoring and magnitude priming. *Cognition*, 106 (1), 13–26. DOI: 10.1016/j.cognition.2006.12.008.

Osman, M. (2004). An evaluation of dual-process theories of reasoning. *Psychonomic Bulletin & Review*, 11, 988–1010. DOI: 10.3758/BF03196730.

Pachur, Th., Todd, P. M., Gigerenzer, G., Schooler, L. J., & Goldstein, G. (2011). The recognition heuristic: A review of theory and tests. *Frontiers in Psychology*, 2, 1–14. DOI: 10.3389/fpsyg.2011.00147.

Petty, R. E., & Cacioppo, J. T. (1986). *Communication and persuasion: Central and peripheral routes to attitude change*. New York: Springer-Verlag.

Plous, S. (1989). Thinking the unthinkable: The effect of anchoring on likelihood esti-mates of nuclear war. *Journal of Applied Social Psychology*, 19, 67–91.

Pohl, R. F. (2011). On the use of recognition in inferential decision making: An over-view of the debate. *Judgment and Decision Making*, 6 (5), 423–438.

Ritov, I. (1996). Anchoring in simulated competitive market negotiation. *Organizational Behavior and Human Decision Processes*, 67 (1), 16–25. DOI: 10.1006/obhd.1996.0062.

Ross, L. (1977). The intuitive psychologist and his shortcomings: Distortions in the attribution process. In L. Berkowitz (Ed.), *Advances in experimental social psychology* (Vol. 10, pp. 173–220). New York: Academic Press.

Ross, M., & Sicoly, F. (1979). Egocentric biases in availability and attribution. *Journal of Personality and Social Psychology*, 37 (3), 322–336. DOI: 10.1037/0022-3514.37.3.322.

Simon, H. A. (1982). *Models of bounded rationality*. Cambridge, MA: The MIT Press.

Sloman, S. A. (1996). The empirical case for two systems of reasoning. *Psychological Bulletin*, 119 (1), 3–22. DOI: 10.1037/0033-2909.119.1.3.

Smith, E. R., & DeCoster, J. (2000). Dual-process models in social and cognitive psychology: Conceptual integration and links to underlying memory systems. *Personality and Social Psychology Review*, 4, 108–131. DOI: 10.1207/S15327957PSPR0402_01.

Stanovich, K. E., & West, R. F. (2002). Individual differences in reasoning: Implications for the rationality debate? In T. Gilovich, D. Griffin, & D. Kahneman (Eds.), *Heuristics and biases: The psychology of intuitive judgment* (pp. 421–440). New York: Cambridge University Press.

Stanovich, K. E., & West, R. F. (2008). On the relative independence of thinking biases and cognitive ability. *Journal of Personality and Social Psychology*, 94, 672–695. DOI: 10.1037/0022-3514.94.4.672.

Strack, F., & Deutsch, R. (2004). Reflective and impulsive determinants of social behavior. *Personality and Social Psychology Review*, 8 (3), 220–247. DOI: 10.1207/s15327957pspr0803_1.

Strack, F., & Mussweiler, T. (1997). Explaining the enigmatic anchoring effect: Mechanisms of selective accessibility. *Journal of Personality and Social Psychology*, 73, 437–446. DOI: 10.1037/0022-3514.73.3.437.

Swets, J., Dawes, R. M., & Monahan, J. (2000). Psychological science can improve diagnostic decisions. *Psychological Science in the Public Interest*, 1 (Whole No. 1).

Tentori, K., Crupi, V., & Russo, S. (2013). On the determinants of the conjunction fallacy: Probability versus inductive confirmation. *Journal of Experimental Psychology: General*, 142 (1), 235–255. DOI: 10.1037/a0028770.

Tversky, A., & Kahneman, D. (1973). Availability: A heuristic for judging frequency and probability. *Cognitive Psychology*, 5 (2), 207–232. DOI: 10.1016/0010-0285(73)90033-9.

Tversky, A., & Kahneman, D. (1974). Judgment under uncertainty: Heuristics and biases. *Science*, 185, 1124–1130. *DOI: 10.1126/science.185.4157.1124.*

Tversky, A., & Kahneman, D. (1983). Extensional versus intuitive reasoning: The conjunction fallacy in probability judgment. *Psychological Review*, 90, 293–315. DOI: 10.1037/0033-295X.90.4.293.

Unkelbach, C., & Greifeneder, R. (Eds.) (2013). *The experience of thinking: How the fluency of mental processes influences cognition and behavior*. New York: Psychology Press.

von Sydow, M. (2011). The Bayesian logic of frequency-based conjunction fallacies. *Journal of Mathematical Psychology*, 55, 119–139. DOI: 10.1016/j.jmp.2010.12.001.

Winkielman, P., Schwarz, N., & Belli, R. F. (1998). The role of ease of retrieval and attribution in memory judgments: Judging your memory as worse despite recalling more events. *Psychological Science*, 9 (2), 124–126. DOI: 10.1111/1467-9280.00022.

Wolford, G. (1991). The conjunction fallacy? A reply to Bar-Hillel. *Memory & Cognition*, 19, 415–417.

Zuckerman, M., Koestner, R., Colella, M. J., & Alton, A. O. (1984). Anchoring in the detection of deception and leakage. *Journal of Personality and Social Psychology*, 47 (2), 301–311. DOI: 10.1037/0022-3514.47.2.301.

13

Decision making under risk: Beyond Kahneman and Tversky's (1979) prospect theory

Ben R. Newell (University of New South Wales, Australia)

BACKGROUND TO THE CLASSIC STUDY

DEFINING A DECISION UNDER RISK

On 24 June 2013 Nik Wallenda took what, for many of us, would be defined as an archetypal risky decision. He stepped out on to a 426-metre-long wire suspended 450 metres above the rocky floor of the Grand Canyon. He had no safety harness and no safety net. Twenty-two minutes and 54 seconds later, after being buffeted by gusty winds all the way across, he reached the end of the wire and the security of the other side. When asked about his amazing feat Nik said that his strong Christian faith allowed him to overcome any fear of dying: 'I know where I'm going to go when I die ... what I do is risky, and if I die, I have peace.' In deciding to step out on to the wire, Nik had presumably gone through a process of assessing the likelihood and value of success (the 'happiness' that achieving the walk would bring him) against the likelihood and (ultimate) cost of failure. This cost was not abstract: his father Kurt died from falling off a tightrope. Clearly, Nik's faith went a long way towards balancing out the potential gains and losses; for him it reduced the riskiness of the situation.

Most of us will never face a decision in which the consequences are as stark as those that faced Nik. Nonetheless, the process of evaluating the likelihood and value of potential outcomes is common to many of the decisions we face. A 'decision under risk' need not involve exposure to danger or harm. Rather, we can think of *risk* more generally as uncertainty about the amount you might gain or lose from making a particular choice. Whether it is the chicken or fish for dinner, the Toyota or the Volkswagen to drive, Rome or Barcelona for a holiday, decisions can be construed as an attempt to assess probabilities associated with different options and choose what is best given the situation.

But how do we know which option is 'best'? Early attempts to formalise a 'decision-quality-benchmark' can be traced to an exchange of letters between Blaise

Pascal and Pierre Fermat, two seventeenth-century French mathematicians with a keen interest in gambling. Their discussions of the gambling game 'points' led to the concept of *mathematical expectation*, which at the time was thought to be the essence of a *rational choice* (see Hacking, 1975; Hertwig, Barron, Weber, & Erev, 2004). Put simply, a choice was thought to be rational if it maximised the *expected value* for the decision maker. Expected value is defined as the sum of the products of the probability of each outcome and the value of that outcome (typically a monetary outcome) for all possible outcomes of a given alternative.

A simple example makes this idea concrete. Consider the expected value of an even-money gamble on rolling 'snake eyes' (a 1 on each of a pair of six-sided dice). Throwing such a pair of dice yields 36 possible outcomes and 'snake eyes' is just one outcome out of that set. With a $100 stake, the calculation of expected value is $(1/36 \times \$100) + (35/36 \times \$0) = \$2.70$. Because this expected value ($2.70) is considerably less than the cost of the stake ($100), it is clearly a poor gamble. Defined this way, expected value was thought to offer both a descriptive and prescriptive account of rationality, but it soon became clear that it was neither (Gigerenzer & Selten, 2001).

Early objections came from Nicolas Bernoulli, a Swiss mathematician, who proposed a monetary gamble, now known as the St Petersburg Paradox, as an example of how the notion of expected value failed to capture how people actually made choices. The St Petersburg example showed that people would be unwilling to pay more than a few dollars for a gamble with infinite expected value (see Newell, Lagnado, & Shanks, 2007). To accommodate this 'paradoxical' finding, Daniel Bernoulli (Nicolas's younger cousin) modified the theory by exchanging the notion of expected 'value' with expected 'utility'. The latter is a subjective construct that entails the evaluation of subjective values rather than actual monetary outcomes. The concept also incorporates an important caveat that is of high psychological relevance: the utility of money declines with increasing gains. Bernoulli (1738/1954) suggested that the relation between utility and monetary value could be captured by a logarithmic function.

Several centuries later von Neumann and Morgernstern (1947) published a theorem for assessing decision making according to the principle of maximising expected utility. They were interested in the mathematical rather than the behavioural implications of their theorem, but an added result of this axiomatisation of expected utility was that it provided researchers with a 'set of rules' for testing the rationality of people's choices. Thus, what began with Pascal's musings about how people should respond in various gambling situations grew into a fully-fledged theory of rational choice. Savage (1954) developed von Neumann and Morgernstern's work further by incorporating the notion of subjectivity into the maximisation of expected utility. Savage proved that a person, whose choices satisfy all of the axioms of the theory, chooses as if she were maximising her expected utility while assigning subjective probabilities to the possible outcomes of a choice.

From the 1950s onwards Expected Utility Theory (EUT) became the dominant theory in the analysis of decision under risk, but it was not without its detractors.

Perhaps most prominent among them was Maurice Allais, who presented a simple yet compelling hypothetical example of how he proposed people's preferences would violate central axioms of EUT (Allais, 1953). Daniel Kahneman and Amos Tversky entered the fray in 1979, building on the theoretical work of Allais (1953), Markowitz (1952), Ellsberg (1961), and others, and presented a whole new series of experimental examples that highlighted the deficiencies of EUT as a descriptive model of human economic behaviour. They argued that these systematic violations were captured and explained by their new theory of choice: Prospect Theory.

DETAILS OF THE CLASSIC STUDY

WHAT IS PROSPECT THEORY?

The beauty of Kahneman and Tversky's 1979 paper (hereafter K&T) is that before introducing the new theory it takes the reader on a journey through several choice problems that provide persuasive challenges to the existing EUT model. Thus, by the time the reader reaches the theory, she is crying out to have these violations – which she has no doubt observed in her own preferences – explained to her. This method of presenting challenges reflects the research practice that Kahneman and Tversky adopted when carrying out this seminal work. Kahneman (2011, pp. 7, 10) recounts that 'Our research was a conversation ... we spent many days making up choice problems and examining whether our intuitive preferences conformed to the logic of choice'. When choices did not conform – and often they did not – they asked why, and through this inquisitorial process developed their alternative theory.

Each of the problems presented in the paper was designed to illustrate violations of EUT. It is beyond the scope of this chapter to examine all 14 choice problems presented in the original paper, so a subset that highlights some of the key points will be discussed here. We begin with a pair of problems that illustrate a violation of EUT first hypothesised by Allais (1953). The notation used to describe each problem follows that used by K&T: the outcomes were all hypothetical and described in terms of Israeli pounds (at the time of the experiments, 3000 Israeli pounds per month was the net median outcome); 0 outcomes were not provided. Thus Problem 1 (below) compares a .80 probability of winning 4000 (and an assumed .20 probability of getting nothing) with winning 3000 for certain (probability of 1.0). K&T described each option as a 'prospect', hence Prospect Theory. The *N* below each problem is the number of participants given each problem and the number in square brackets is the percentage of participants choosing each option; the asterisk indicates a statistically significant difference in proportions. To begin an examination of your own preferences, consider the pair of hypothetical choices offered in the following two problems:

Problem 1

A: (4000, .80) or B: (3000, 1.0)

N = 95 [20] [80]*

Problem 2

C: (4000, .20) or D: (3000, .25)

N = 95 [65]* [35]

What are your intuitive responses? If you are like the majority of people you prefer option B in Problem 1 but option C in Problem 2. Why? Option B in Problem 1 appears more attractive because it offers a *certain* outcome; K&T observed that people tend to overweight certain outcomes relative to merely probable ones – a *certainty effect*. In Problem 2, neither option provides a certain outcome, but the relatively small difference in probabilities appears to be offset by the relatively larger reward offered by option C, making it more preferable.

Why is this modal set of preferences irrational under EUT? A preference for B over A means that your expected utility for a value (U) of 3000 for sure is greater than your expected utility for a .8 chance of 4000 [U(3000) > .8 U(4000)]. A preference for C over D implies [.2 U(4000) > .25 U(3000)]. However, the substitution axiom of EUT states that if B is preferred to A, then this preference should be maintained provided the ratio of probabilities is constant. It can be seen that Problem 2 is simply a version of Problem 1 in which the probabilities of winning in each option have been divided by 4 (i.e., .80/4 = .2 and 1.0/4 = .25) – thus the ratios are constant, but preferences reverse, implying that one can simultaneously demonstrate [U(3000) > .8 U(4000)] and [U(3000) < .8 U(4000)] – a violation of the principle. As K&T noted: 'Apparently, reducing the probability of winning from 1.0 to .25 has a greater effect than the reduction from .8 to .2' (K&T, p. 266).

K&T then considered what happened to this certainty effect when the prospects involved losses rather than gains. Consider Problems 3 and 4, which are the same as 1 and 2 but now offer losses:

Problem 3

A: (−4000, .80) or B: (−3000, 1.0)

N = 95 [92]* [8]

Problem 4

C: (−4000, .20) or D: (−3000, .25)

N = 95 [42] [58]

The reversal in preferences as a function of outcome sign is striking, especially the comparison between Problems 1 and 3: a clear preference for the sure gain of 3000 is replaced by an overwhelming preference for a risky loss of 4000. This occurs despite the lower expected value of the risky loss (i.e.,−4000 × .80 = −3200 compared to −3000). K&T described these reversals as a *reflection effect* because preferences for positive prospects were the mirror image of those for negative prospects. The key insight here was that: 'the same psychological principle – the overweighting of certainty – favors risk aversion in the domain of gains and risk seeking in the domain of losses' (K&T, p. 269).

With the importance of certainty, and these differences in behaviour framed as losses and gains clearly illustrated, K&T set out to describe what they termed the *isolation effect*. Consider the following pair of problems, presented to two different groups of participants:

Problem 5

In addition to whatever you own, you have been given 1000. You are now asked to choose between:

A: (1000, .50) or B: (500, 1.0)

N = 70 [16] [84]*

Problem 6

In addition to whatever you own, you have been given 2000. You are now asked to choose between:

C: (−1000, .50) or D: (−500, 1.0)

N = 68 [69]* [31]

The first thing to notice here is a replication of the *reflection effect*: people are risk-averse when faced with gains – preferring the sure thing in Problem 5, but are attracted to the risk when faced with losses in Problem 6. But there is something else going on here too. The *final states of wealth* in the two problems are identical. This is the case because in Problem 6 you are given an additional 1000 (compared to Problem 5) to begin with, therefore the problems can be rewritten as:

A = (1000) + (1000 × .50) = 1500 and B = 1000 + 500 = 1500

C = (2000) − (1000 × .50) = 1500 and D = (2000-500) = 1500

And therefore:

A = (1000 × .50; 1000 × .50) = C and B = (1500) = D

The modal pattern of preferences suggests that participants do not take the initial bonus or windfall into account when evaluating the prospects, perhaps because it is common to both options in the problem. Thus, people *isolate* the aspects of the problems that differ and ignore those that are common. In essence, K&T explain the violation via an appeal to *changes in states of wealth* entailed by the different options rather than the final states of wealth, which are equivalent. The key idea here is that people perceive prospects as gains and losses relative to a neutral *reference point* that does not necessarily accommodate initial starting wealth.

Armed with these psychological insights, K&T then present their alternative theory. Prospect Theory is still deeply rooted in the underlying logic of EUT (i.e., maximising expectation), but proposes crucial modifications whereby both the utilities and probabilities of outcomes undergo systematic cognitive distortions. The theory comprises two phases: editing and evaluation. The editing phase proposes several cognitive operations (coding, combination, segregation, cancellation) which serve to reformulate options in order to make subsequent evaluation more straightforward. The isolation effect described in Problems 5 and 6 is an example of cancellation editing. As we shall see in the critique section, one of the critiques of Prospect Theory was that this editing phase was rather ill-specified and lacked parsimony. In contrast, the evaluation phase was much more thoroughly developed and presented two formal functions for explaining departures from standard EUT: the *value function* and the *weighting function*.

The value function attempted to explain how the 'objective' monetary utilities of outcomes are transformed into 'subjective' values. The function captures two principal features of people's choices illustrated in the gambles reviewed above: (1) people tend to evaluate prospects in terms of gains and losses relative to a neutral reference point; and (2) people tend to be risk-averse in the domain of gains and risk-seeking in the domain of losses. This leads to the S-shaped curve shown graphically in Figure 13.1. It has a concave function in the domain of gains (top-right quadrant), illustrating the diminishing marginal utility of gains (something that Bernoulli had noted with his proposed logarithmic utility function). A similar diminishing function is reflected in the convex shape of the curve for losses (bottom-left quadrant). The steeper line for losses below the midpoint (relative to that for gains directly above it) captures what is perhaps the most well-known aspect of Prospect Theory that: 'losses loom larger than gains' (K&T, p. 279) – the idea that the aggravation associated with a loss of $100 is greater than the pleasure associated with gaining the same amount. Specifically, K&T speculated that people would be reluctant to take a symmetric gamble with equal chances of winning and losing the same amount (e.g., $100, .50; -$100, .50) precisely because of their aversion to the loss.

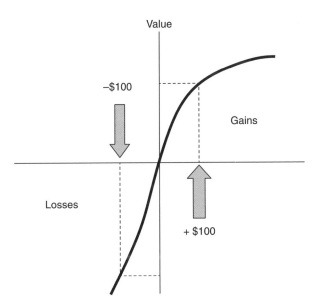

Figure 13.1 The value function of prospect theory. Adapted with permission from Figure 3 of Kahneman, D. and Tversky, A. (1979) Prospect theory: An analysis of decision under risk. *Econometrica* 47, 263–91. Copyright of the Econometric Society.

The weighting function explained how 'objective' probabilities of outcomes are transformed into subjective 'decision weights'. These weights are measures of the impact of events on the desirability of prospects rather than estimates of the pure likelihood of those events. In order to capture the *certainty effect* (see Problems 1–4) K&T proposed that this weighting function would not be 'well behaved' near the end points (low or high probabilities). They also illustrated with this final example how low probabilities in general tend to be *over-weighted* relative to their objective probability.

Problem 7

A: (5000, .001) or B: (5, 1.0)

N = 72 [72]* [28]

Problem 8

C: (–5000, .001) or D: (–5, 1.0)

N = 72 [17] [83]*

The overwhelming preference for the low-probability gain in Problem 7 shows that people weight the probability of a large gain more highly than the expected value of the prospect – this is in effect what people do when buying lottery tickets. In contrast, in Problem 8 the preference reverses: people prefer to take the sure loss than risk the large one – this is akin to paying insurance premiums (see also Markowitz, 1952). Note that this pattern of preferences is the reverse of what was observed in Problems 5 and 6: when very low probabilities are involved, people are risk-seeking in the domain of *gains* and risk-averse in the domain of *losses*. Taken together these patterns of preferences led to the weighting function depicted in Figure 13.2. Its key

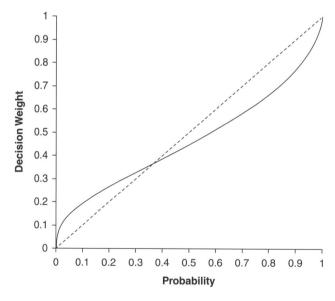

Figure 13.2 The weighting function of prospect theory. Adapted with permission from Figure 4 of Kahneman, D. and Tversky, A. (1979) Prospect theory: An analysis of decision under risk. *Econometrica* 47, 263–91. Copyright of the Econometric Society.

Table 13.1   The fourfold pattern of choice that prospect theory can explain

	Gains	Losses
Small probabilities	Risk-seeking	Risk-aversion
Medium and large probabilities	Risk-aversion	Risk-seeking

features are the overweighting of small probabilities, the underweighting of moderate to large probabilities, and extreme behaviour close to zero or one.

In summary, Prospect Theory retains the assumption of EUT that 'things' are multiplied in order to maximise expectation, but rather than those 'things' being objective utilities and probabilities, they are subjective values and decision weights. In doing so, the theory captures what has become known as the fourfold pattern of choice behaviour illustrated in the gamble problems considered here and summarised in Table 13.1.

IMPACT OF THE CLASSIC STUDY

Perhaps the most salient impact of Prospect Theory was the award of the Nobel Prize for Economics to Daniel Kahneman in 2002. The dedication acknowledged the joint contribution of the late Amos Tversky and Kahneman 'for having integrated insights from psychological research into economic science, especially concerning human judgment and decision-making under uncertainty'. The theory was so influential because it offered perhaps the first really compelling alternative to the standard 'rational agent' model of decision under risk so beloved by economists. A measurable impact of the paper is its citation count: somewhere between 9,000 (*Web of Science*, 24/9/13) and 27,000 (*Google Scholar*, 24/9/13) citations since its publication in 1979. The profound impact on economics was driven in large part by the fact that the paper was published in a leading economics journal (*Econometrica*) rather than a psychology one. This ensured that both psychologists, who were already familiar with Tversky and Kahneman's work on judgment (see Chapter 12), and economists took notice of the paper. The work inspired many researchers from both disciplines to refine, build on, and develop satisfactory *psychological* accounts of decision making under risk (e.g., Kahneman & Tversky, 2000).

Camerer (2000) discusses several examples in which the predictions of Prospect Theory appear to receive support from observations in the field that go beyond the hypothetical gambles offered to participants in the lab. For example, an oft-noticed effect in US race-track betting is the 'end-of-the-day-effect' whereby punters shift bets towards longshots and away from favourites as the racing day unfolds. This shift occurs because by the end of the day punters are typically out of pocket and are looking to cover their losses – to break even. Camerer argues that such behaviour is consistent with the setting of a zero profit 'reference point' for the day, and thus turning to greater risk-seeking as one moves further into the domain of losses. In a different gambling context, Smith, Levere, and Kurtzman

(2009) also found evidence for a 'break-even' hypothesis. Smith et al. analysed strategies of over 2,000 online poker players and found that players played noticeably less cautiously after experiencing a big loss. Much like the race-track bettors wanting the longshot to win, poker players appear to put false hope in receiving lucky cards in order to recoup earlier losses and maintain a break-even reference point. In a very different domain, Pope and Schweitzer (2011) argue that a key tenet of Prospect Theory – loss aversion – is observed in the putting performance of professional golfers. In an analysis of 2.5 million putts, Pope and Schweitzer demonstrate that when golfers make 'birdie' putts (ones that would place them 1 point below par for the hole – a desirable result) they are significantly less accurate than when shooting comparable putts for par. Such behaviour is interpreted as loss aversion because missing par (taking more shots to complete a hole than one 'should') is recorded as a loss relative to the normative 'par' reference point and thus golfers focus more when they are faced with a putt to maintain par.

Although debate remains about the prominence and relevance of biases seen in the lab for behaviour observed in the real world (e.g., Levitt & List, 2008), the work on Prospect Theory is credited as the watershed for the discipline now known as behavioural economics. Behavioural economics – the study of _human_ economic behaviour, as opposed to that of a strictly rational economic agent – is currently enjoying a heyday. Several governments (the USA, the UK, Australia) are seeking policy advice from psychologists and economists who have developed behavioural 'nudges' based on simple insights about people's reactions to gains and losses, evaluations relative to reference points and the desire for the status quo – all implications of Prospect Theory (e.g., John et al., 2011; Thaler & Sunstein, 2008). Thus the impact of Prospect Theory both within and without the ivory towers of academia cannot be overstated.

CRITIQUE OF THE CLASSIC STUDY

A major aspect of Prospect Theory is the editing phase in which the decision maker constructs a representation of the options, probabilities, and outcomes that are relevant to a particular decision. Although candidate processes and heuristics were proposed for how such editing took place, the ideas remain rather unconstrained and in some cases appear to lead to unsupported predictions about behaviour. Take, for example, the setting of the _reference point_ on the valuation scale. Prospect Theory assumes this reference point to be the status quo (no change) and it is typically assigned a subjective value of zero. However, this assumption will not always hold and can be affected by the context in which options are presented. Kahneman (2011) offers the following illustration:

Problem 9

A: one chance in a million to win $1 million

B: 90% chance to win $12 and a 10% chance to win nothing

C: 90% chance to win $1 million and a 10% chance to win nothing

Although winning nothing is a possibility common to all three options, such an outcome would be felt much more intensely in Option C than it would in A and B. Thus assuming that winning nothing is the reference point and assigning it a zero value in all three options – as Prospect Theory would – seems demonstrably at odds with our intuitions. Such context-dependent shifts in the reference point are even more apparent in decisions involving multiple possible outcomes. Consider the gambles offered in Problem 10 (adapted from Lopes & Oden, 1999):

Problem 10

A: ($200, .04; $150, .21; $100, .50; $50, .21; $0, .04)

B: ($200, .20; $150, .20; $100, .20; $50, .20; $0, .20)

What seems to happen in these situations is that people evaluate prospects in terms of their *ranks*, that is, what is the *best* I can get, the *second best*, *third best*, and so on. Thus someone might prefer A because it offers higher odds of winning at least something (i.e., the .50 for $100) and low odds of winning nothing (i.e., the .04 for $0) even though the odds of winning the highest amount ($200) are lower than in option B. (Note that the expected value of A and B is identical: $100). Such behaviour is indicative of labile reference points and the joint notions of an 'aspiration level' ('What is the best I can get?') and a 'security level' ('What is the chance that I will lose $X or more?'). More broadly, this idea of 'rank dependence' is included in several alternative psychological models of decision under risk (e.g., Birnbaum, 2004, 2008; Lopes & Oden, 1999). These models also often incorporate the related idea that people treat probabilities cumulatively rather than independently. The original formulation of Prospect Theory proposed that people assess the probability of each outcome independently. However, examples like Problem 10 suggest that when faced with multiple option gambles, people evaluate the cumulative probability of winning *at least something* given the available options. In essence, these models have a weighting function that applies to the cumulative probability of doing as well or better than an outcome. Tversky and Kahneman (1992) included such a function in their own *cumulative* version of prospect theory (CPT), and such functions also feature in several other models, such as Birnbaum's (2004, 2008) transfer of attention exchange (TAX) and Lopes and Oden's (1999) security-potential aspiration model (S/PA), both of which, under certain circumstances, provide better accounts of decisions under risk than either the original or the cumulative versions of Prospect Theory (e.g., Birnbaum, 2008; Lopes & Oden, 1999).

An additional insight from thinking about people's aspirations when making choices is the potential *emotional* impact of different outcomes. Specifically, several researchers have argued that prospect theory fails to incorporate notions of *regret* and *rejoicing* (e.g., Bell, 1982; Loomes & Sugden, 1982; Starmer, 2000; see also Mellers, Schwartz, Ho, & Ritov, 1997). If a decision turns out badly (the outcome seems worse than other possible outcomes), we suffer more than just the disutility of the outcome – we also regret the decision. Similarly, if a decision leads to an outcome that seems better than other alternatives, we appear to revel or rejoice in the outcome, over and above the simple utility associated with that gain. Theories that attempt to account for such patterns have been useful in advancing our thinking about decisions under risk, but notions of regret and rejoice seem insufficient for providing a full account of choice behaviour, particularly as such theories often do not make predictions that diverge from those of prospect theory (Baron, 2008; Kahneman, 2011; Newell et al., 2007; although see Rottenstreich and Hsee (2001) and McGraw, Shafir, & Todorov (2010) for discussions of when and how emotional outcomes might lead to divergent predictions).

The influence of Prospect Theory is also highly apparent with the resurgence of interest in the last 10 years or so into what has been termed 'decisions from experience' (Barron & Erev, 2003; Camilleri & Newell, 2011; Hertwig et al., 2004; Rakow & Newell, 2010). Prospect Theory was proposed for choices in which outcomes and probabilities are clearly stated (or described) to participants. For example, in Problem 1 above there is no ambiguity about the prospects on offer. In contrast to these described problems, many of the decisions we commonly face do not have a convenient look-up table of relevant probabilities and unambiguous outcomes (cf. Knight, 1921). Recall Nik Wallenda and his tightrope walk: the probability of success was something he needed to determine based on his *experience* in similar situations; it was not something he could look up in a book. One of the reasons such 'decisions from experience' have garnered so much attention is that when people are forced to learn about probabilities and outcomes from experience, choices often diverge markedly from the predictions of Prospect Theory.

The standard 'decision from experience' experiment is very simple: participants are presented with two unlabelled buttons on a computer screen and are asked to click on either one on each trial of a multi-trial experiment. A click on the button reveals an outcome which the participant then receives; the probability of the outcome occurring is pre-programmed by the experimenter but the participant does not know what the probability is – she has to learn from experience. Thus an experience version of Problem 1 would have two buttons, one paying out 3000 every time it is clicked and the other 4000 on 80% of clicks and 0 on 20%. Recall that when Problem 1 is presented in a described format, the overwhelming preference is for the certain reward (3000). What happens when the same problem is learned from feedback? Contrary to the dictates of the *certainty effect*, participants now come to prefer the 4000 button (Barron & Erev, 2003). Furthermore, if the prospects are converted into losses, so now one button offers -3000 on every click and the other -4000 on 80% of clicks, participants learn to prefer the certain loss of 3000. In other words, under experience there is a striking reversal of the *certainty effect* and participants appear to be risk-seeking in the domain of gains and risk-averse in the domain of losses – the opposite of what Prospect Theory predicts. One way to explain this pattern is by assuming that people tend to *under*weight the smaller (i.e., 20%) probability of getting nothing in the gain frame – leading to a choice of the 4000, .80 – and similarly *under*weight the smaller possibility (20%) of losing nothing in the loss frame – leading to a choice of the –3000. In essence, where Prospect Theory predicts *over*weighting, we see *under*weighting.

Despite the fact that the underweighting pattern is very strong in decisions from experience, the reason for its presence is still not completely understood. Current explanations range from the feedback having a 'diffusing' effect that lessens the 'threat' of low probability negative events (e.g., Barron, Leider, & Stack, 2008) to the possibility that repeated feedback reduces attention to individual choices (e.g., Yechiam, Erev, & Barron, 2006). Some researchers have tried to examine the reasons why decisions from experience and description diverge (the so-called 'description–experience gap'; Hertwig & Erev, 2009; Rakow & Newell, 2010) by disentangling the choice and information acquisition aspects inherent in an experience-based choice. In Barron and Erev's (2003) task, the only way to learn about an option is to choose it, even if one fears this choice is sub-optimal. Therefore, the description–experience gap may emerge because description permits a 'pure' choice, whereas experience requires a different pattern of 'choice' in order to learn about the options.

In an effort to overcome this issue, Hertwig et al. (2004) divided experiments into a sampling and a choice phase. In the sampling phase, participants could click on either button as many times as they liked in order to discover what each option offered – but these samples did not affect their overall payment. Payment was determined in the subsequent 'choice' phase, in which participants clicked on their preferred option to play 'for real' and receive the payoff. This sampling paradigm dissociates exploration (finding out about options) from exploitation (choosing an option for reward) – the two aspects which are intertwined in the feedback paradigm. Intriguingly, even under these sampling conditions a large 'gap' between experience and description was observed. This finding led Hertwig et al. (2004) to call for a new theory of risky choice because Prospect Theory is unable to explain the observed pattern of choices.

Whether such a new theory is actually required has been the subject of much recent debate. Several researchers have investigated when, why, and how decisions from description and experience diverge and various explanations have been offered for the 'gap' (e.g., Camilleri & Newell, 2011, 2013; Fox & Hadar, 2006; Hau, Pleskac, & Hertwig, 2010; Rakow, Demes, & Newell, 2008; Ungemach, Stewart & Chater, 2009). While a consensus may not yet have been reached, the 'new' focus on experience-based decision making is a welcome return to questions that vexed researchers from the 1930s to the 1960s (e.g., when and why do people maximise versus probability match: Goodnow, 1955; Humphreys, 1939; Peterson & Ulehla, 1965). However, far from a regress, bringing the roles of experience, sampling, memory, and learning to the fore further facilitates the integration of 'typical' judgment and decision-making phenomena with related areas in cognitive psychology (cf. Bröder & Newell, 2008; Weber & Johnson, 2009). Thus although decisions from experience initially caught people's attention because they showed patterns of choice at odds with Prospect Theory, their study has gone far beyond this observation and opened the door to a rich repertoire of fundamental theoretical issues.

CONCLUSIONS

How Prospect Theory advanced thinking and how thinking has subsequently advanced

The principal contribution of Prospect Theory to the analysis of decision under risk is that it offers a viable alternative to Expected Utility Theory, a theory that had been so dominant for so long. Prospect Theory is viable and plausible because it captures – and predicts – several robust departures from EUT that only become apparent when one considers what people *actually* do rather than what they *should* do when faced with a risky choice. One of the simplest and most enduring messages is perhaps the influence of *framing* on people's decisions. The gamble problems, and even simple word problems, such as the famous Asian Disease problem (see Tversky & Kahneman, 1981), demonstrated the susceptibility of choice to frames that emphasised different aspects of a problem (e.g., gains versus losses, or lives *saved* versus lives *lost*). This insight that mathematical equivalence is not the same as psychological equivalence is very important, not least in situations in which people need to understand and communicate risk, for example, in medical settings (Li, Rakow, & Newell, 2009; McNeil, Pauker, Sox, & Tversky, 1982), in legal settings (Koehler, 2001), and in environmental settings (Newell & Pitman, 2010; Weber, 2006). Recent work has sought to clarify when and why asymmetric reactions to losses and gains are observed and suggest a more nuanced account of 'loss aversion' than that offered by Prospect Theory (Yechiam & Hochman, 2013).

The ways in which thinking has advanced since the publication of K&T are manifold. As discussed in the critique section, these range from models that incorporate ideas about cumulative probabilities and the role of emotions, to situations in which probabilities need to be learned via experience rather than description. There have also been attempts to understand better the *processes* people engage in when making decisions under risk. For example, the *Priority Heuristic* proposed by Brandstätter and colleagues seeks to explain risky choice via the adoption of simple rules for searching information, stopping search, and deciding, that do not involve the concept of value maximisation (Brandstätter, Hertwig, & Gigerenzer, 2006; but see Johnson, Schulte-Mecklenbeck, & Willemsen, 2008, for contrary evidence). In a similar, and perhaps even more radical vein, Stewart and colleagues have developed models that eschew completely the notion of underlying psycho-economic scales for utility (Stewart, 2009; Stewart, Chater, & Brown, 2006). Their decision-by-sampling account attempts to explain (rather than just describe) key phenomena like the certainty effect via an appeal to a series of binary ordinal comparisons with a sample of attribute values from the immediate context and from long-term memory. Such accounts question a central tenet of Prospect Theory, the idea that decision makers attempt to calculate value when choosing between options (Vlaev, Chater, Stewart, & Brown, 2011). It will be very interesting to see if this new class of 'comparison-only' models has the same impact and legacy on our understanding of decision under risk as Prospect Theory.

AUTHOR'S NOTE

Preparation of this chapter was supported by funding from the Australian Research Council (DP 110100797; FT110100151). I thank Adrian Camilleri, Sule Guney, Christin Schulze, David Groome, and Michael Eysenck for insightful comments on an earlier draft of the chapter.

FURTHER READING

Kahneman, D., & Tversky, A. (Eds.) (2000). *Choices, values, and frames.* Cambridge, UK: Cambridge University Press.

An edited collection of papers that brings together much of the work inspired by Prospect Theory.

Rakow, T., & Newell, B. R. (2010). Degrees of uncertainty: An overview and framework for future research on experience-based choice. *Journal of Behavioral Decision Making, 23,* 1–14.

An introduction to the description–experience 'gap' in risky choice.

Thaler, R., & Sunstein, C. (2008). *Nudge: Improving decisions and about health, wealth and happiness.* London: Penguin.

An accessible account of how insights from behavioural economics can be used in policy development.

Vlaev, I., Chater, N., Stewart, N., & Brown, G. D. A. (2011). Does the brain calculate value? *Trends in Cognitive Science,* 15, 546–554.

A discussion of approaches that do and do not assume value calculation in decisions under risk.

REFERENCES

Allais, M. (1953). La psychologie de l'homme rationnel devant le risque: critique des postulats et axiomes de l'école Américaine. *Econometrica,* 21, 503–546.

Baron, J. (2008). *Thinking and deciding.* New York: Cambridge University Press.

Barron, G., & Erev, I. (2003). Small feedback-based decisions and their limited correspondence to description-based decisions. *Journal of Behavioral Decision Making,* 16, 215–233.

Barron, G., Leider, S., & Stack, J. (2008). The effect of safe experience on a warnings' impact: Sex, drugs, and rock-n-roll. *Organizational Behavior and Human Decision Processes,* 106, 125–142.

Bell, D. E. (1982). Regret in decision making under uncertainty. *Operations research,* 30 (5), 961–981.

Bernoulli, D. (1954). Exposition of a new theory on the measurement of risk. *Econometrica,* 22, 23-36. (Translation of Bernoulli, D. 1738. Specimen *theoriae novae de mensura sortis.* Papers Imp. Acad. Sci. St. Petersburg, 5, 175-192).

Birnbaum, M. H. (2004). Tests of rank-dependent utility and cumulative prospect theory in games represented by natural frequencies: Effects of format, event framing, and branch splitting. *Organizational Behavior and Human Decision Processes,* 95, 40–65.

Birnbaum, M. H. (2008). New paradoxes of risky decision making. *Psychological Review,* 115, 463–501.

Brandstätter, E., Gigerenzer, G., & Hertwig, R. (2006). The priority heuristic: Making choices without trade-offs. *Psychological Review*, 113, 409–432.

Bröder, A., & Newell, B. R. (2008). Challenging some common beliefs: Empirical work within the adaptive toolbox metaphor. *Judgment and Decision Making*, 3, 205–214.

Camerer, C. F. (2000). Prospect theory in the wild: Evidence from the field. In D. Kahneman & A. Tversky (Eds.), *Choices, values, and frames*. Cambridge, UK: Cambridge University Press.

Camilleri, A. R., & Newell, B. R. (2011). When and why rare events are underweighted: A direct comparison of the sampling, partial feedback, full feedback and description choice paradigms. *Psychonomic Bulletin & Review*, 18, 377–384.

Camilleri, A. R., & Newell, B. R. (2013). Mind the gap? Description, experience, and the continuum of uncertainty in risky choice. *Decision making: Neural and behavioural approaches – progress in brain research*. Oxford, UK: Elsevier.

Ellsberg, D. (1961). Risk, ambiguity and the Savage axioms. *Quarterly Journal of Economics*, 75, 643–679.

Fox, C. R., & Hadar, L. (2006). 'Decisions from experience' = sampling error + prospect theory: Reconsidering Herwig, Barron, Weber & Erev (2004). *Judgment and Decision Making*, 1, 159–161.

Gigerenzer, G., & Selten, R. (2001). Rethinking rationality. In G. Gigerenzer & R. Selten (Eds.), *Bounded rationality: The adaptive toolbox* (pp. 1–12). Cambridge, MA: The MIT Press.

Goodnow, J. J. (1955). Determinants of choice-distribution in two-choice situations. *The American Journal of Psychology*, 68, 106–116.

Hacking, I. (1975). *The emergence of probability: A philosophical study of early ideas about probability, induction and statistical inference*. Cambridge, UK: Cambridge University Press.

Hau, R., Pleskac, T. J., & Hertwig, R. (2010). Decisions from experience and statistical probabilities: Why they trigger different choices than a priori probabilities. *Journal of Behavioral Decision Making*, 23, 48–68.

Hertwig, R., & Erev, I. (2009). The description–experience gap in risky choice. *Trends in Cognitive Science*, 13, 517–523.

Hertwig, R., Barron, G., Weber, E., & Erev, I. (2004). Decisions from experience and the effect of rare events, *Psychological Science*, 15, 534–539.

Humphreys, L. G. (1939). Acquisition and extinction of verbal expectations in a situation analogous to conditioning. *Journal of Experimental Psychology*, 25, 294–301.

John, P., Cotterill, S., Moseley, A., Richardson, L., Smith, G., Stoker, G., & Wales, C. (2011). *Nudge, nudge, think, think: Experimenting with ways to change civic behaviour*. London: Bloomsbury Academic.

Johnson, E. J., Schulte-Mecklenbeck, M., & Willemsen, M. C. (2008). Process models deserve process data: Comment on Brandstätter, Gigerenzer and Hertwig (2006). *Psychological Review*, 115, 263–272.

Kahneman, D. (2011). *Thinking, fast and slow*. Basingstoke: Macmillan.

Kahneman, D., & Tversky, A. (1979). Prospect theory: An analysis of decision under risk, *Econometrica*, 47, 263–291.

Kahneman, D., & Tversky, A. (2000). *Choices, values, and frames*. Cambridge, UK: Cambridge University Press.

Knight, F. H. (1921). *Risk, uncertainty and profit*. New York: Hart, Schaffner and Marx.

Koehler, J. J. (2001). When are people persuaded by DNA match statistics? *Law and Human Behavior*, 25, 493–513.

Levitt, S. D., & List, J. A. (2008). Homo Economicus evolves. *Science*, 319 (5865), 909–910.

Li, S. Y. W., Rakow, T., & Newell, B. R. (2009). Personal experience in doctor and patient decision making: From psychology to medicine. *Journal of Evaluation in Clinical Practice*, 15, 993–995.

Loomes, G., & Sugden, R. (1982). Regret theory: An alternative theory of rational choice under uncertainty. *Economic Journal*, 92, 805–824.

Lopes, L. L., & Oden, G. C. (1999). The role of aspiration level in risky choice: A comparison of cumulative prospect theory and SP/A theory. *Journal of Mathematical Psychology*, 43, 286–313.

Markowitz, H. (1952). The utility of wealth. *Journal of Political Economy*, 60, 151–158.

McGraw, A. P., Shafir, E., & Todorov, A. (2010). Valuing money and things: Why a $20 item can be worth more and less than $20. *Management Science*, 56, 816–830.

McNeil, B. J., Pauker, S. G., Sox, H. C., & Tversky, A. (1982). On the elicitation of preferences for alternative therapies. *New England Journal of Medicine*, 306, 1259–1262.

Mellers, B. A., Schwartz, A., Ho, K., & Ritov, I. (1997). Decision affect theory: Emotional reactions to the outcomes of risky options. *Psychological Science*, 8, 423–429.

Newell, B. R., & Pitman, A. J. (2010). The psychology of global warming: Improving the fit between the science and the message. *Bulletin of the American Meteorological Society*, 91, 1003–1014.

Newell, B. R., Lagnado, D. A., & Shanks, D. R. (2007). *Straight choices: The psychology of decision making*. Hove, UK: Psychology Press.

Peterson, C. R., & Ulehla, Z. J. (1965). Sequential patterns and maximizing. *Journal of Experimental Psychology*, 69, 1–4.

Pope, D., & Schweitzer, M. (2011). Is Tiger Woods loss averse? Persistent bias in the face of experience, competition and high stakes. *American Economic Review*, 101, 129–157.

Rakow, T., & Newell, B. R. (2010). Degrees of uncertainty: An overview and framework for future research on experience-based choice. *Journal of Behavioral Decision Making*, 23, 1–14.

Rakow, T., Demes, K. A., & Newell, B. R. (2008). Biased samples not mode of presentation: Re-examining the apparent underweighting of rare events in experience-based choice. *Organizational Behavior and Human Decision Processes*, 106, 168–179.

Rottenstreich, Y., & Hsee, C. K. (2001). Money, kisses, and electric shocks: On the affective psychology of risk. *Psychological Science*, 12, 185–190.

Savage, L. J. (1954). *The foundations of statistics*. New York: Wiley.

Smith, G., Levere, M., & Kurtzman, R. (2009). Poker player behavior after big wins and big losses. *Management Science*, 55, 1547–1555.

Starmer, C. (2000). Developments in non-expected utility theory: The hunt for a descriptive theory of choice under risk. *Journal of Economic Literature*, 38, 332–382.

Stewart, N. (2009). Decision by sampling: The role of the decision environment in risky choice. *The Quarterly Journal of Experimental Psychology*, 62, 1041–1062.

Stewart, N., Chater, N., & Brown, G. D. A. (2006). Decision by sampling. *Cognitive Psychology*, 53, 1–26.

Thaler, R. H., & Sunstein, C. R. (2008). *Nudge: Improving decisions about health, wealth, and happiness*. New Haven, CT: Yale University Press.

Tversky, A., & Kahneman, D. (1981). The framing of decisions and the psychology of choice. *Science*, 211, 453–458.

Tversky, A., & Kahneman, D. (1992). Advances in prospect theory: Cumulative representation of uncertainty. *Journal of Risk and Uncertainty*, 5, 297–323.

Ungemach, C., Chater, N., & Stewart, N. (2009). Are probabilities overweighted or underweighted when rare outcomes are experienced (rarely)? *Psychological Science*, 20, 473–479.

Vlaev, I., Chater, N., Stewart, N., & Brown, G. D. (2011). Does the brain calculate value? *Trends in Cognitive Sciences*, 15, 546–554.

von Neumann, J., & Morgernstern, O. (1947). *Theory of games and economic behaviour* (2nd edn). Princeton, NJ: Princeton University Press.

Weber, E. U. (2006). Experience-based and description-based perceptions of long-term risk: Why global warming does not scare us (yet). *Climatic Change*, 77, 103–120.

Weber, E. U., & Johnson, E. J. (2009). Mindful judgment and decision making. *Annual Review of Psychology*, 60, 53–85.

Yechiam, E., & Hochman, G. (2013). Losses as modulators of attention: Review and analysis of the unique effects of losses over gains. *Psychological Bulletin*, 139, 497–518.

Yechiam, E., Erev, I., & Barron, G. (2006). The effect of experience on using a safety device. *Safety Science*, 44, 515–522.

14

Language: Beyond Chomsky's (1957) syntactic structures

Trevor Harley (University of Dundee) and Siobhan MacAndrew (University of Abertay)

BACKGROUND TO THE CLASSIC STUDY

WHO KILLED PSYCHOLINGUISTICS? LET'S ALL BLAME CHOMSKY

It is rare for a book review to be more famous that the book upon which it is based, but such a situation arose with Noam Chomsky's (1959) review of B. F. Skinner's *Verbal Behavior* (1957). We can date the start of the cognitive revolution from around the time this review was published. Although Chomsky cannot take all the credit – the widening appeal of information theory and the rise of the computer were also important – his review did act as a manifesto for the emerging cognitive movement. In his review, the cracks of the foundations of behaviourism as a complete account of how the human mind works were exposed for all to see. In exposing these cracks, the research emphasis shifted from behaviour in general to language in particular. The book review punctuated a period framed by two extraordinarily influential books, *Syntactic structures* (1957) and *Aspects of the theory of syntax* (1965). The three works taken together provide a classic triptych of early cognitive science and a refutation of all approaches to cognition that ignore processes intervening between input and output, as well as completely redefining the discipline of linguistics. An unfortunate and presumably unintended side-effect was delaying the development of the scientific study of language processing: that is, of a subject we now call *psycholinguistics*.

It is, however, one thing to stipulate that there are processes intervening between stimulus and response, and quite another to specify what those processes might be. The problem of process under-specification has dogged cognitive models since their inception, and continues to do so. The difficulty surfaces explicitly from time to time. One criticism of many cognitive and neuropsychological models is that they are nothing more than 'boxology', naming magical boxes in a flow chart to carry out tasks between input and output.

DETAILED DESCRIPTION OF THE CLASSIC STUDY

The details of Chomsky's approach to language and psychology were first spelled out in detail in *Syntactic structures* (1957). The difference between Chomsky's work and what came before is of sufficient magnitude as to constitute the beginnings of a paradigm shift (Kuhn, 1962), and indeed a double paradigm shift, because it contributed to a major change of direction in both psychology and linguistics.

Psychology at the time was dominated by behaviourism and animal models of psychology. In the extreme behaviourism of Watson and Skinner, the mind was a construct best dispensed with. It could not be measured or observed, and, said the behaviourists, scientists should stick with the measurable and observable. Hence psychology was restricted to the measurement of stimulus and response and the connection between them. Skinner's classic book *Verbal Behavior* (1957) attempted to show how the same principles of operant conditioning that had been used to explain animal behaviour could be extended to account for language use and learning. Some aspects of the theory may seem derisory to us now (e.g., taking volume, speed, and repetition of speech as measures of language response strength), but in the context of the time they made perfect sense and formed a perfectly reasonable and respectable attempt to produce a mature theory of language.

Linguistics at much the same time was dominated by structuralism, exemplified by the work of Leonard Bloomfield and Zellig Harris. Structuralism emphasised the analysis of the units of language. Linguists collected bodies of language utterance known as corpora and analysed how utterances could be decomposed into smaller units, specifying the interconnection between these units. Linguists were also concerned with different languages and how these could be analysed, having moved on from the historical analysis of the relations between languages.

Chomsky's great contribution in *Syntactic structures* (1957) was to link psychology and linguistics, and to attempt to reveal underlying patterns in the structural description of language. In doing so, he specified an account of how sentences could be constructed by a grammar – hence the name *generative grammar* for this sort of approach. A very good example is that a sentence (S) can be formed (among many other ways) from a noun phrase (NP) and a verb phrase (VP); furthermore, in transitive sentences, the VP can be further decomposed into the verb and another noun phrase (the object). The noun phrase in turn can comprise a determiner (the, a, an, etc.) and noun. So, for example, we can have a sentence such as:

The aardvark chases the echidna.

represented by the units:

Determiner noun verb determiner noun

and importantly these units can then be grouped progressively in turn into:

NP V NP

NP VP

S

Not only have we produced a description of the *sentence*, we have produced a *structure*, and in doing so have shown how sentences can be generated by grammatical rules of the form, in this case:

S -> NP + VP

However, Chomsky argued that the power of the grammar limited to these sorts of rules was inadequate to account for the complexity and infinite nature of human language, and therefore that we needed to augment the power of the grammar. To this aim, Chomsky specified *transformational* processes (at least in the early version of generative grammar) that translated a syntactic deep structure to a syntactic surface structure. The deep structure of a sentence was generated by the semantic component of language, while the surface structure provided an input to the phonological component. There were two important ideas for psychology. The first idea was the *autonomy of syntax*: the idea that syntactic processes operate independently of other processes, such as semantics and phonology. (Syntax concerns the order of the words of the language, and how we convey grammatical information such as number and tense; semantics concerns meaning, and phonology concerns sound.) So although we might start with a semantic input and end with a phonological output, the language module does not permit anything other than syntactic processes at the syntactic level. In a slightly different form this idea is still important and influential in modern theories of language processing. For example, the cutting-edge debate in models of parsing is between the garden-path model, which does not allow anything other than syntactic influences on decision making in parsing, and constraint-based models, which allow all available sources of information to influence the selection of a syntactic structure. The second important idea was the *derivational theory of complexity* (DTC), which states that more complex syntactic structures are more difficult to process. Complexity was defined in terms of the number of syntactic transformations necessary to arrive at the surface form. For example, we can take a *kernel sentence* such as *The aardvark chases the echidna*, and turn it into a passive negative *The echidna was not chased by the aardvark*, by applying two transformations (passivisation and negative). Such a sentence should be more difficult to process than a sentence constructed by just one transformation, which in turn should be more difficult than a kernel sentence. Later, in *Aspects of the theory of syntax* (1965), Chomsky removed the idea of optional transformations, and instead made the famous distinction between the underlying deep structure of the language and its cognitive shallower surface structure. The distinction was subsequently couched in terms of I-language, or internalised language, and E-language, or external language. Nevertheless, the distinction between some kind of underlying linguistic representation and more transparent linguistic realisation with the two mediated by rules has always remained central to Chomsky's approach.

IMPACT OF THE CLASSIC STUDY

THE COMPETENCE–PERFORMANCE DISTINCTION

But what status do these transformations and other notions from Chomsky's early work actually play in psychological models of language processing? Early psycholinguists treated Chomsky's theory as a performance account of how we use language. Soon after the publication of generative grammar, psychologists developed new empirical tools that enabled us to measure what had previously been considered to be hidden psychological processes. Chief among these were measures of memory load, and particularly the measurement of reaction time – still the chief armament in the cognitive psychologist's arsenal. The central assumption of the reaction time experiment is that differences in reaction time between controlled conditions reflect fundamental differences in cognitive processing. While early studies using offline measures such as memory load provided limited support for Chomsky's model, more sophisticated studies using online measures such as reaction times showed that we do not produce utterances by transforming deep structures into surface structures, and that the assumption that syntactic processing is independent of other processing (initially semantic) is highly questionable (although it still provides a focus of research in modern psycholinguistics). For example, transformationally more complex sentences are not always more difficult to process (see Harley (2014) for a more detailed account and the theory's failings). In general, there was little clear support for either the autonomy of syntax or derivational complexity. Hence it was soon agreed by all that generative grammar was a *competence* model of language. One aspect of the fall-out from these early experiments was eventually a strong delineation between the disciplines of linguistics (dealing with competence) and psycholinguistics (dealing with performance).

But regardless of the details of the processing model, a clear consequence of taking a model based on generative grammar as an account of human language processing was a theoretical motivation for the computational model of mind, which underpinned the cognitive revolution. In a computational model, rules process information, with the nature of the content of what is manipulated being unimportant. The mind is like a meat factory, taking an input, grinding its way through regardless of what meat goes in, and delivering a nice pie at the end. But if the processes that mediate syntactic representations (and other types of linguistic representation) are not transformations, what are they?

CRITIQUE OF THE CLASSIC STUDY

A SHIFT FROM EMPIRICISM TO RATIONALISM

Chomsky's approach to language had several important consequences, and we now focus upon some of these.

The first consequence is that theoretical, computational considerations appear to drive us towards accepting some form of rationalism. Chomsky noted that the input a child hears is *impoverished* in several senses: adult speech is fast, poorly segmented, and full of errors. Of particular importance, adult language does not contain the types of utterance necessary for a child to be able to work out the underlying grammatical rules of the language. According to the poverty of the stimulus argument, the child cannot acquire language from mere exposure to positive instances of noisy real-world language. Instead, Chomsky argued, they must sift the input using some built-in structure, originally called the *Language Acquisition Device* (LAD), and later *Universal Grammar.*

The second consequence of Chomsky's work was that the processes whereby children acquire language became central to the study of the mind. As we have just noted, Chomsky argued that no matter how much positive or negative reinforcement a child has, they will never be able to learn human language by exposure alone. Chomsky focused on the types of syntactic structure different grammars of differing power could produce, and showed that humans produce sentences of a complexity that is too great to be produced by the sort of grammar that can be taught by conditioning alone. The most famous example is that of multiply embedded clauses, which can go on and on:

The cat chased the mouse.

The cat the dog chased chased the mouse.

The cat the dog the flea bit chased chased the mouse.

And so on. Never mind that no one actually produces a sentence like this; in principle, a competent adult speaker of English will accept that sentences like these, with any number of embeddings, are in fact legal sentences (although we might dispute this claim). There is the important point here that limitations of processing created by psychological constructs such as working memory are considered by Chomsky to be issues of *performance.* On the other hand, the intuitions of linguists about what would be an acceptable string is a *competence* issue that provides the only acceptable data for studying language itself.

If children cannot acquire powerful enough grammars by simple reinforcement, what else is needed? There has been an industry devoted to child language and linguistic power, and the most famous product of that industry is Gold's theorem (Gold, 1967), which states that to learn certain types of utterance, mere exposure to positive instances of an acceptable syntactic structure is insufficient; children need additional information in the form of explicit teaching of non-sentences ('no Elizabeth, "The cat the dog the flea chased chased the mouse" is not a sentence of English'). Early on it was assumed that parents just do not police their children's speech and correct syntax in this way. However, there has been much debate about the power of real-world language, and indeed observations of actual data in language development show that the linguistic input to the child is much more rich and directed than was once supposed (although there are huge cultural differences).

As mentioned above, Chomsky argued that what was needed to acquire language is the innate Language Acquisition Device. That is, children come pre-packed with linguistic knowledge that makes the task of learning a specific grammar from input alone possible. In particular, children have a general framework for grammar in the form of *parameters*, and exposure to a specific syntax sets the switches of these parameters (for example, the details of word order). This account also explains for Chomsky why all human languages are, according to him, essentially the same. As Stephen Pinker once famously remarked, any Martian examining our behaviour would rapidly conclude that we are all speaking essentially the same language (Pinker, 1995). For these reasons, linguists have been preoccupied with the search for linguistic universals – features of language that are common to all and that describe the structure of the set of parameters and their set of possible values rather than the details of the value to which these switches are set. However, as we saw above, it is not necessarily the case that children need innate help to acquire language. Furthermore, children across cultures share cognitive and environmental constraints that might shape and restrict the types of language found. At the very least, given the level of debate in the literature, we must say that the case for language-specific information is 'not proven'. But what then is the role of cognition in language and vice versa?

The third consequence of Chomsky's contribution is an understanding of the nature of computational roles, context, and the role of language in cognition. For the early behaviourists, all behaviours were functionally identical: what mattered was not *what* we were exposed to, but *how* we were exposed to it. Although later studies, such as that of Garcia et al. (1955), showed that were biological constraints on the strength of associations that could be formed (for example, it is easier to condition an animal so as to relate nausea to taste than other types of stimulus), in Skinner's time it was believed that all that mattered for the organism was its conditioning history. What was being conditioned didn't matter. One of Chomsky's great achievements was in appearing to show that language was *special*. Chomsky argued that language was a separate mental faculty (and by later argument, made use of dedicated brain regions). This general approach has been extremely influential in psychology, and is currently known as the *modularity of mind*, as put forward most famously by Fodor (1983). The modularity of language and of the components of language has been one of the most important themes in the history of psycholinguistics (Harley, 2014): the question 'to what extent are language processes encapsulated?' has dominated research. When we hear or see a word, is the process of identifying that word purely driven by the data, or are perceptual processes influenced by semantic knowledge and our expectations? When we parse a sentence, are the processes of parsing restricted to syntactic information, or again can semantic and contextual influences affect the online construction of the parse tree? Such issues are still very much at the fore of psycholinguistic research.

One consequence of Chomsky's view that language is a special faculty was the conclusion that language must be unique to humans. In the early animal language debate there was generally a great deal of scepticism from many linguists that the sort of language used by chimpanzees and other apes, regardless of format (ideograms, ASL, etc.), when attempts were made to teach them a human-like language, was truly syntactic. The study of whether or not animals are capable of using language has captivated popular imagination, with apes such as Washoe and Kanzi promoted as examples of what animals can achieve in the right conditions. Most researchers agree that much depends on exactly how language is defined, and many accept that there is a dichotomy rather than a continuum in the definition of language.

However, even for Chomsky, the scope of ideas that has defined human uniqueness has declined over the years. Now, it appears, all we are left with is the idea that only rules involving *recursion* are uniquely specific to humans. Put another way, recursion, apart from a few nuisance variables such as brain size, is all that distinguishes humans from the rest of the animal kingdom. Recursion is when a rule is defined in terms of itself: for a definition of recursion, see recursion. Recursion is what gives language its immense power: it enables us to define those multiple-centre embedded sentences discussed above. But more than these sentences, which seem at times to be no more than a linguistic game, recursion gives us a way of thinking about ourselves: according to many writers on consciousness, recursion gives us the ability to model ourselves thinking about ourselves thinking about ourselves thinking about ... (of course, any resemblance to infinitely multiply embedded sentences is not accidental). Recursion also enables us to construct sophisticated models of other people: she thinks that I think that she thinks.... These ideas mean that the computational power of human grammar is directly related to full human consciousness. And according to recent research by Chomsky and associates, animals are not capable of thinking recursively (Hauser, Chomsky, & Tecumseh-Fitch, 2002). In the world of Chomsky, language, self, consciousness, and human identity are necessarily intertwined.

Chomsky's work is very much in the rationalist tradition. There is something defeatist about rationalism: if you can't explain something easily, it must depend on innate information. Defeatism stifles research.

What alternatives are there to this approach? In addition to the shift from linguistic intuition to psycholinguistic processing, two significant approaches have come to prominence in psychology over the last few decades. We believe that in many ways these new ideas underlie a more plausible approach to psychology than the rule-based, innate knowledge using linguistics models pioneered by Chomsky.

The more established of the two is connectionism. The basic idea of connectionism is that computation is carried out by systems that are more brain-like (although not too much emphasis should be put on biological plausibility). Instead of computation making use of explicit rules, it makes implicit use of rules by a system that detects statistical regularities in the environment, and these regularities look like rules. Connectionist models comprise large networks of many massively interconnected simple units of processing. In a typical model, a pattern is presented to input units, and activation spreads throughout the network to activate a set of output units; this pattern of activation is compared with a target pattern, and the error reduced by adjusting the connection strengths between units using an algorithm such as *back-propagation*. The process is repeated many times until the error reaches a predetermined acceptable level. Connectionist models have contributed, among other things, to our understanding of reading, speech perception, semantics, speech production, the development of the past tense, Alzheimer's disease, and aphasia (see Harley, 2014, for a more detailed review).

There are several important properties of these models. First, the model learns how to optimally store the information it needs from the environment. Second, the representations used are complex (for example, semantic information might be encoded as a pattern of activation over many hundreds or thousands of semantic features). Third, as mentioned, rules are not explicitly encoded, but arise from statistical regularities in the input. There has been a great deal of debate in the literature about the extent to which these regularities are sufficient and correspond to explicit rules. Fourth, connectionism is very much in the empiricist tradition. Obviously we have to provide a network architecture and, if necessary, a learning rule, but the general approach taken is to see how much the model can do without information being explicitly supplied in advance (corresponding to innate information). Fifth, it is possible to modify the architecture to account for other aspects of development. For example, it has been shown that rather than presenting all information at once when learning (a rather unrealistic assumption), there are advantages to a network 'starting small' and only attempting to learn a subset of the information eventually required. What is more such an arrangement leads to other features of, for example, linguistic development that are difficult to explain in any other way. Sixth, models uncover regularities, rather than relying on hard coding. Finally, the emphasis in connectionist cognition is on general rules and general architectures: there is nothing special about language – it makes use of the same general learning rules as do other areas of cognition.

A more recent development is embodied cognition, which emphasises how cognitive processes take place in the world and are related to the brain. To take a simple example: when we think of throwing a ball, parts of the brain responsible for the action of throwing become active. Embodied cognition emphasises the interaction of mind, brain, and environment in a complex way.

CONCLUSIONS

Our polemic clearly cannot detract from Chomsky's massive contribution to cognitive science. There is no doubt that Chomsky is a 'Great Man', in Carlyle's sense, but science eventually still proceeds when other Great Men come along. The general idea that we need to think of internal rules that mediate input and output came to early prominence because of him. In addition, his contribution led to the rather paradoxical position that language was identified (by him) as a separate faculty in the mind, but also that led to the rise of language research in a way that language came to dominate cognitive psychology. Even now in cognitive science courses the interaction between linguistics and psycholinguistics, a branch of cognitive psychology, is a bit blurred.

No one could deny the importance of Chomsky for the development of linguistics. But although the distinction was blurred in the early days, there is now a very clear distinction between linguistics and psychology: essentially, psychology studies performance, linguistics studies competence. Now, of course, there is a psychological aspect to performance: making a judgement about the grammaticality of linguistic strings is a psychological process, and to that extent things like the grammaticality judgement task are considered to be diagnostic of certain types of acquired impairment. So psychology has a role to play even in the study of competence.

We do not wish to detract from these enormous achievements, but if one considers the direction psychology has taken in the last 30 years or so, we can see that:

1. Psychologists are interested in performance issues – how we actually produce, understand, and store language, rather than competence issues about how the rules describing language, derived from intuitions about linguistic acceptability, are best described.

2. There has been an increasing emphasis on the processes involved in cognition.

3. Rather than throwing our hands up in despair when faced with a complex task (e.g., language acquisition) and concluding that we need to adduce innate knowledge to accommodate the limitations, we should consider what caregivers actually do when speaking to children – that is, we should turn the linguistic into the psycholinguistic. We can also benefit from considering computational constraints on language acquisition – for example, the advantage of starting small (Elman, 1993).

4. Reports of intuitions can be wrong. Nothing ever beats a good experiment.

5. Rather than focusing on the extent to which language is a separate module, recent approaches emphasise the relationship between the mind and the body – the so-called 'embodied cognition' approach.

We are also left with a slightly uncomfortable feeling about the status of psycholinguistics as a discipline. If Chomsky is correct and language is a special, distinct faculty of the mind, then it isn't of general interest to psychologists concerned with fundamental processes in psychology. If, on the other hand, he is incorrect and language just makes use of general purpose mechanisms, why are we not studying those fundamental processes instead of placing so much emphasis on their linguistic manifestation? In part, connectionist models generally take the latter approach, stressing the role of general learning mechanisms. This important question is discussed in more detail by Harley (2010).

One more recent trend, made possible by having a body of research in many aspects of psycholinguistics to synthesise, as well as the development of easier and more accurate brain imaging techniques, such as fMRI, has been to construct sophisticated accounts of the complete language system, and particularly how they are related to the brain. We are approaching an era where psychological models of language are now as sophisticated as linguistic theories of language knowledge.

FURTHER READING

Chomsky, N. (1957). *Syntactic structures.* The Hague/Paris: Mouton.

Chomsky, N. (1959). Reviews: 'Verbal behavior by B. F. Skinner'. *Language*, 35, 26–58.

Chomsky, N. (1965). *Aspects of the theory of syntax.* Cambridge, MA: The MIT Press.

Harley, T. A. (2014). *The psychology of language* (4th edn). Hove, UK: Psychology Press.

REFERENCES

Chomsky, N. (1957). *Syntactic structures.* The Hague/Paris: Mouton.

Chomsky, N. (1959). Reviews: 'Verbal behavior by B. F. Skinner'. *Language*, 35, 26–58.

Chomsky, N. (1965). *Aspects of the theory of syntax.* Cambridge, MA: The MIT Press.

Elman, J. L. (1993). Learning and development in neural networks: The importance of starting small. *Cognition*, 48, 71–79.

Fodor, J. A. (1983). *The modularity of mind.* Cambridge, MA: The MIT Press.

Garcia, J., Kimeldorf D. J., Koelling R. A. (1955). Conditioned aversion to saccharin resulting from exposure to gamma radiation. Science 122, 157–158.

Gold, E. M. (1967). Language identification in the limit. *Information and Control*, 16, 447–474.

Harley, T. A. (2010). *Talking the talk.* Hove, UK: Psychology Press.

Harley, T. A. (2014). *The psychology of language* (4th edn). Hove, UK: Psychology Press.

Hauser, M.D., Chomsky, N., Tecumseh-Fitch, W. (2002). The faculty of language: What is it, who has it, and how did it evolve? *Science*, 298, 1569–1579.

Kuhn, T. (1962). *The structure of scientific revolutions.* Chicago, IL: University of Chicago Press.

Pinker, S. (1995). The language instinct. Harmondsworth: Penguin.

Skinner, B. F. (1957). *Verbal behavior.* Acton, MA: Copley.

15 Cognitive neuropsychology of language: Beyond Marshall and Newcombe's (1973) patterns of paralexia

Max Coltheart (Macquarie University, Sydney Australia)

BACKGROUND TO THE CLASSIC STUDY

In the summer of 1971 the International Neuropsychology Symposium met at the Swiss ski resort of Engelberg for its annual meeting, and there John Marshall and Freda Newcombe presented a paper on acquired dyslexia (impaired reading caused by brain damage), which was subsequently published in the *Journal of Psycholinguistic Research* two years later with the title 'Patterns of Paralexia: A Psycholinguistic Approach' (Marshall & Newcombe, 1973). This paper has had an enormous impact not only on the experimental psychology of reading, but also on the modern development of a whole discipline, cognitive neuropsychology.

I will explain how and why the paper has been so influential shortly, but first I will describe what the paper itself contains.

DETAILED DESCRIPTION OF THE CLASSIC STUDY

The paper begins with a detailed and scholarly review of the previous 80-odd years of research on acquired dyslexia, focusing in particular on the many different types of reading errors that have been reported in such cases. This research yielded a rich and fascinating set of observations, but very little by way of scientific explanation and hence much mystery. Why are some patients' reading errors typically focused on the right ends of words (e.g., reading *obtained* as 'oblong' or *beware* -> 'because'), whereas in other patients it is the *left* ends of words that are subject to error (*light* -> 'night', *gnome* -> 'income')? What could cause the type of error in which all of the stimulus letters are in the response, but in incorrect positions (*broad* -> 'board')? Why are some patients unable to recognise printed words as wholes, immediately and automatically, and so have to resort to sounding them out by grapheme-phoneme rules to read them aloud, which produces errors with irregularly-spelled words, such as reading *island* as 'iz-land'? And, finally, what could *possibly* have gone wrong that would give rise to semantic errors in reading aloud? Here the patient, shown a single word and given as much time as he or she needs to read it aloud, produces semantically-related reading errors such as *garden* -> 'flowers', *little* -> 'small', or *wed* -> 'marry'.

Marshall and Newcombe imposed order on this near-chaos by doing two things. The first was to insist that acquired dyslexia was not a single homogeneous condition, and that instead there were distinct subtypes of acquired dyslexia that differ in terms of their characteristic symptoms, especially their characteristic error types. The second was to offer explanations of each of these subtypes by interpreting their different characteristic symptoms in terms of a single model of the normal reading processes, with the different subtypes of acquired dyslexia corresponding to impairments to different processing components of that model.

THREE SUBTYPES OF ACQUIRED DYSLEXIA

In their paper Marshall and Newcombe report data from six men with reading impairments due to brain damage. Five of them had suffered missile wounds to the left hemisphere of the brain while serving in the Second World War (they were being tested about 25 years after suffering these injuries). The sixth man had sustained a closed head injury in a road accident two months before his reading was tested.

If acquired dyslexia is not a homogeneous condition, then it will be unenlightening – indeed, misleading – to average data across the members of a group of patients: what is essential is to study each individual patient separately. So this kind of work requires a single-case study approach, not a group study approach. And if it is correct that different subtypes of acquired dyslexia are due to impairments of different processing components of a model of the reading system, it is important, first, to manipulate various psycholinguistic variables (e.g., concreteness, part of speech, letter confusability) when testing reading, since these different variables affect different processing components of the reading system and, second, to carefully analyse the types of reading error the patients make. Finally, if one wants to obtain a detailed characterisation of which psycholinguistic variables affect a particular patient's reading and which do not, it is essential that the testing of reading be as extensive as possible; the reading of one of Marshall and Newcombe's patients was tested with more than 4,000 words, testing being spread out over a period of five years. These four features of their work in this paper – a single-case study approach, selection of stimulus variables on theoretically-motivated grounds, detailed analysis of error types, and very extensive testing of patients – characterises the type of research typical of the discipline that came to be known as *cognitive neuropsychology*. The nature of this discipline is discussed further below.

In their paper, Marshall and Newcombe defined three subtypes of acquired dyslexia, and the reason they chose to report data from these six patients was because each patient illustrated one of these subtypes (two patients for each subtype).

Two of the patients, GR and KU, were examples of a subtype of acquired dyslexia that Marshall and Newcombe named *deep dyslexia*. This is the subtype of acquired dyslexia in which semantic errors in reading aloud are seen. GR's reading errors included *city* -> 'town', and KU's included *diamond* -> 'necklace'. This is not the only reading symptom these patients showed. There were also visual errors, such as *shallow* -> 'sparrow', and morphological errors, such as *strength* -> 'strong'. And their reading accuracy was affected by concreteness (concrete nouns were read much better than abstract nouns) and by part of speech (content words were read much better than function words). Since this first report of deep dyslexia, much more work on this subtype of acquired dyslexia has been done: it is the subject of a book (Coltheart, Patterson, & Marshall, 1980), and a *Google Scholar* search with the term 'deep dyslexia' returned more than 4,700 hits on 12 March 2014.

Two other patients, JC and ST, were examples of a subtype of acquired dyslexia that Marshall and Newcombe named *surface dyslexia.* These patients often seemed unable to recognise words directly as wholes when attempting to read aloud, and seemed instead to have to assemble a word's phonology piecemeal by using grapheme-phoneme rules. This led to errors with words that disobey these rules, such as reading *listen* as 'Liston' (here JC added the gloss 'that's the boxer'), or *island* as 'iz-land') and also to incorrect stress assignment, such as responding to *begin* and *omit* by reading them with first-syllable stress, rather than the correct second-syllable stress. There has been considerable study of surface dyslexia since Marshall and Newcombe's identification of it as a subtype of acquired dyslexia; it is the subject of a book (Patterson, Marshall, & Coltheart, 1985), and a *Google Scholar* search with the term 'surface dyslexia' returned more than 5,500 hits on 25 December 2013.

The remaining two patients, JL and AT, were examples of a subtype of acquired dyslexia that Marshall and Newcombe named *visual dyslexia*. This third subtype of acquired dyslexia was described less clearly and in less detail than the other two. The characteristic reading error here is the visual error, but it isn't clear exactly what the authors meant by this term. When one considers errors such as *dug* -> 'bug' (JL) or *lit* -> 'hit' (AT), one might think of these as visual errors in the sense that one letter is being misidentified as another, visually similar, letter (*b* for *d*; *h* for *l*). But errors such as *was* -> 'saw' or *rut* -> 'tug' (JL) and *broad* -> 'board' or *angel* -> 'angle' (AT) are not visual errors in this letter-identification sense. They are errors that involve correct identification of a letter's identity but erroneous processing of its position. It is therefore not clear which of these two clearly different types of error is meant to define the visual dyslexia subtype. It is perhaps because of this ambiguity that there have been very few published studies of visual dyslexia as it was characterised by Marshall and Newcombe: perhaps no more than half a dozen papers. Indeed, Shallice and Rosazza (2006) recently referred to it as 'the forgotten visual dyslexia'. Coltheart and Kohnen (2012) went even further, suggesting that when one considers more recently discovered subtypes of acquired dyslexia, puta- tive cases of visual dyslexia can all be subsumed under one or other of these new subtypes, and therefore that there is no need for the subtype 'visual dyslexia'.

INTERPRETING SUBTYPES OF ACQUIRED DYSLEXIA IN TERMS OF A MODEL OF NORMAL READING

Having described the characteristics of three subtypes, Marshall and Newcombe went on to offer a theoretical interpretation of each one. 'We shall interpret dyslexic mistakes in terms of a *functional analysis* of normal reading processes' (Marshall & Newcombe, 1973, p. 188), which meant that they needed to offer a model of what these normal reading processes actually are. The model they offered can be seen in Figure 15.1.

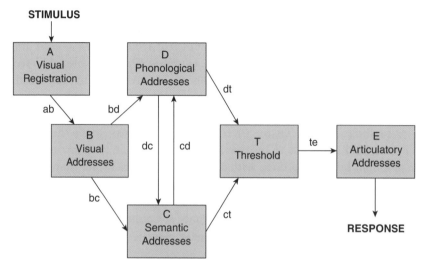

Figure 15.1 The dual-route model of reading proposed by Marshall and Newcombe (1973)

A key feature of this model is that there are two routes from vision (component A) to articulation (component E), that is, two routes from print to speech. There is the ABDTE route that goes via the Phonological Addresses component and does not use the Semantic Addresses component, and there is the ABCTE route that goes via the Semantic Addresses component and does not use the Phonological Addresses component. Hence here we have a dual-route model of reading. This represents one of the major contributions of the Marshall and Newcombe paper, because the dual-route conception of the functional architecture of the reading system is now unanimously accepted by theorists of reading, and this conception began with the Marshall–Newcombe paper.[1] Current theoretical modellers of reading certainly disagree greatly with respect to the details of how each of the two reading routes

---

[1]Although a dual-route conception of reading was independently proposed in the same year, by Ken Forster and Susan Chambers (1973).

is supposed to work, but all agree that there are two routes. Furthermore, it is widely held that this broad consensus has arisen in part from the need for any model of reading to explain how subtypes of acquired dyslexia arise.

Marshall and Newcombe's next task was to use this model to interpret the three subtypes of acquired dyslexia. Using models of normal cognitive processing to interpret patterns of disordered cognitive processing, as Marshall and Newcombe did here, is an enterprise that has stood the test of time (it is fundamental to cognitive neuropsychology), although I will argue that the specific details of their interpretations of their three subtypes of acquired dyslexia have not.

First, consider visual dyslexia. All that Marshall and Newcombe offer by way of a model-based interpretation of this form of acquired dyslexia is a discussion of letter-confusability effects. However, it can be presumed – though the authors do not explicitly state this – that they considered that in visual dyslexia the impairment is of Component B (the Visual Addresses component). Here it is hard to see how a single impairment of that model component could produce errors of the type *lit* -> 'hit' and also errors of the type *broad* -> 'board'.

Next, consider deep dyslexia. Semantic errors 'are within component C' (Marshall & Newcombe, 1973, p. 193). At first sight, this seems to be saying that in deep dyslexia component C is damaged, but in fact that is not what Marshall and Newcombe meant: their view instead was that semantic access within component C is *intrinsically* imprecise (their word for this was 'unstable') *even when the whole system is intact*. Morphological errors such as *strength* -> 'strong' are attributed to an impairment of component B; presumably this would also be the explanation of visual errors. Pathway *bd* must also be impaired in deep dyslexia since, if that were not so, correct reading-aloud responses could be achieved and hence potential semantic errors blocked. No model-based interpretation of the part-of-speech or concreteness effects was offered.

There are a number of difficulties with this analysis of deep dyslexia. A specific difficulty is this: if the Semantic Addresses component is intrinsically inexact even in the normal language-processing system, and is also, as they argue, modality-free, then how could error-free picture naming occur in intact subjects? There is very general agreement that pictures are named via the route Picture Recognition -> Semantics -> Phonology. If that were so and normal access to Semantics is intrinsically semantically inexact, intact subjects should make semantic errors in picture naming that resemble the semantic errors that deep dyslexics make in reading aloud, and this is not the case.

A more general difficulty is this: if visual and morphological errors occur because of an impairment of the visual component B, whereas semantic errors arise because there is an impairment of pathway bd and the semantic component C is intrinsically semantically inexact, these are two independent factors, and so should occur independently: in particular, we should see patients who make abundant semantic errors in reading aloud but do not make visual or morphological errors. But this pattern has not been reported in any cases of acquired dyslexia (Coltheart, 1980a). This result, and other failures of dissociation (such as the failure to observe patients making semantic errors but showing no part-of-speech or concreteness effects) led to the radical suggestion, independently made in the late 1970s by Eleanor Saffran and by me (Saffran, Bogyo, Schwartz, & Marin, 1980; Coltheart, 1980b) that deep dyslexics are not reading with a damaged version of the normal left-hemisphere system (as Marshall and Newcombe argued), but are instead reading with a rudimentary and intact right-hemisphere reading system. Subsequent brain-oriented investigations have offered support for this right-hemisphere hypothesis. If this hypothesis is correct, then deep dyslexia, unlike all other known subtypes of acquired dyslexia, is not relevant to models of the normal reading process.

Finally, consider Marshall and Newcombe's model-based interpretation of surface dyslexia. Here more detailed consideration of the data from their two surface-dyslexic patients could have been used by them to reveal one way in which their model (i.e., Figure 15.1) was inadequate as a model of normal reading, and so could have led them to improve their model.

The first point to note is that the term 'Addresses' in Figure 15.1 is meant to refer to a system of *word* representations: 'The figure illustrates that, in reading individual words visual addresses (B) must be associated with stimulus entries on a primary visual register [and] that both phonological (D) and semantic (C) addresses must in turn be associated with individual visual-address...' (Marshall & Newcombe, 1973, p. 188). It follows from this that the function of pathway *bd* is to activate word-specific representation in the phonological system D from word-specific representations in the visual system B.

The second point to note is that Marshall and Newcombe are inconsistent in how they characterise pathway *bd*, because they also want it to be a grapheme-phoneme conversion pathway. That is how they interpret surface dyslexia: 'If functional pathway *bc* is usually unavailable (visual addresses->semantic addresses), subjects will have to read via putative grapheme-phoneme correspondence rules (pathway *bd*)'. And here they even anticipate much subsequent work by pointing out that no system of grapheme-phoneme rules will yield the correct response for all English words, because for any such system a number of English words will violate these rules: these are the irregular or exception words of English.

So, if pathway *bd* is specific to words, and if one wants a grapheme-phoneme pathway, one must add to this model a visual component that represents graphemes (this isn't component B) and a phonological component that represents phonemes (this isn't component D), with a pathway of communication between these. Without this, not only is there no way of interpreting surface-dyslexic regularisation errors such as *listen* -> 'Liston' or *island* -> 'iz-land', but there is also no way of explaining how intact readers can read non-words aloud. This point was clear to the other inventors of the dual-route model, Forster and Chambers, for whom the two routes from print to speech were a grapheme-phoneme conversion route and a dictionary lookup route. On the other hand, Forster and Chambers did not distinguish between dictionary lookup as the looking up of a word's *semantics* from its printed form and dictionary lookup as the looking up of a word's *phonology* from its printed form, whereas Marshall and Newcombe did make this distinction (in the form of the distinction between their pathway *bc* and their pathway *bd*). As the dual-route model has developed over the past 40 years, both of these ideas have been incorporated, as one can see in recent versions of the dual-route model, such as the one shown in Figure 15.2 (Coltheart, Rastle, Perry, Langdon, & Ziegler, 2001), which contains not only Marshall and Newcombe's *bd* and *bc* pathways but also the grapheme-phoneme pathway of Forster and Chambers (1973).

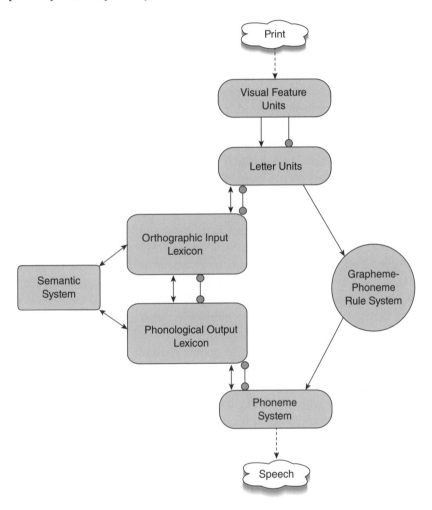

Figure 15.2 The DRC dual-route model of reading, Coltheart et al. (2001)

IMPACT AND CRITIQUE OF THE CLASSIC STUDY

One can identify numerous developments in cognitive psychology over the past 40 years that directly sprang from Marshall and Newcombe's ground-breaking paper. I will discuss the most prominent of these.

THE DISCOVERY OF OTHER SUBTYPES OF ACQUIRED DYSLEXIA – AND OF SUBTYPES OF ACQUIRED DYSGRAPHIA

As soon as a distinction is made between a word-specific (i.e., lexical) route from print to phonology and a non-lexical route from print to phonology that depends upon grapheme-to-phoneme rules – a distinction that Marshall and Newcombe's work on surface dyslexia might have suggested to them – one immediately is prompted by that distinction to wonder whether there could be a form of acquired dyslexia in which the lexical word-specific route is intact but the non-lexical grapheme-to-phoneme rule route is not. That impairment would produce a patient who could read words well (including irregularly-spelled words) but who read non-words badly. This form of acquired dyslexia was duly reported by Jacqueline Dérouesné and Marie-France Beauvois (1979); it is known as phonological dyslexia, and numerous other cases of this subtype have since been reported.[2] Further work on acquired dyslexia using the single-case approach, model-based choice of test materials, careful analysis of error types, and extensive testing of each patient – that is, using the methods pioneered by Marshall and Newcombe – have led to the discovery of still other subtypes. In their recent review, Coltheart and Kohnen (2012) describe eight different subtypes of acquired dyslexia that have been documented in the literature.

Next, imagine running a model like the one in Figure 15.2 backwards: that is, providing it with a string of phonemes as its input and wanting a string of letters as its output; and suppose the grapheme-to-phoneme rules could also work in reverse (i.e., could convert phonemes to graphemes). Here, what the model is doing is spelling, and in fact here we have a dual-route model of spelling, since the model is using two procedures to convert phonemes to letters: looking up spellings in a dictionary of word-specific information, and using phoneme-grapheme rules. Such dual-route models of spelling have indeed been proposed (see, for example, Shallice, 1981). And if the way people spell can be described in this way, we might expect that different kinds of brain damage could impair spelling in different ways: that is, there would be subtypes of acquired dysgraphia. Single-case studies of people in whom spelling had been impaired by brain damage have shown that this is so. Some dysgraphic patients can correctly spell words that have regular relationships between phonemes and graphemes, but when asked to spell 'blood' will write *blud*: this is called *surface dysgraphia*. Other dysgraphic patients can correctly spell words, including those that have irregular relationships between phonemes and graphemes, but cannot spell simple non-words: this is called *phonological dysgraphia*. And still other dysgraphic patients produce semantic errors when writing to dictation, such as the patient who, when given

---

[2]Crisp and Lambon Ralph (2006) have proposed that phonological dyslexia and deep dyslexia should not be regarded as distinct types of acquired dyslexia, but as points along a single continuum of acquired dyslexia. However, since, by definition, all patients who make semantic errors in reading aloud are classified as deep dyslexics and all patients who make no semantic errors in reading aloud but are impaired at non-word reading are, by definition, classified as phonological dyslexics, the categorical distinction here seems sharp enough.

'chipmunk' to write wrote *squirrel*: this is called *deep dysgraphia*. These different subtypes of acquired dysgraphia are reviewed by Coltheart and Kohnen (2012). So the Marshall–Newcombe approach has illuminated the study of spelling disorders as well as the study of reading disorders.

THE APPLICATION OF THESE METHODS TO THE INVESTIGATION OF DEVELOPMENTAL DYSLEXIAS AND DYSGRAPHIAS

If the mental information-processing system used by skilled readers and spellers is a multicomponent system (such as the systems depicted in Figures 15.1 and 15.2), then when children are learning to read and spell they are learning the individual components of some multicomponent system. That raises the possibility that in children who are having difficulties in learning to read (or spell), these difficulties could be specific to acquiring particular components of the system, with the other components being acquired in a normal way. So: might there be, for example, a subtype of developmental dyslexia that could be called *developmental phonological dyslexia*, in which a child is specifically having difficulties learning the grapheme-phoneme rules component of the reading system? And might there be another subtype of developmental dyslexia that could be called *developmental surface dyslexia*, in which a child is specifically having difficulties learning to recognise words as orthographic wholes and mapping these word-specific orthographic representations onto their whole-word phonological forms? John Marshall thought so, and with his students Jane Holmes and Christine Temple did provide evidence for this view, a view that has been confirmed in subsequent studies. So developmental dyslexia is no more homogeneous a condition than acquired dyslexia; and comparable studies of developmental dysgraphia show that it is no more homogeneous a condition than acquired dysgraphia: there are subtypes of developmental dyslexia and dysgraphia too (see Coltheart and Kohnen (2012) for brief reviews of subtypes of developmental dyslexia and dysgraphia).

GOING BEYOND WRITTEN-WORD PROCESSING TO OTHER BASIC DOMAINS OF COGNITION: COGNITIVE NEUROPSYCHOLOGY

If modular modelling of cognitive systems is not just appropriate for reading and spelling, but is quite generally appropriate for the modelling of every basic cognitive process, then the approach that Marshall and Newcombe took to understanding acquired dyslexia could be extended to the understanding of acquired disorders of every basic cognitive process for which plausible modular models of normal processing existed. Many people were stimulated by Marshall and Newcombe's paper to begin doing just this kind of work in a variety of basic domains of cognition, and this type of work soon was given a name: *cognitive neuropsychology*. Cognitive neuropsychology is the use of data from case studies of people with disorders of cognition in order to learn more about normal cognition and the use of models of normal cognition to understand data from case studies of people with disorders of cognition: exactly what Marshall and Newcombe did with respect to disorders of reading.

Even though cognitive neuropsychologists typically study people with brain damage, and despite the impression that might be given by the prefix 'neuro' in the term 'cognitive neuropsychology', cognitive neuropsychology is not about the brain: it is about information-processing models of cognition. Of course, many scientists are interested in the neural structures subserving cognition, and investigation of the brain in people with acquired disorders of cognition is one obvious way to pursue such an interest. But this is not cognitive neuropsychology, it is cognitive neuroscience – two different disciplines that are sometimes confused.

In the decade after the Marshall and Newcombe paper was published, many people began doing cognitive neuropsychology, so much so that, less than ten years after their paper appeared, I and others established the journal *Cognitive Neuropsychology* in 1984. A classic textbook for the field followed in 1988 (Ellis and Young's *Human Cognitive Neuropsychology*) with chapters covering cognitive-neuropsychological work in many basic domains of cognition, including face recognition, object recognition, visuospatial processing, spoken-language production, spoken-language comprehension, reading, spelling, and memory.

Extensions to higher-level domains of cognition: Cognitive neuropsychiatry

I have been referring to 'basic domains of cognition' because these are the kinds of domains that are typically chapter headings in undergraduate textbooks of cognitive psychology. They can be contrasted with higher-level domains of cognition that are much harder for cognitive psychologists to investigate and so about which we know much less. Some examples of these are belief formation and evaluation, body image and the sense of ownership of one's own body and its parts, and the sense of agency of one's own actions. Even though we have at best only rudimentary theories about how these kinds of cognitive processes might work, it is clear that brain damage can cause selective breakdowns even at these high levels of cognition – breakdowns such as delusions, hallucinations, phantom limb sensations, or 'hysterical' paralyses. Might it be possible to apply the methods of cognitive neuropsychology – the methods pioneered by Marshall and Newcombe – to the understanding of even these high-level breakdowns, and to use data from such studies to develop theories of how these high-level cognitive abilities are normally carried out?

John Marshall thought so. During the 1990s he published cognitive-neuropsychological work on hallucinations (Halligan, Marshall, & Ramachandran, 1994), supernumerary phantom limbs (Halligan, Marshall, & Wade,1993), delusions such as somatoparaphrenia (the belief that one of your limbs is not yours but someone else's – Halligan, Marshall, & Wade, 1995), and 'hysterical' paralysis (Marshall, Halligan, Fink, Wade, & Frackowiak, 1997). What distinguishes this type of cognitive-neuropsychological work is that the symptoms being studied are psychiatric in nature. So it is useful to have a term defining the application of cognitive neuropsychology to the understanding of psychiatric types of cognitive disorder. When in 1996 Marshall published, with Peter Halligan, a book (*Method in Madness* – Halligan & Marshall, 1996) describing various case studies of such high-level disorders, the term he used was *cognitive neuropsychiatry*. That has become a standard term describing this kind of work. The discipline of cognitive neuropsychiatry has flourished over the past 20 years, and it too has its own journal, *Cognitive Neuropsychiatry*, which began publication in 1996.

The journal's website makes it plain that cognitive neuropsychiatry is a sub-field of cognitive neuropsychology, thus indicating its debt to Marshall and Newcombe (1973): the site says: '*Cognitive Neuropsychiatry* seeks to promote the study of cognitive processes underlying psychological and behavioural abnormalities, including psychotic symptoms, with and without organic brain disease. The journal publishes high quality empirical and theoretical papers (original papers, short reports, case studies and reviews) in fields of clinical and cognitive neuropsychiatry and which have a bearing on the understanding of normal cognitive processes.'

THE FUTURE: SCHIZOPHRENIA AND AUTISM?

One message from Marshall and Newcombe (1973) is that clinical syndromes such as 'acquired dyslexia' or 'developmental dyslexia' are not suitable objects of scientific study, because any set of patients classified as exhibiting the same syndrome may have nothing in common beyond that syndrome name. What one should be studying is not the syndrome, but the *symptom*. For example, if several patients with acquired dyslexia are selected because there is some reading symptom that they all have in common (for example, all of them make semantic errors in reading aloud), which is precisely what Marshall and Newcombe did, then one can use data from these patients to try to explain how semantic errors could arise from damage to some model of the normal reading system, and that may increase our understanding of both the patients' reading difficulty and the model of normal reading.

Later, Marshall pointed out another compelling reason why research must focus on the symptom rather than the syndrome. Referring to a model like that in Figure 15.1, he noted that even so simple a model had quite a large number of elements: six boxes and eight arrows. Suppose it were true that brain damage could impair just one of these 14 elements while sparing all of the others. If that is true, then the number of different patterns of impairment that could arise – that is, the number of distinct syndromes – is 2^{14}-1. That is 16,383. We don't want to distinguish between 16,383 distinct syndromes of acquired dysexia, and even if we did, this would be a pointless exercise because the probability of coming across a patient with any particular one of these syndromes is 1/16,383, and the probability of coming across two patients with the same syndrome is less than one in 3 million.[3]

_____

[3]How, then, does one generalise from the study of one patient with acquired dyslexia to the study of another such patient? The answer is that it is assumed that all patients with acquired dyslexia have in common the cognitive architecture of the system they were using for reading before the occurrence of their brain damage. Here generalisations are inferences, from the patient data, about the nature of that pre-damage cognitive architecture, that is about the nature of the normal reading system.

There are many cognitive disorders for which this stricture – study the symptom, not the syndrome – has been taken on board. But there are two notable exceptions: schizophrenia and autism. For both of these disorders, research is currently almost entirely syndrome-based. Publications in this area characteristically state, in their *Participants* section, something like: 'Participants were XX people who had all received a clinical diagnosis of schizophrenia' (or, in the case of autism, 'a clinical diagnosis of autism'). The most commonly used instrument for making these clinical diagnoses is the American Psychiatric Association's *Diagnostic and Statistical Manual*' (DSM), the most recent version of which, DSM-V, was published in 2013.

According to DSM-V's criteria for diagnosing a person with schizophrenia, if a person has just the two symptoms 'delusions' and 'diminished emotional expression', that is sufficient for the diagnosis of schizophrenia. But so are just the two symptoms 'hallucinations' and 'disorganised behaviour'. And so are just the two symptoms 'disorganised speech' and 'avolition' (lack of initiation of behaviour). These three types of patient have no symptoms in common, yet any study of schizophrenia could include all three types of patient. If in such a study the aim was to investigate, say, the genetic basis of schizophrenia, or the neurochemical basis of schizophrenia, or even the cognitive basis of schizophrenia, such aims are incoherent. How could there be a single genetic (or neurochemical, or cognitive) defect that in some people resulted in delusions and diminished emotional expression, in others hallucinations and disorganised behaviour, and in others disorganised speech and avolition? That's why syndrome-based research on schizophrenia, though it is the norm, makes no sense when viewed from the perspective of Marshall and Newcombe (1973).

The same is true of autism. If the only symptoms that child A shows are 'Avoids eye contact and gesturing in social situations, lacks emotional reciprocity, has never developed language, has stereotypes repetitive motor mannerisms, is preoccupied with parts of objects, and exhibits inflexible adherence to behavioural routines', that is sufficient for the child be given a DSM-V diagnosis of autism. If the only symptoms child B shows are this different (though somewhat similar) list 'Has failed to develop peer relations, does not share attention with other people, has idiosyncratic language use, cannot manage conversation exchange, preoccupied with restricted interests and lack of social reciprocity', that is sufficient for the child be given a DSM-V diagnosis of autism. Here, the two children A and B have no symptom in common, yet they are given the same diagnosis. So what could it mean to say 'I am studying the nature of autism' or 'I am studying what causes autism' if there is no symptom in common to all the children you are studying? Brock (2011) discusses this issue and the possibility of future work that would seek to subtype the syndrome of autism in just the same way as Marshall and Newcombe showed us 40 years ago how the sydrome of acquired dyslexia could be subtyped.

Hints are emerging that there may be a general shift away from syndrome-based research to symptom-based research here. Thomas Insel, the Director of the National Institutes for Mental Health (NIMH), the largest funding body for mental-health research in the world and one that funds a very large amount of research on schizophrenia and on autism, issued a statement on 29 April 2013 (Insel, 2013) saying that NIMH will from now on 'be re-orienting its research away from DSM categories' and towards research on specific symptoms, even when patients with that symptom cross diagnostic categories. That is, the symptom matters here, and the syndrome does not.

So perhaps the voices of John Marshall and Freda Newcombe have now even reached the hallowed halls of the NIMH. And if that is the case, perhaps at some time in the future we will understand schizophrenia and autism as well as we currently understand acquired dyslexia – thanks to John and Freda.

ACKNOWLEDGEMENTS

I thank Ken Forster, Naama Friedmann, David Howard, Saskia Kohnen, Eva Marinus and the two editors of this volume for their valuable comments on an earlier draft.

FURTHER READING

Coltheart, M. (2012). The cognitive level of explanation. *Australian Journal of Psychology*, 64, 11–18.

Explains why there needs to be both a cognitive and a neural level of description for the types of cognitive phenomenon described in this chapter.

Coltheart, M., & Kohnen, S. (2012). Acquired and developmental disorders of reading and spelling. In M. Faust (Ed.), *Handbook of the neuropsychology of language*. Oxford, UK: Blackwell.

An up-to-date summary of the currently-recognised subtypes of acquired and developmental dyslexia and dysgraphia.

Coltheart, M., Langdon, R., & McKay, R. T. (2011). Delusional belief. *Annual Review of Psychology*, 62, 271–298.

Delusional belief is the most advanced area of cognitive neuropsychiatry (just as acquired dyslexia is the most advanced area of cognitive neuropsychology), and this is an account of current work on the cognitive neuropsychiatry of delusion.

Ellis, A. W., & Young, A. W. (1988). *Human cognitive neuropsychology*. Hove, UK: Psychology Press.

The best overview of the whole field of cognitive neuropsychology.

Heilman, K. H. (2006). Aphasia and the diagram makers revisited: An update of information processing models. *Journal of Clinical Neurology*, 2, 149–162.

Cognitive neuropsychology flourished in the second half of the nineteenth century but almost completely vanished from the beginning of the twentieth century until the late 1960s. This paper is a valuable account of nineteenth-century cognitive neuropsychology.

REFERENCES

American Psychiatric Association (2013). *Diagnostic and statistical manual* (5th edn). Arlington, VA: APA.

Brock, J. (2011). Complementary approaches to the developmental cognitive neuroscience of autism – reflections on Palfrey et al. (2011). *Journal of Child Psychology and Psychiatry*, 52, 645–656.

Coltheart, M. (1980a). Deep dyslexia: A review of the syndrome. In M. Coltheart, K. Patterson, & J. C. Marshall (Eds.), *Deep dyslexia*. London: Routledge & Kegan Paul.

Coltheart, M. (1980b). Deep dyslexia: A right hemisphere hypothesis. In M. Coltheart, K. Patterson, & J. C. Marshall (Eds.), *Deep dyslexia*. London: Routledge & Kegan Paul.

Coltheart, M., & Kohnen, S. (2012). Acquired and developmental disorders of reading and spelling. In M. Faust (Ed.), *Handbook of the neuropsychology of language*. Oxford, UK: Blackwell.

Coltheart, M., Patterson, K., & Marshall, J. C. (Eds.) (1980). *Deep dyslexia*. London: Routledge & Kegan Paul. (2nd edn, 1987).

Coltheart, M., Rastle, K., Perry, C., Langdon, R., & Ziegler, J. (2001). DRC: A Dual Route Cascaded model of visual word recognition and reading aloud. *Psychological Review*, 108, 204–256.

Crisp, J., & Lambon Ralph, M. A. (2006). Unlocking the nature of the phonological-deep dyslexia continuum: The keys to reading aloud are in phonology and semantics. *Journal of Cognitive Neuroscience*, 18, 348–362.

Dérouesné, J., & Beauvois, M. F. (1979). Phonological alexia: Three dissociations. *Journal of Neurology, Neurosurgery & Psychiatry*, 42, 1115–1124.

Ellis, A. W., & Young, A. W. (1988). *Human cognitive neuropsychology*. Hove, UK: Psychology Press.

Forster, K. I., & Chambers, S. M. (1973). Lexical access and naming time. *Journal of Verbal Learning and Verbal Behavior*, 12, 627–635.

Halligan, P. W., & Marshall, J. C. (1996). *Method in madness: Case studies in cognitive neuropsychiatry*. Hove, UK: Psychology Press.

Halligan, P. W., Marshall, J. C., & Ramachandran, V. S. (1994). Ghosts in the machine: A case description of visual and haptic hallucinations after right hemisphere stroke. *Cognitive Neuropsychology*, 11, 459–477.

Halligan, P. W., Marshall, J. C., & Wade, D. T. (1993). Three arms: A case study of supernumerary phantom limb after right hemisphere stroke. *Journal of Neurology, Neurosurgery, and Psychiatry*, 56, 159–166.

Halligan, P. W., Marshall, J. C., & Wade, D. T. (1995). Unilateral somatoparaphrenia after right hemisphere stroke: A case description. *Cortex*, 31, 173–182.

Insel, T. (2013). Transforming diagnosis, www.nimh.nih.gov/about/director/2013/transforming-diagnosis.shtml (retrieved 25 December 2013).

Marshall, J. C., & Newcombe, F. (1973). Patterns of paralexia: A psycholinguistic approach. *Journal of Psycholinguistic Research*, 2, 175–199.

Marshall, J. C., Halligan, P. W., Fink, G. R., Wade, D. T., & Frackowiak, R. S. (1997). The functional anatomy of a hysterical paralysis. *Cognition*, 64, B1–B8.

Patterson, K. E., Marshall, J. C., & Coltheart, M. (Eds.) (1985). *Surface dyslexia: Cognitive and neuropsychological studies of phonological reading*. Hove, UK: Lawrence Erlbaum Associates.

Saffran, E. M., Bogyo, L. C., Schwartz, M., & Marin, O. S. M. (1980). Does deep dyslexia reflect right-hemisphere reading? In M. Coltheart, K. Patterson, & J. C. Marshall (Eds.), *Deep dyslexia*. London: Routledge & Kegan Paul.

Shallice, T. (1981). Phonological agraphia and the lexical route in writing. *Brain*, 104, 413–429.

Shallice, T., & Rosazza, C. (2006). Patterns of peripheral paralexia: Pure alexia and the forgotten visual dyslexia? *Cortex*, 42, 892–897.

Index

NOTE: page numbers in *italic* type refer to figures and tables